A long way from home

CATHY GLASS

A long way from home

How many heartbreaks can a little girl take?

Certain details in this story, including names, places and dates, have been changed to protect the family's privacy.

HarperElement
An imprint of HarperCollins*Publishers*
1 London Bridge Street
London SE1 9GF

www.harpercollins.co.uk

First published by HarperElement 2018

3 5 7 9 10 8 6 4 2

A catalogue record of this book is
available from the British Library

ISBN 978-0-00-827589-1

Printed and bound in Great Britain by
CPI Group (UK) Ltd, Croydon, CR0 4YY

MIX
Paper from
responsible sources
FSC™ C007454

This book is produced from independently certified FSC paper
to ensure responsible forest management

For more information visit: www.harpercollins.co.uk/green

ACKNOWLEDGEMENTS

A big thank you to my family; my editors, Carolyn and Holly; my literary agent, Andrew; my UK publishers HarperCollins, and my overseas publishers who are now too numerous to list by name. Last, but definitely not least, a big thank you to my readers for your unfailing support and kind words. They are much appreciated.

Some stories have to wait to be told to gain the full picture and a better understanding of what happened. Anna's story is one of them.

PART I

CHAPTER ONE

LANA

Although the children weren't babies, they appeared as helpless as the day they were born. Dressed only in nappies and ragged T-shirts, they were sitting or lying on the hard floors, or incarcerated in their cots. Their large eyes stared out blankly from emaciated faces. Some children were obviously disabled, others not, but all were badly undernourished and clearly developmentally delayed. The four rooms in the orphanage were hot and airless in the middle of summer. Flies circled around the broken ceiling fans and buzzed against the grids covering the windows. The only toys in any of the rooms were a few balls and a handful of building bricks, but no child played with them. And the silence was deafening and unnatural. Not one of the thirty or so infants cried, let alone spoke.

'This nice one,' the care worker said in broken English, pausing at a cot containing a Down's syndrome boy. 'He no give you trouble.'

Elaine looked with renewed horror at the child rocking back and forth in the cot. A few wisps of fair hair covered his otherwise bald head, open sores bled on his lips and his face was so pale it was doubtful he had ever felt the sunlight. He stared blankly into the distance. Elaine went to speak to him but the care worker was already moving briskly to the next cot. 'Or this one,' she said, tapping the metal bars of the cot and ignoring the fact that the child had been sick.

Elaine fought back tears and looked to her husband to say something.

Ian cleared his throat. The care worker – a large, brusque woman – seemed to be in charge. He didn't know what role she played and didn't want to upset her and risk their chance of a child. 'I'm sorry, we don't understand,' he said, almost apologetically. 'We were supposed to adopt a particular child. She's called Lana. We have a photograph of her here in our paperwork.' He went to unclip his briefcase.

The care worker tapped his arm. 'No. No. Lana, that baby dead. You choose another baby. We have plenty.'

Elaine's hand shot to her mouth. 'Dead? When?' she cried.

'We weren't told,' Ian said.

The care worker shrugged. 'You on plane.'

'She died yesterday?' Elaine asked, horrified.

'Maybe too late to tell you. You choose another baby. Plenty. Over here.' She led the way to another cot on the far side of the room.

'I want to go,' Elaine said, taking Ian's arm.

'We are leaving,' he said to the care worker, who was waiting for them by the cot.

'You come here and see baby. Talk to it.'

'No!' Elaine cried.

'You no want baby?' the care worker asked, a mixture of incredulity and impatience.

'Not like this,' Ian said. 'We came here for Lana and you tell us she is dead. We are very upset.'

'But you can choose another baby,' she said, as though they were in the wrong.

'No,' Ian said firmly. 'We can't.'

'Suit yourself,' she said, clearly offended. Leaving the cot, she headed out of the room and towards the main door, a bunch of keys jangling at her hip. They followed. 'Lots of other parents come here and take our babies,' she snapped.

'But not us,' Ian said, annoyed.

They waited while she unlocked the door. Ian hung back as Elaine stepped outside. 'Where's the doctor we've been dealing with?' he asked. 'He was supposed to meet us here.'

The care worker shrugged, either not understanding or refusing to answer.

'Dr Ciobanu,' Ian tried again. 'We spoke to him on the phone. Is he here?'

She shook her head. 'You go now. I'm busy.'

'You tell him we came?' he said, but she pushed at his arm, signalling for him to leave.

Ian and Elaine stepped outside and the large metal door clanged shut behind them. A lone child screamed from inside.

Elaine burst into tears and Ian put his arm around her. 'I don't believe it,' she sobbed. 'All this time, working towards the adoption, and that heartless woman tells us our baby is dead.' Although they'd never met little Lana, they'd felt a bond with her ever since they'd first received her details and photograph, and considered her their daughter. This was supposed to have been the final stage in the adoption process that had begun nearly two years before and had included a detailed social worker's report, references, medicals, and endless form filling and expectation. Today they should have met Lana for the first time, given the doctor their paperwork and signed the forms for court. And while they waited for the court hearing they would have visited Lana each day, loving her more and more. But that had all come to an abrupt and distressing end. Their baby had died.

Ian gently guided his wife to the taxi they had waiting.

'No baby?' the taxi driver asked, seeing their faces as they got into the back.

'No. The baby died,' Ian replied, his voice shaking with emotion.

'Oh dear. It happens in this country,' the driver said matter-of-factly. 'Many babies die here.'

Ian nodded as Elaine wiped her eyes. They knew about the high infant mortality rate and the shocking conditions in some of the state-run orphanages that had contributed to their decision to adopt from this country.

The driver glanced at them in the rear-view mirror, started the car and pulled away. 'I find you a healthy baby,' he said. 'My cousin knows a lady who finds couples babies. You no worry. She find one for you, and she very cheap.'

'That's kind of you, but no thank you,' Ian said politely. They'd been warned about these types of arrangements by other couples who had adopted from this country. There were many parents on the internet who were happy to share their experiences of international adoption to help others. While not always illegal, these private adoptions were fraught with problems, and money was demanded at each stage of the process. Yet ironically they'd followed the correct procedure and look where it had got them!

'You think about it,' the driver said. 'I give you my telephone number when we stop.'

'OK,' Ian said, without the strength to protest.

The air conditioning in the reception of their three-star hotel was a welcome relief after the heat outside. Ian and Elaine, desperate to be alone, caught the lift straight up to their room on the third floor. The maid had been in and everything was clean and tidy and the bed made. It was such a stark contrast to the poverty outside that Elaine felt a familiar stab of guilt.

'I don't think we're meant to have children,' she said, utterly defeated and sitting on the bed.

Ian sighed and poured himself a glass of water from the flask that was refreshed daily. 'I don't know,' he said, as dejected as his wife. 'I expected to face some hurdles, most of those we've been talking to who adopted from here did, but I never imagined this. To arrive and be told our child is dead, and then be shown other children, is heartless beyond belief.'

'Do you think what she's doing is legal?' Elaine asked.

'Who knows?'

'Those poor children. She kept calling them babies but they weren't. Some of them could have been six or seven, and most of them were disabled.'

'I suppose they are the ones no one wants to adopt,' Ian said sadly. 'That care worker probably thought as Lana had died we'd be desperate and grateful for any child.'

'I feel awful but I really can't take on a disabled child. I told our social worker that right at the beginning.' Her voice caught. 'I'm just not cut out for it.'

'I know, love, me neither. We've been honest, and it wasn't fair to put us in that position.' He sat beside her on the bed and rested his head back, exhausted.

They were having to deal with so many emotions: bereavement, shock, disappointment and anger. At forty-two and thirty-eight respectively, this had been Ian and Elaine's last chance of a family. Elaine was infertile, IVF had failed, and they were considered too old to adopt a baby or very young child in their own country, the UK.

'I think we should just go home and forget about it,' Elaine said, leaning her head on Ian's shoulder.

'Yes, I agree. But I'm going to speak to that Dr Ciobanu first and tell him what I think. I don't want other couples going through what we have.'

Half an hour later, when Ian felt up to it, he telephoned the orphanage but was told by a care worker that Dr Ciobanu wasn't there, so he left a message (which he wasn't sure the care worker understood), saying he'd call back later. After two hours, having heard nothing, Ian tried again and was told bluntly, 'No doctor.' But later that evening, with plans to change their flights to the following day so they could return home as soon as possible, they received a phone call from Dr Ciobanu.

Ian steeled himself to say what he had to; he wasn't an aggressive man and avoided confrontation, but this needed to be said. Yet before he had a chance, Dr Ciobanu said, 'Mr Hudson, I'm sorry I wasn't there to meet you today but my wife was taken to hospital.'

Thrown, Ian said, 'Oh, I see. I hope it's nothing serious.'

'It wasn't, thank you. A funny turn. She is home now. If you come to the orphanage tomorrow morning you can meet your child.'

'I don't understand,' Ian said, shocked and confused. 'We were told our baby was dead.' Elaine moved closer to the handset so she, too, could hear.

'Yes, Lana died,' the doctor said evenly. 'She was a sickly baby so perhaps it was for the best that it happened here, rather than when you got home. I have another child. She is not sickly. You come here tomorrow and I will arrange it.' Ian glanced at Elaine, not knowing what to say. 'You come tomorrow and we go ahead,' he repeated. Taken completely unawares, Ian looked at Elaine for direction. 'You come here tomorrow at eleven and meet Anastasia. Now I have to go to my wife. Good night.' The line went dead.

CHAPTER TWO

ANOTHER CHANCE?

Elaine and Ian were up most of that night discussing what had happened and what they should do. Prior to the doctor's phone call they'd decided to bring forward their flight and return home childless, yet now they were being offered the chance of another child, reigniting their hopes of having a family of their own. They were calmer now but still had big concerns. This new child, Anastasia, had appeared very quickly, and with no background information they were imagining all sorts of horrifying scenarios, including that she could have been abducted from her natural family or the parents might have been put under pressure or even paid to give her up. Yet while the care worker they'd seen the day before probably didn't have the authority to find them another child, Dr Ciobanu certainly did. He was a recognized professional in the adoption process in this country and had been recommended to them by other couples who had successfully adopted through him.

Ian and Elaine talked themselves round in circles. They knew nothing about Anastasia, yet other couples had told them not to place too much emphasis on any details given before they'd seen the child, especially the child's birthday.

Record keeping was haphazard in this country, and if a woman gave birth in a remote village it could take her weeks to register the child or get to the orphanage. Also, children going for adoption were portrayed in the best possible light, as developing countries such as this one relied on international adoption to take their orphaned and abandoned children. There was a lot to consider, but in the early hours they decided they would visit Dr Ciobanu as he'd asked and at least hear what he had to say about Anastasia, and take it from there.

'Perhaps it will be all right,' Elaine said hopefully as she finally drifted off to sleep.

'Whatever the outcome, I will always love you,' Ian replied.

They were awake again at 5 a.m., showered and dressed, and then went down for breakfast as soon as the restaurant opened at 6.30 a.m. On the way through the lobby Ian stopped off at reception and booked a cab to pick them up at 10.30. The hotel had been recommended by Dr Ciobanu and the cab firm it used had experience of ferrying couples who were adopting.

There were only four others in the restaurant having breakfast at that time, all businessmen in suits. The hotel had thirty rooms, and although it had been recommended by the doctor, as far as Elaine and Ian knew they were the only would-be adopters staying at present. Some of the staff knew why they were there, and when they'd checked in the receptionist had said she would arrange for a cot to be put in their room once the adoption had gone through.

Unsurprisingly, Elaine had little appetite that morning and only managed half a croissant and a cup of coffee. Ian, who showed his anxiety in different ways, had scrambled eggs on toast, but kept checking his phone and nervously straightening the napkin on his lap. Neither of them spoke. Not only were they exhausted from the emotion of the day before and too little sleep, but there was also nothing left to say. Either they still had a chance of adopting or they'd return home as they'd arrived – a couple and not a family.

During breakfast an email came through to Ian's phone from one of the families they'd got to know online who were also going through the process of adopting. They were eager to know how the meeting with Lana had gone. 'I'll reply later,' Ian said. 'I can't face it now.'

After breakfast, they returned to their hotel room and tried to read the books they'd brought with them, but concentrating was near impossible. At 10.20 they were in the lobby waiting for the cab. They knew that little happened on time in this country – sometimes it happened earlier but more often late. The cab arrived at 10.40; not the same driver as the day before but he knew why they were there. Elaine and Ian would have liked to be left to their thoughts during the journey, but the driver was chatty and direct.

'You going to adopt?' he asked almost as soon as they got in.

'We're not sure,' Ian replied.

'Why not?' He glanced in the rear-view mirror, puzzled. Elaine moved out of his line of vision so she didn't have to talk.

'Our baby was very sick and died,' Ian said.

'Oh. I'm sorry. They find you another one?'

'Possibly.'

'Boy or girl?'

'Girl,' Ian said.

'I have children, a boy and a girl,' the driver continued amicably as he drove. 'You meet your child today?'

'Maybe, we don't know yet,' Ian replied. Elaine gazed out of her side window. Although international adoption was well known in this country, it was still a source of interest to the locals, possibly because adoption wasn't part of their culture, hence all the state-run orphanages. They didn't adopt or foster and didn't really understand why anyone would.

'Many couples adopt from here,' the driver said as he drove.

'Yes, I know,' Ian agreed.

'This is your first trip here?'

'Yes.'

'Some couples come back two, three times to adopt. They must like our children a lot.' He grinned and Ian met his gaze in the mirror with a polite smile. 'I take one couple three times to orphanages,' he continued. 'They from America. They adopt brothers and sisters. Six in all! Very good people with lots of money.'

Ian nodded. 'But we don't have lots of money. We saved up to make this trip.'

'You good people too.'

Yet while it was a strain having to make conversation, hearing about successful adoptions was heartening and proof that the system did work. Perhaps they had just been very unlucky and it would work out in the end. Perhaps.

It was 11.15 when the cab pulled up in the lane outside the orphanage. Ian opened the door to get out. 'You wait here?' he asked the driver.

'Yes. No rush. Very important you spend time with your child.'

There wasn't a meter running – cab journeys were quoted in advance and included any waiting time. Elaine joined Ian in front of the high metal gate as the driver wound down his window and lit up a cigarette. A wire-netting fence ran all around the perimeter of the orphanage, with a patch of land separating it from the building. This strip of land would have made a good outside children's play area had it not been so badly overgrown. Ian rattled the metal gate – the only way of attracting attention, as there wasn't a bell – and they waited. There'd been some rain in the night, and although the sun wasn't out the humidity had risen. Elaine knocked away a fly.

'They come soon,' the driver said, and sounded his car horn.

The door to the orphanage opened and the care worker who'd dealt with them the day before came out, keys on the short chain at her waist. Elaine took a deep breath. She really didn't like the woman. Without acknowledging them, the care worker nodded to the driver and unlocked the gate. 'Thank you,' Ian said, and they waited just inside while she locked the gate. They then followed her up the cracked cement path and in through the main door, which again she locked behind them.

'You wait here,' she said brusquely, and disappeared down the corridor, her shoes clipping heavily on the hard, tiled floor. A solitary child screamed in the distance and Ian threw Elaine a reassuring smile.

A few minutes later Dr Ciobanu appeared from the corridor. Although they'd never met him, they recognized him from his photograph online. In his mid-forties, of average height and build, he was wearing a dark suit with an open-neck shirt.

'Pleased to meet you,' he said pleasantly and, smiling, shook Elaine's hand, then Ian's. 'So you decided to give me another chance?' Ian nodded awkwardly. 'No worries,' he said, clapping Ian on the arm. 'Come through to my office and we can talk.'

His office overlooked the front of the orphanage, and through the window they could see their cab waiting in the lane. Dr Ciobanu motioned for them to sit down. The room was small and cramped, with an old wooden table acting as a desk in the centre, and three chairs. Filing cabinets lined one wall and a fan stood on top of one beside an open bottle of water. 'Would you like a drink?' the doctor offered, going to the bottle.

'No, thank you,' they both said politely. The bottle would very likely have been refilled with tap water, and while this was safe for locals to drink – they'd built up a resistance to its bacteria – it upset foreigners' stomachs.

Placing his tumbler of water on the table, Dr Ciobanu opened the top drawer of a filing cabinet and removed a folder. 'Your paperwork,' he said, returning to sit behind the table. He carefully opened the file before him. Elaine and Ian saw the top page was their initial application sent a year ago, with passport-sized photographs of both of them.

'I have the rest of the paperwork you need in my briefcase,' Ian said.

Dr Ciobanu nodded and then, folding his arms, leaned forward in earnest. 'I am sorry you were disappointed yesterday. It is not good practice to have a couple arrive and find the child is no longer with us. It is a pity I could not be here to tell you personally. We are very short-staffed and my two care workers have no time for breaking bad news gently.'

He threw them a knowing smile and Ian, at least, started to relax.

'As I said last night on the phone,' the doctor continued, 'Lana was a very sick baby. We did our best to save her but it wasn't enough. She died peacefully in her sleep.'

'What was the matter with her?' Elaine asked, her voice slight.

'She wouldn't feed, something wrong in her gut, but you needn't worry about that. We have to look to your future.' His gaze went from one to the other, gauging their reaction, and Ian nodded. 'I do not have a photograph yet of Anastasia. She has only just been given up for adoption. But she is healthy and you can see her shortly. Her mother works abroad a lot, as many single women here have to. She has been leaving her with us since she was a baby. Now the mother has met a man who is going to marry her, so she will be leaving this country for good for a better life.'

'And she can't take her child with her?' Elaine asked, horrified.

'No. It happens,' Dr Ciobanu said matter-of-factly. 'The man may not even know she has a child. The mother believes her daughter will be better off here in the orphanage, as many parents in this country do.' He sighed with exasperation, as though he didn't agree with this. 'I will explain to the mother that her daughter will have a better life being adopted by you, rather than being left here.'

'So the child isn't free for adoption yet?' Ian asked.

'No, but she soon will be. I will speak to the mother today and get her to sign the forms, which I will take to the court personally.' Elaine and Ian knew that this wasn't so unusual. Part of the doctor's role was as an adoption facilitator –

arranging and completing the formalities of adoption as well as advising the adopters on procedure. 'The court will set a hearing date and once the adoption has gone through you will be issued with a new birth certificate, passport and visa for the child.' This was standard and what would have happened with Lana's adoption had she lived.

'How long will all this take if we decide to go ahead?' Ian asked. 'With Lana we were already a long way through the process. It would have been completed in three to four weeks. I have to work; we can't stay here indefinitely.' He hoped this didn't sound abrupt but they had to be practical.

The doctor gave a small shrug. 'It shouldn't take too long. The legal system in this country can run slowly at times, but I will do everything in my power to speed things up.' Which didn't really tell them much.

'How old is the child?' Elaine finally thought to ask, overwhelmed.

'Two and a quarter,' the doctor said, glancing at a hand-written note tucked into their file. 'Don't worry, I will make sure you have all the correct paperwork for her, including a medical.'

'She's a lot older than Lana,' Elaine said.

'Yes, but she is strong and healthy. Why don't you come and meet her? I am sure you will be happy.' Dr Ciobanu immediately stood. He was used to having his word acted on, although he came across as caring. Ian and Elaine knew he only charged the minimum for his services, while some adoption facilitators were growing rich on the proceeds of international adoption, although no money reached the natural parents. It was illegal to give them anything – gifts or money.

Elaine's heart missed a beat as she tucked her hand into Ian's and they followed Dr Ciobanu out of his office. Could it possibly be? The moment they'd anticipated, worked towards and dreamed of for so long? Was it possible that after all the ups and downs and disappointments, they were going to meet a child who could be theirs? Ian's hand tightened in hers and Elaine knew he was as nervous as she was.

CHAPTER THREE

ANXIOUS

'Anastasia!' Dr Ciobanu announced brightly, leading them to a cot in the second nursery room. Ian and Elaine met the child's inquisitive gaze with a mixture of awe and apprehension. Clearly not a baby, but an apparently healthy, bouncing child with personality and gusto. She was pulling on the bars of the cot as though demanding to be let out, and was so different to the nine-month-old baby they'd come to adopt, it took them a minute to adjust.

'Say hello to your new mummy and daddy,' Dr Ciobanu told her.

Anastasia babbled something in her own language.

'What did she say?' Elaine asked.

'It was just baby talk,' the doctor replied. 'Don't worry, she will quickly learn English and forget her life here.'

'Hello,' Elaine said tentatively, taking a step closer to the cot. Ian joined her. Anastasia looked at them and they looked back. It was one of the most touching and surreal moments of their lives as they were presented with this little stranger who could shortly become their daughter. 'Why is she in a cot?' Elaine asked, without taking her gaze from Anastasia.

'To keep her safe,' Dr Ciobanu replied. 'She is an active child and would be gone from here given the chance.'

'I don't blame her,' Ian quipped, which helped ease the tension.

'I'll get her out and you can see how active she is,' Dr Ciobanu said. Reaching over the cot side, he lifted out the child and set her on the floor. As soon as her bare feet touched the ground she made a dash for the exit. Dr Ciobanu called out something in her language and she stopped. 'You mustn't go out. It's not safe,' he repeated to her in English. She threw him an almost defiant look, but it was so quaint on the face of a cherubic two-year-old that they all laughed.

She was like a life-sized porcelain doll, Elaine thought, with her pale skin, clear blue eyes and fair hair, and wearing a little floral dress that was really far too small. But she did look healthy and robust, which was so important after what had happened to poor little Lana. Moving away from the door, Anastasia went to the closest cot and, peering through the bars, began talking to the child. He was very disabled and lay motionless on his back, staring up at the ceiling, his misshapen limbs jutting out at odd angles.

'He's blind and deaf,' Dr Ciobanu said with a heartfelt sigh. 'We do what we can, but …' He left the sentence unfinished.

It was as heartbreaking now for Elaine and Ian to see these children as it had been the day before. Although they hadn't been in this room, it was similar to the others, and the major-ity of the children in the cots seemed to have a severe physical and/or mental disability. Elaine felt a pang of guilt for want-ing a healthy child, but she knew her limitations – she couldn't cope with a badly disabled child. That took a very special person. For some moments they watched, spellbound, as Anastasia went from cot to cot, babbling to the infants in her own language and gently stroking their foreheads or holding their hands through the bars. Only a few responded by shifting their gaze to her; most lay unresponsive and continued to stare blankly into space as though they weren't aware she was even there.

'Can we take Anastasia outside and play ball for a while?' Elaine asked. The room was oppressive.

'Possibly tomorrow,' Dr Ciobanu said. 'Today is just for you to meet her. I will speak to the mother and then you can come back tomorrow and play with Anastasia.' Which they had to accept, and it seemed reasonable that the doctor would want to speak to the mother first to gain her consent to start the adoption process. 'Don't worry,' he said, clapping Ian on the shoulder. 'All will be well, I promise you.'

They continued to watch Anastasia for a while longer as she went from cot to cot. How Elaine would have loved to pick her up and carry her home there and then, for the bonding process had begun and she was already feeling protective towards her.

Dr Ciobanu made a move to go. 'So you come back tomorrow,' he said.

'Yes, of course. What time?' Ian asked.

'I'll phone you in the morning in your hotel room to let you know.' He then called down the corridor for a care worker. 'Anastasia can stay out of her cot for now,' he said to them. 'She can help. She likes to help.'

A different care worker appeared, but seemed no less harsh and abrasive in her manner than the other one. Dr Ciobanu said something to her in their own language and then called

Anastasia, presumably to go with the care worker. Anastasia pretended not to hear and stayed by the cot. 'Now, please,' the doctor said firmly, then repeated it in her own language. Anastasia dutifully turned and went over to the care worker. Elaine's heart clenched.

'Goodbye, love,' she called after her. 'See you tomorrow.' But Anastasia didn't reply, because of course she hadn't understood.

'You can teach her English when you visit,' Dr Ciobanu said, beginning towards the door. 'She will learn quickly. She is bright.'

'Yes,' Ian agreed, much happier now.

Anastasia and the care worker were already out of sight as the doctor led the way to the main door. 'Do you want our paperwork now?' Ian asked, having brought it with them in his briefcase.

'Tomorrow will do. We have plenty of time.'

'But not too long, I hope,' Ian said.

The doctor smiled. 'Don't worry. You enjoy your stay here, see some of our beautiful country and let me take care of the rest.' He unlocked the door and they followed him down the path, where he let them out of the main gate, saying hello to their cab driver.

'So you'll phone us tomorrow morning to let us know what time we have to come?' Ian confirmed. He would have liked a firm time but had to accept that things ran differently in this country.

'Of course.' Dr Ciobanu shook their hands and then returned inside as Elaine and Ian climbed into the back of the cab.

'You look happier,' the driver said.

'We are,' Ian replied, taking Elaine's hand.

'You met your daughter?' the driver asked, starting the engine.

'We did,' they chimed. For although they hadn't actually had that conversation, they both instinctively knew that to adopt Anastasia was the right decision. They were beside themselves with joy.

The driver dropped them off at their hotel and they went briefly to their room to freshen up, then had a light lunch in the hotel, including a glass of wine to celebrate. While they ate, Ian messaged those who knew they were there and were waiting for news, telling them only that they had met their daughter and everything was fine. They would fill in the details about Lana's passing and Anastasia when they returned home. For now, this was the update their friends were waiting for, and his and Elaine's phones buzzed with messages of congratulations and good luck.

They spent the afternoon walking around the local area, gazing into shop windows and down side alleys, and visiting the street market. They took lots of photographs. Although it was their first visit to the country, they'd read up about it and researched online and wanted pictures of the area to show Anastasia when she was older. The social worker who'd assessed them for their suitability to adopt and compiled their Home Study report had emphasized how important it was for adopted children to know their roots. She said they had to be completely honest with the child from the start and recommended they compile a Life Story Book and Memory Box, which they'd already begun, having taken photographs of the departure board at the airport and saved their boarding cards. They'd take photographs of Anastasia tomorrow and, if they were allowed, of the orphanage too. They'd keep the clothes she wore here and anything else significant or of sentimental value that would help give her a better understanding of her past. Elaine had also begun a diary of their journey through the adoption process, confiding their hopes and feelings from when they'd made that first phone call enquiring about adoption. Anastasia would know as much about her past as possible, just like the social worker had said, although possibly not about Lana. She must never feel second best.

That evening, after dinner, they sat in their hotel room with a phrase book and tried to learn some of the language, but it was a very difficult language to learn and they laughed at their feeble attempts to pronounce the words. Thankfully Dr Ciobanu spoke very good English, and it was important that Anastasia learned English as soon as possible, so learning the local language for them was fun rather than necessary.

They were in bed early and slept well. Nevertheless, they were downstairs at 7 a.m. having breakfast, excited at the prospect of spending time with Anastasia, and not wanting to miss Dr Ciobanu's phone call. As soon as they'd finished eating they returned to their room. Although Dr Ciobanu had both their mobile numbers, the network service in this country was notoriously haphazard and expensive, and they knew that most professions preferred to use landlines where possible.

The morning slowly ticked by. The maid knocked on their door to make up their room but they thanked her and told her not to bother today. The phone stayed perversely silent and by noon, when Dr Ciobanu still hadn't called, doubt and anxiety set in.

'He definitely said he'd phone in the morning,' Elaine said, 'and the morning has gone now.'

'Perhaps he got held up or called away,' Ian offered.

'Or perhaps Anastasia's mother has refused to give consent and is taking Anastasia with her,' Elaine said, voicing her worst fears. 'If so, I can't go through this again, Ian. I can't. We forget about it and go home.'

'We don't know that,' Ian said, trying to be rational. 'Let's assume for now that no news is good news.'

Elaine wasn't reassured. 'Dr Ciobanu said we could visit this afternoon but before long it's going to be too late. We can't just sit here waiting indefinitely.'

'But we know from other couples that there is a lot of waiting and hanging around,' Ian reminded her.

'But that was waiting for the court date,' she said, irritable from worry.

'All right, calm down. We'll give him another hour and then I'll phone at one o'clock.'

The hour passed, the phone didn't ring and their unease increased.

'Shall I phone or will you?' Elaine snapped at 1.05.

'I will,' Ian said, but went to use the bathroom first.

Elaine would have liked to give Dr Ciobanu a piece of her mind for causing them all this extra stress. International adoption was emotional and fraught even when it ran smoothly. But neither she nor Ian would criticize the doctor to his face, as they were relying on him to give them what they wanted more than anything in the world – a child of their own. He could keep them waiting for as long as he wanted and they had to put up with it.

Returning from the bathroom, Ian sat beside Elaine on the edge of the bed and pressed the speaker button on the phone so they could both hear the conversation. He keyed in the number to the orphanage and to their surprise it was answered straight away by Dr Ciobanu.

'It's Ian Hudson,' he said, a slight tremor in his voice.

'Hello. How are you?' the doctor asked jovially, apparently oblivious to the worry he'd caused them. Elaine wrung her hands in her lap.

'We're OK,' Ian said. 'But we were expecting you to phone this morning about our visit this afternoon.'

'Yes, come here tomorrow with your paperwork.'

'Not today?' Ian asked.

'No. I have a visitor from the government coming this afternoon. Tomorrow is good.' Which again they had to accept.

'All right. So everything went well with the mother?'

'Yes.'

'She has consented to the adoption?'

'Yes, of course. You and your wife will have to learn to trust me. I know what I am doing.'

'Yes, I'm sure you do. I'm sorry,' Ian said quickly. 'We're just very anxious, having lost Lana. We couldn't bear another loss.'

'And you won't have to. Come here tomorrow at two and you can spend time with your daughter.'

'Thank you so much.'

'You're welcome.'

CHAPTER FOUR

ANASTASIA

With their confidence in Dr Ciobanu restored, and looking forward to seeing Anastasia again, Elaine and Ian passed the following morning with a visit to the local supermarket. It wasn't a large shop but it was crammed full of every type of good imaginable, including groceries, pharmaceuticals, underwear and socks, toys, beer, hardware and numerous miscellaneous items. There was also a box of Christmas decorations, even though it was only August. They bought bottled water, and some bread and ham for their lunch, as it was too expensive to keep eating in the hotel and there weren't any cheap restaurants or cafés close by. They also found a colouring book, crayons and a doll for Anastasia. Lana would have been too young for these – they had packed nappies, baby food and first-year toys for her, which were still in the suitcase. They'd also brought with them clothes to fit Lana that would be far too small for Anastasia. They'd have to buy more here before the adoption, as they knew the children often arrived at court only with what they stood up in.

They returned to their hotel room to eat their picnic-style lunch, and then with Elaine carrying the bag of toys for Anastasia and Ian his briefcase containing the paperwork for Dr Ciobanu, they waited in the lobby for the cab. They'd booked it for fifteen minutes earlier than it needed to be, to allow time for it being late, so in fact it arrived to collect them on time. 'I've cracked it!' Ian joked to Elaine, and she laughed conspiratorially. How much happier they were now.

It was the same driver they'd had on their first trip to the orphanage and he greeted them like long lost friends, shaking their hands warmly and asking how they were. 'Perhaps we're tipping him too much,' Ian whispered to Elaine as they climbed into the cab.

But it was rather nice – reassuring – to see a familiar friendly face in a country where they knew no one and didn't speak the language. He was eager to know what had happened since he'd last seen them, when they'd arrived at the orphanage to be told Lana was dead. Ian briefly explained about meeting the doctor and Anastasia the day before and that the adoption was going ahead. The driver was very pleased for them and didn't seem to mind that they weren't using the lady his cousin knew. 'So I'll be seeing lots of you,' he said, for he knew the procedure. Couples usually visited the child most days while they waited for the adoption to go through.

He parked outside the orphanage, and as Ian and Elaine got out he wished them luck and confirmed he would be waiting for them when they came out – it didn't matter how long they were. Trying to summon a cab outside the towns and cities was highly unreliable and most cab drivers were happy to wait for hours if necessary. It added a little to their income and saved the clients a lot of aggravation.

Ian rattled the gate to alert the staff to their presence and the driver gave a blast of the car horn. A few moments later Dr Ciobanu appeared.

'Good afternoon,' he called brightly, coming down the path. He unlocked the gate and warmly shook their hands and said hello to the driver. 'So are we all good?' he asked Ian and Elaine as they followed him inside.

'Yes, thank you,' they replied.

'You slept well? And the hotel is comfortable?' he asked, showing them into his office.

'Yes, it's fine, thank you,' Ian said. Although staying in the hotel was purely practical. They'd been warned that the cheaper guest houses were very basic and unclean and the court wouldn't be happy knowing the child would be taken to one of them. There would be at least a week between the adoption order being granted and the adoption papers, her passport and visa being issued. During which time Anastasia would be with them. While many children lived in far worse conditions than those found in guest houses, the courts expected better from the adoptive parents.

The orphanage was quiet as usual, and Ian and Elaine sat at the table in Dr Ciobanu's office as he offered them a glass of water, which they politely refused. He sat opposite them, their folder and other paperwork on the table in front of him. 'So I have spoken to Anastasia's mother,' he said, taking a sip of his water. 'She has agreed to you seeing the child for an hour each day before the adoption, but she has requested you do not take her outside.'

'OK,' Ian said. 'Can I ask why?'

'It's normal. The mothers are concerned you may abduct or harm the child.' They nodded. 'She has also asked that she has new clothes. Again, this is usual. She is very poor and what we have at the orphanage is basic. You have brought some with you?'

'Yes,' Elaine said. It was on their instruction sheet. 'But they were for Lana. They are far too small for Anastasia. We were looking at some children's clothes this morning at the local supermarket but they didn't have much choice.'

'No. I will give you the address of a proper children's shop in town. You can go there.' He scribbled the address on the notepad, tore it off and passed it to Elaine. 'It's about a twenty-minute cab ride from your hotel. The driver will know where it is.'

'Thank you,' Elaine said, and tucked the paper carefully into her bag.

'The clothes you brought with you for the other child you can donate to the orphanage,' Dr Ciobanu said. 'We rely on donations.'

'Yes, of course,' Ian said, although he would have liked to have been asked rather than instructed. They both knew the doctor wasn't being rude; it was just the way so many people in this country talked. They issued instructions rather than requests, so it could sound very curt and abrupt.

'Give me your paperwork now, please,' Dr Ciobanu said. 'You have brought the originals?'

'Yes,' Ian said. Unclipping his briefcase, he handed the file to the doctor. In it was their Home Study report compiled over eight months by their social worker, Certificate of Eligibility to adopt, medical reports, references, bank and mortgage statements (showing they could afford to look after a child) and police checks. All of which had been notarized and translated. Ian had another complete set in his briefcase in case any went missing. Photocopies of the documents had already been sent, but the court required the originals.

They waited patiently as Dr Ciobanu turned the pages, checking everything was there. 'Good,' he said, flicking through the last few. 'It seems to be in order. Now you need to sign these forms so I can process them.' He opened the second file and placed various forms in front of them, which they both signed. They weren't translated but Ian and Elaine knew what they were and had been expecting them. 'Your request to adopt Anastasia,' Dr Ciobanu confirmed, 'and in this one you appoint me to represent you and act on your behalf.' The last form was a donation to the orphanage and an amount equivalent to £500 had been entered. Again, this was standard and they'd been expecting it.

'Do you want the donation now?' Elaine asked. The doctor nodded. She opened her handbag and took out an envelope containing the local currency and passed it to him.

'And the second payment for you arrived in your account?' Ian asked.

'I haven't checked but I am sure it has,' the doctor said. They'd had to send an initial payment for the doctor's services when they'd first instructed him and then a second payment to cover the court fees before they arrived. But these fees were small compared to what they'd already spent at home on their Home Study, Certificate of Eligibility, notarization, medicals, etc. All in all, including accommodation and travel, they estimated they would spend in the region of £25,000 for the adoption. A lot of money to them, but obviously worth every penny.

'So now you have time with Anastasia,' Dr Ciobanu said. Standing, he tucked the envelope into his inside jacket pocket.

'I will bank this later and give you a receipt. Come this way. Anastasia is in the playroom.'

Their hopes rose at the mention of a playroom, but fell again as soon as they entered the room. It was very small and mostly empty. The only furniture was a beanbag in one corner, on which Anastasia sat waiting. Beside her were a few old and broken toys.

'Hello, love,' Elaine said, going over and sitting beside her on the floor. Anastasia was wearing the same dress as the day before.

'I'll leave you to it then,' Dr Ciobanu said. 'Let someone know when it is time for you to go.'

'Thank you,' Ian said. Dr Ciobanu closed the door behind them.

'How are you, love?' Elaine asked gently. Ian joined them on the floor, setting his briefcase to one side.

Anastasia stared at them and then tugged at the carrier bag looped over Elaine's arm.

'Oh, you'd like to see what I have in here, would you?' Elaine asked, pleased. 'Of course. These are for you.' She took out the doll and placed it in Anastasia's lap. 'Doll,' Elaine said. 'For Anastasia. Can you say doll? Doll.' She knew that children learned language through imitation and repetition, but Anastasia was more interested in what else was in the carrier bag.

'Crayons,' Elaine said, handing her the packet of wax crayons. 'And a colouring book.' She set it on the floor and stuffed the empty carrier bag into her pocket. Although Anastasia was only two and a quarter, Elaine and Ian had friends with children of a similar age who managed to hold a crayon and make large swirls of different colours. But Anastasia had never seen a crayon close up before, let alone used one. She spent some moments examining the packet and then, selecting the red crayon, put it in her mouth.

'No, love,' Elaine said, stopping her. 'It's not to eat. It's a crayon, we use it for colouring in. I'll show you.' She took another crayon from the packet and passed one to Ian, and together they began colouring in the first picture in the book, which was of a teddy bear wearing a spotted hat and scarf.

Anastasia watched intently for a while, then lost interest and, dropping the crayon, picked up the doll. 'Doll,' Elaine said. 'You like the doll?' Anastasia stared at them as though wondering who on earth these strangers were and why they were here.

'It must be so difficult for her,' Ian said. 'I hope Dr Ciobanu has tried to explain to her what is happening.'

'I would think he has,' Elaine said, concentrating on Anastasia.

Suddenly Anastasia jumped up and, still holding the doll, ran to the window. Ian and Elaine followed her. The only redemptive feature of the room was a large window that looked out to the woods at the back of the orphanage. There were bars at the window and the glass was dirty, but it gave more natural light than the small grids in the nursery rooms and the view was encouraging. Anastasia reached one hand through the bars and banged on the glass with her little fist, then looked up at them imploringly. She didn't need language to make herself understood.

'We can't go outside,' Elaine said gently. 'One day we will after we've been to court.' Anastasia banged on the glass again and then held up the doll so she could have a glimpse of the outside. It was touching and upsetting. Anastasia hadn't spent all her life in the orphanage as many of the other children had – some of it had been with her mother – so she knew a very different world lay out there. 'Come on, let's do some colouring,' Elaine encouraged, but Anastasia remained glued to the window.

'I don't think she has been in this room before,' Ian said. 'She's fascinated by the window.'

'No,' Elaine agreed. 'I get the feeling she spends most of her time in that cot or helping in those so-called nurseries.' Elaine's eyes filled. Although they'd been aware of the conditions at these orphanages, it still hurt and angered them to see it for themselves.

'But we mustn't say anything,' Ian reminded her. 'They don't like criticism.' Which was one of the reasons change in social care had been slow.

Elaine bent down to Anastasia's height. 'We'll take you out as soon as we can, love. We are going to visit lots and lots of places when we go home. Parks, the seaside, the zoo, activity centres and, when you are older, museums and castles. But for now we have to stay here. Let's play with the doll.' Elaine gently drew Anastasia from the window and to the beanbag, where she sat beside her.

It was a very basic, cheap-looking doll, but it was all the store had. Its dress was held on by Velcro and Elaine now showed Anastasia how to dress and undress the doll. Anastasia liked the tearing noise the Velcro made and spent some time sticking and unsticking it. Then she spotted Ian's briefcase and made a grab for that.

'Do you want to see inside?' he asked, smiling. Anastasia tugged at the flap. 'OK, I'll show you, but you can't have what's in it. They are very important papers, about you.'

Ian unfastened the clip and allowed Anastasia to peer in, but he needn't have worried about her wanting the papers and files – they were of no interest to a two-year-old, regardless of how important they might be. Anastasia was up again and at the window.

'Come on and we'll do some crayoning,' Elaine said, going over. Anastasia tapped on the glass and looked at her imploringly again. 'We can't go out,' Elaine said, shaking her head to signal no. 'Let's play with the doll again.' But even as she said it, it was clear that all the child's hopes lay in being allowed to go out. 'What about these toys?' Elaine said, going over to the broken toy cars and four plastic building pots that were already in the room. Anastasia glanced over to where Elaine pointed and then returned her attention to the window.

'I don't know what else to do,' Elaine said to Ian. 'We'll have to buy some more interesting toys when we go shopping.' Then she had a thought. Opening her handbag, she took out her mobile phone and went into the Photo Gallery. 'Look, Anastasia, pictures!'

The child's interest was piqued. She turned from the window to look, then allowed Elaine to lead her to the beanbag where she sat between them and they spent a pleasant ten minutes going through the photographs.

'Well done,' Ian said to Elaine. 'When she's finished with yours we can look at the photos on my phone.'

So the hour passed with photographs, some colouring, sticking and unsticking the Velcro on the doll's dress, and visits to the window. While Ian and Elaine had thought an hour was a very short time to spend with their future daughter when it had first been mentioned, now it seemed appropriate. They were emotionally exhausted and had also used up their resources so that Anastasia had grown bored with what they had to offer. As well as gazing out of the window she kept looking towards the door, perhaps wondering when it would be opened. When the hour was up and they told her it was time for them to go and went to find someone to tell them they were leaving, she didn't resist. Far from it. She seemed pleased to see the care worker again and ran to her side, but of course what is familiar feels safe to a young child. Elaine and Ian said goodbye to Anastasia, and the care worker issued an instruction to Anastasia. Without looking back, she ran off into one of the rooms and the care worker saw them out.

As they collapsed into the back of the cab the driver said, 'First few visits always difficult. You and child strangers. It will get better. I bring a lot of couples here and they look like you to begin with – shell-shocked.'

Ian and Elaine laughed, relieved. 'That's the word – shell-shocked,' Ian said. 'You speak a lot of sense.'

'You tell my wife that!' the driver replied with a cheeky grin.

CHAPTER FIVE

SHOCKED AND SADDENED

B ack in their hotel room, Ian and Elaine went over the time they'd spent with Anastasia, holding a post-mortem on the things they felt they'd got right and those they hadn't.

'It will get easier each time we see her,' Ian said. It wasn't just the driver who'd said this, but other families who'd adopted. They'd warned them not to expect too much during the first week of introductions and to just go with what the child felt comfortable with. This had also been covered during the three-day preparation course they'd had to attend in the UK as part of their adoption assessment.

Ian booked cabs for the following day, one for 9.30 a.m. to take them to the children's store Dr Ciobanu had recommended in town, and the other to the orphanage for 2 p.m. Using public transport wasn't an option, as buses were infrequent and unreliable. They were going to donate Lana's belongings to the orphanage as Dr Ciobanu had suggested, so that night as Ian showered before bed Elaine sorted through their suitcases, carefully taking out what they'd packed for Lana that couldn't be used for Anastasia: clothes, nappies, baby toys, packets of milk and food, dummy and so on. There was a lot; they'd brought extra in case they got delayed in the country, and had distributed it between both their cases. Now, as Elaine carefully put Lana's belongings into carrier bags she kept finding herself overcome with emotion and had to stop to wipe away her tears. Although other children would bene-fit from their donation, these things had been bought specifi-cally for Lana. Elaine remembered the joy she'd felt when choosing the little clothes and toys and carefully packing them in the cases. There were other first-year baby items at home and Elaine would sort out those when they returned.

By the time Ian came out of the shower the items they were donating to the orphanage were in carrier bags ready for the next day, apart from one teddy bear – a special bear they'd had personalized with Lana's name.

'Do you think we could visit Lana's grave?' Elaine asked Ian as she held the bear. 'I'd like to put this on her grave if possible.'

'That's a lovely idea. We'll ask Dr Ciobanu,' Ian said, giving her a hug. Elaine wasn't the only one with tears in her eyes.

The following morning they woke feeling refreshed and in a positive frame of mind. They knew there would be a lot of waiting around as the legal wheels turned in international adoption, but today they'd be busy and productive. A different cab driver took them to the children's store in town and showed them where to catch a cab back, reassuring them that it would be easy to find a cab at the stand so he didn't need to wait. The shop selling children's goods was one of four large stores set side by side and back from the main road. They were clearly upmarket, with dazzling, brightly lit window displays, and their goods would only be affordable to a few. The other three sold furniture, carpets and electrical goods.

Inside the children's store, Ian and Elaine wandered up and down the aisles of carefully laid out merchandise. It was so unlike any of the other local shops they'd seen during their stay so far, with smartly dressed assistants on hand to help. It sold everything imaginable for babies and young children: good-quality goods, mostly imported and therefore very expensive. Using the calculator on Ian's phone, they converted the prices into pounds as they went. Most of the goods were at least double what they would have paid at home but they weren't surprised that Dr Ciobanu had sent them to such an expensive store. It was widely thought in countries that practised international adoption that those adopting must be very wealthy, although in fact most had average incomes and had saved up to finance the trip, forgoing holidays and similar, remortgaging their home or taking out a bank loan. But of course compared to the locals they were wealthy.

They needed clothes for Anastasia and bought seven outfits to see her through the next three to four weeks, assuming they could be washed, and some toys, all of which Ian paid for on his credit card.

That afternoon they had the same cab driver as on their first and previous day's visits to the orphanage, and he told them his name was Daniel – Danny for short. Ian was carrying the bags of Lana's belongings and Elaine the items they were taking that day for Anastasia: three sets of clothes, underwear, pyjamas, sandals and some of the toys – an activity centre and two jigsaw puzzles. They'd decided not to take everything they'd bought for her in one go, as it could be overwhelming for Anastasia and also it would have to be stored somewhere in the orphanage.

Danny parked outside the orphanage, sounded the car's horn to draw attention, and Ian and Elaine were let in by the care worker they'd seen the day before, who managed a small nod. They'd only seen two care workers so far in the orphanage for all thirty children.

'Dr Ciobanu?' Ian asked the care worker once they were inside and pointed to his office. 'Is he here?' She shook her head. 'These are for the orphanage,' Ian said, showing her the carrier bags of Lana's belongings. 'Clothes and toys for the children.'

She nodded. 'I take them,' she said, apparently understanding.

'Thank you.' He passed her the carrier bags.

'These clothes are for Anastasia,' Elaine said, holding up the bag containing her clothes. 'Where shall I put them?'

'I take them,' the care worker said again, and Elaine handed her the bag. They'd left the teddy bear with Lana's name on it in their hotel room and they'd ask Dr Ciobanu when they next saw him if it would be possible to put it on Lana's grave.

'Where is Anastasia?' Elaine now asked.

The care worker nodded in the direction of the 'playroom' and they went in. She wasn't there. The stained and faded beanbag and small heap of broken toys sat forlornly where they'd been the day before. 'The care worker has probably gone to fetch her,' Ian said, looking round.

A minute or so later a child's footsteps could be heard running down the corridor, then Anastasia flew into the room. She looked pleased to see them.

'Hello, love,' Elaine said, going to her. 'How are you?' The care worker closed the door behind her.

Anastasia spotted the carrier bag Elaine held and, remembering that a similar bag had held gifts the day before, tugged at it.

'Yes, they are for you,' Elaine said, smiling, and took out the activity centre. 'Come on, let's sit down and we'll show you how it works.'

Intrigued, Anastasia went with them and sat beside Elaine on the beanbag as Ian sat on the floor on the other side of her. Elaine placed the activity centre on Anastasia's lap and together she and Ian began showing her how it worked, pressing the various brightly coloured keys to give a letter of the alphabet, number or colour, followed by a four-note tune. Anastasia tapped a few of the keys and then peered into the carrier bag to see what else was in there. Elaine took out one of the jigsaw puzzles and remarked to Ian, 'I wonder where her doll, crayons and colouring book that we brought in yesterday are?' They'd left them in the playroom.

'Perhaps she has them in her cot?' Ian suggested.

'Doll?' Elaine asked Anastasia, hoping the child might recognize the word from the day before. But she was more interested in the puzzle.

They showed her how the pieces went together and then Anastasia wanted to see what else was in the bag. Elaine took out the second puzzle, but as she and Ian began to assemble it the child lost interest again. With the carrier bag empty, Anastasia picked up Elaine's handbag.

'I know what you're after,' Elaine said, smiling. 'You want to see the photographs on my phone. Shall we do the jigsaw first and then look at photographs?'

But Anastasia didn't like that idea and was most insistent on opening Elaine's handbag, babbling in her own language. Elaine set the jigsaw to one side and took out her phone. She then went through the photographs as she had done the day before, telling Anastasia what they were and repeating simple words like 'house' and 'ball', hoping Anastasia would try to say the words.

Having got to the end of Elaine's photos, Anastasia began tugging on Ian's arm, signalling that she wanted to see the photographs on his phone. He laughed indulgently and took out his phone. Anastasia wanted to hold it and he let her. She began pressing the keys and then didn't want to return it. Fearing the phone might get broken or his messages and contacts erased, Ian gently eased it from her hand. She wasn't happy and jumped up from the beanbag and ran to the window, where she banged on the glass. Not wanting to upset her, Ian relented and held out his phone. Anastasia returned to the beanbag and then spent some minutes pressing various buttons before losing interest and discarding it in favour of the activity centre.

Anastasia clearly had a personality and will of her own, but that was good, wasn't it? It showed she was intelligent and developing normally. Elaine had read that children of Anastasia's age sought greater autonomy and exerted their will power, which could lead to tantrums, hence the expression 'the terrible twos'. But all in all they felt their time with Anastasia had gone well. They had a lot to learn as new parents as well as getting to know Anastasia. She hadn't been as agitated and unsettled as she had been the day before, and while she'd gone to the window a number of times, it had been easy to persuade her away. She seemed more comfortable around them (they weren't complete strangers any more), and although she hadn't settled to an activity for very long, it was early days yet and many two-year-olds have short attention spans.

When the hour was up, Ian and Elaine felt they could have stayed a little longer, but mindful of what Dr Ciobanu had said about keeping to the hour, they began to pack away. Anastasia wanted to keep the activity centre, which was fine. They went to find a care worker to say they were going. 'This toy is for Anastasia,' Elaine said, pointing to the activity centre. The care worker nodded as though she understood. 'Do you know where her doll and crayons are?' Elaine asked. The care worker frowned, puzzled, either not knowing or not understanding. 'Doll?' Elaine said, and mimed a small baby in her arms. The care worker shook her head. 'Crayons?' Elaine said, moving her hand as though drawing. The care worker shrugged. Anastasia babbled something in her own language and the care worker shrugged and shook her head.

'Don't worry,' Ian said to Elaine. 'If they don't turn up we'll ask Dr Ciobanu where they are when we see him.' It wasn't that the toys had been expensive – they hadn't been – but they'd been the first gifts they'd given to Anastasia and for this reason the doll especially would have sentimental value in years to come.

As they began to say goodbye, to their delight, instead of sending Anastasia away while the care worker saw them out, she was allowed to go with them to the gate. Elaine offered Anastasia her hand to hold as they walked but she refused, which was hardly surprising, as she barely knew them. They said goodbye to her at the gate and then waved as Anastasia watched them get into the cab. The care worker locked the gate.

'Nice-looking kid,' Danny said, and they both agreed.

That evening Ian and Elaine felt confident enough that everything was going as planned to message their family and friends with an update. Elaine's parents were dead but she had a sister who, while not living close, had been very supportive and was eagerly awaiting news. Ian's parents lived closer but had expressed reservations about their plans to adopt from abroad; however his brother and his family had wished them well. Ian messaged his parents that everything was fine and not to worry, and sent his brother a few extra details about the orphanage and their time with Anastasia. They also updated the friends they'd made online in the international adoption support group forums.

They slept well, and the next day continued the routine that was likely to see them through to the court hearing when Anastasia would become theirs. In the morning they walked to the local supermarket where they stocked up on bottled water and bought fresh bread, cheese and cooked meats for their lunch, and in the afternoon they took the cab to the orphanage. When they arrived Anastasia was in one of the dresses they'd bought for her and the new sandals. She looked lovely and more like their child now that she was wearing what they had chosen for her. 'We'll have to buy her a hairbrush and some bands and I'll braid her hair,' Elaine said as they settled in the playroom. Every mother wants to see her child looking smart and their hair neat. Anastasia's hair was long and unkempt.

There was still no sign of the doll, crayons or colouring book, but Anastasia had the activity centre they'd left with her the day before, so they played with that, plus the new toys in the bag they'd brought with them. These included a toy mobile phone, which sounded a recorded message when the numbers were pressed. The hope was that Anastasia would play with this rather then their phones, but their hope was short-lived. Although she liked pressing the buttons and listening to the recorded messages – *Hello, how are you?* and similar – it didn't contain the photographs that Elaine's and Ian's phones did. Anastasia was very insistent that she should play with both their phones, and of course, wanting her to be happy, they let her.

Another of the toys they'd brought with them was a basket of play food and they told her the names of the food in English as she picked them up – apple, pear, bun, jar of jam and so on – repeating the words so that Anastasia would eventually start to use them as she began to learn English.

At the end of the hour, Anastasia was allowed to see them to the gate again. Elaine and Ian felt their time with her had been positive and they were starting to build a relationship. They'd noticed that Anastasia didn't often make eye contact and she wasn't ready for a hug or kiss yet, but given that they'd only just come into her life, this wasn't surprising. They'd read all about bonding and it had been covered in the preparation course, and mentioned by other adoptive parents. They were aware it would take time for Anastasia to trust them and allow herself to feel affection.

The next day, when Anastasia was brought to them, she was barefoot and wearing a faded T-shirt and shorts, not one of the outfits they'd bought for her.

'Where are her clothes?' Elaine asked the care worker – the same one they'd given the clothes to. She shrugged as though she didn't know or understand. 'Or care,' Ian later said to Elaine.

Ian had their phrase book with him and found the word for clothes. He said it a few times but the care worker shrugged and upturned her hands, suggesting she hadn't a clue what he was talking about. He showed her the word in the phrase book, wondering if he wasn't pronouncing it correctly, but she shrugged again. Anastasia was holding the activity centre and she ran off into the playroom, while the care worker disappeared down the corridor into one of the nursery rooms where a child had begun to scream.

'We'll ask about the clothes later,' Ian said to Elaine as they went to the playroom.

Anastasia was sitting on the beanbag expectantly and, while she had the activity centre, there was no sign of the toy phone or puzzle they'd left in the room the day before. Dr Ciobanu had said she'd be the only one using this room for now. They were rotating the toys they brought with them with the idea that Anastasia would have something different to play with each day, but where were they? There was still no sign of the doll, crayons and colouring book either. As Elaine settled beside Anastasia on the beanbag, Ian said he'd go to see if he could find a care worker and ask again about the missing clothes and toys.

He found the one they'd seen earlier in a nursery room dressing a child – presumably the one who'd been screaming – and Ian thought she was rough, although she was clearly rushing, as they were so short-staffed. 'Sorry to trouble you,' he said. 'But Anastasia's toys are missing as well as her clothes.'

She ignored him and kept her back turned. He took a step in and said, 'If you tell me where you keep Anastasia's toys and clothes, I can fetch them, as you are busy.'

'You go,' she said rudely, not looking at him. 'I have to see to the child.'

Not wishing to upset her further, Ian returned to the play-room. At the end of the hour Ian asked the same care worker if Dr Ciobanu was in and she shook her head. 'When will he be in his office?' he asked.

She shrugged, but then said, 'Children lose their things,' suggesting she had understood and knew why they wanted to see him.

Ian didn't pursue it with her, but the following day Anasta-sia was wearing the first dress they'd bought her, although the activity centre was nowhere to be seen. They asked the care worker – the other one – where her toys were but were met with the same dismissive shrug, which said she didn't know or understand. Dr Ciobanu wasn't in, and as Elaine played with Anastasia in the playroom Ian went to see if the missing toys were in Anastasia's cot. They weren't, and he noticed the mattress cover was grubby, as indeed were most of the covers in the other cots. The room smelled of urine and sweat, and as Ian glanced around at the children he felt guilty for worrying about a few missing toys when there was so much misery around him. On returning to Elaine he said, 'The sooner we get Anastasia out of here the better.'

When they left that afternoon Ian asked the care worker when Dr Ciobanu would be in.

'Not here,' the care worker said.

'I know. When will he be here?'

She shrugged.

'I'll phone him,' Ian said to Elaine, frustrated. Apart from wanting to find Anastasia's belongings, he wanted to know if they had a court date yet.

As it turned out, Ian didn't have to phone Dr Ciobanu, for just as they got into their cab a car drew up behind them and Dr Ciobanu got out. 'Please wait, we need to speak to him,' Ian said to Danny.

Anastasia had retuned inside by now with the care worker and Dr Ciobanu greeted them warmly and shook their hands.

'Your time with Anastasia is going well?' he asked them.

'Yes, thank you,' Ian said.

'She waves you off at the gate?'

'She comes to the gate, yes.'

'Good. I tell the care workers to bring the children out to say goodbye. It's nice for the parents.'

'Thank you.'

'And everything is going to plan so you have no need to worry,' he reassured them in his usual upbeat manner.

'Good,' Ian said. 'But I need to talk to you about something.'

'Yes?' And what Ian and Elaine learned next shocked and saddened them deeply.

CHAPTER SIX

LANA'S BEAR

'Dr Ciobanu,' Ian began, choosing his words carefully. 'I'm sorry to trouble you, I know you're very busy, but we bought Anastasia new clothes as you asked, and yesterday she was in old clothes that weren't hers. Apart from one dress, the rest seem to have vanished. Also, we've been buying her toys but we can't find them anywhere. They are not in the playroom or her cot. We've asked the care workers but they don't seem to understand. Where do you keep her things?'

Immediately the doctor's expression changed and he looked annoyed. Ian thought he was annoyed at them for bothering him. 'I'll speak to the care workers,' he said bluntly.

'We don't want to cause any trouble. We'd just like to know where her belongings are.'

'You need to take her toys to your hotel with you. You won't get them back.'

'Oh, why not?' Elaine asked. 'What about her clothes?'

'I'll try to find them,' he said curtly, 'but don't hold your breath.' With a nod signalling the conversation was over, he unlocked the gate.

Ian and Elaine looked at each other, confused, but not wishing to upset the doctor further, they returned to the cab.

'Doctor not happy?' Danny asked, having seen the exchange.

Ian let out a sigh, then explained that they couldn't find Anastasia's clothes and toys and the doctor seemed to have taken it personally.

'He will,' Danny said, turning in his seat to look at them. 'He annoyed because it happens a lot. Parents bring nice new clothes and toys for their child, and sometimes charities donate play equipment, but it all goes.'

'Where to?' Elaine asked.

'The workers in the orphanages take them home for their children and their families and friends' children. Not just this orphanage but others too.'

'But that's stealing!' Elaine exclaimed. 'We bought those things for Anastasia.'

'Yes, it is wrong of them, but you have to understand the people who work in the orphanages are very poor. They can't afford to buy their children nice clothes and toys, and they don't see why the orphans should have them. Also, many of the children are disabled so they think it's a waste, as they can't play with the toys. One charity gave a slide, sandpit and things for outside. The next day it was all gone. You need to look after Anastasia's things, take them away with you, or you won't see them again.'

'How very sad,' Ian said. 'Thank you for explaining.'

The missing toys didn't reappear and neither did the other two outfits. From then on Elaine and Ian did as suggested and took the toys away with them and then brought some back the next day. Anastasia didn't protest at having her toys taken away from her as a child in a normal family would, as she'd had little experience of owning things. They couldn't do the same with her clothes – keep dressing and undressing her

– so they had to accept that the other two outfits they'd left had gone for good, and they kept the rest back for the court date and afterwards, when she would be with them in the hotel until they all flew home. Dr Ciobanu didn't mention it again and neither did Ian and Elaine.

The doctor wasn't at the orphanage much as he had to divide his time between a number of orphanages and other work in the community. As they neared the end of the second week, having not had a chance to see Dr Ciobanu again, Ian left a written message on the table in his office asking him if he could phone him, as they were concerned they hadn't got a firm court date yet. Dr Ciobanu phoned their hotel room that evening but it wasn't the news they'd been hoping for.

'The judge is going on holiday,' Dr Ciobanu said. 'I am trying to fit you in before he goes but the court is very busy.'

Ian and Elaine knew delays happened, but it was still frustrating and it added to their anxiety that something could go wrong that would stop them from adopting Anastasia. Ian had taken a month off work – he was an engineer in a railway company – and a month should have been enough if everything went to plan.

'If we can't go to court before the judge goes on holiday, how long before he comes back?' Ian asked Dr Ciobanu.

'He'll be away for three weeks.' Ian's heart sank. Elaine was watching him as he spoke and knew it was bad news.

'Isn't there another judge who could hear our case?' Ian asked.

'Lots of people take their holidays during August, judges included,' Dr Ciobanu said. 'But don't worry, I'll try my best to have your case fitted in before then. I'll phone you with the date.'

'Thank you,' Ian said, and replaced the handset.

They weren't greatly reassured. They'd seen enough of Dr Ciobanu to know he tended to reassure people by telling them what they wanted to hear.

'If we don't get to court before the judge goes away, I'll have to phone work and ask for unpaid leave,' Ian said to Elaine. Ian's boss knew about the adoption and had been sympathetic when Ian had asked to take all his annual leave in one go, which needed special permission. Elaine, a legal secretary, had left her permanent job the day before they flew out. During their adoption assessment the social worker had said that one parent should be at home at least for the first year after the adoption to give the child continuity and time to settle in. Elaine hadn't minded at all. She had waited a long time to be a mother and wanted what was best for her child and to make the most of every minute. Later, when Anastasia was old enough and went to school, Elaine could take some part-time work. Legal secretaries were always needed and with her experience she would find work easily.

Ian and Elaine felt they were bonding quickly with Anastasia, probably faster than she was with them. But that was to be expected. They had spent two years working towards this point, whereas Anastasia had had barely two weeks so far to adjust. Dr Ciobanu had told them that the care workers had explained to Anastasia what was happening, but Ian and Elaine doubted they'd had the time or patience to explain thoroughly or answer her questions and reassure her. He'd also told them that her attachment to her mother (or anyone else) was very weak, so she'd have no problem bonding with them once they were home, and wouldn't miss anyone there.

Ian and Elaine had got to know some of the staff at the hotel, especially their waitress who served them each morning at breakfast. Her name was Maria and she told them she was improving her English so she could work in the UK where the wages were much higher. She practised her English on them as she served them and knew why they were there. She had a five-year-old daughter who was looked after by her mother during the twelve-hour shifts she worked six days a week. But it was only when Maria showed them a photograph of her daughter that she said her name was Lana. This in itself was not such a huge coincidence, as it was a very popular name, but its significance immediately struck Ian and Elaine. On a waitress's wages, Maria would never be able to afford to buy her daughter nice toys, let alone a personalized bear, as they had done for Lana. They hadn't had a chance to approach Dr Ciobanu about putting the bear on Lana's grave and if they were honest the need for doing this was lessening, as they moved on and bonded with Anastasia.

'I think I'd like Maria's daughter to have Lana's bear,' Elaine said to Ian later. He readily agreed.

The following morning Elaine brought the bear in its original store gift bag down to breakfast and gave it to Maria. 'For your daughter,' Elaine said. We thought our child would be called Lana but we were wrong. We'd like you to have it.' There was no need to go into any more detail about the child they'd lost.

Maria looked at them, surprised and delighted, then, as she took out the bear, her eyes filled and her face crumbled. 'For

Lana? It's beautiful. I could never afford to buy her this. She will love it so much. Thank you.' She took Elaine's hand and then Ian's and kissed them. 'Thank you from the bottom of my heart.'

Elaine and Ian swallowed hard and knew they'd done the right thing.

They began extending their time with Anastasia and running over the hour. Dr Ciobanu wasn't there to tell them not to and the care workers didn't seem to mind. In fact, it probably did them a favour not having to watch Anastasia, who was one of the few non-disabled children and by far the most active. So the hour became one and a half hours and then two. Anastasia always appeared pleased to see them and eager to look inside the carrier bag of toys to discover what they'd brought for her today. She wasn't a tactile child but that would come with time, and although she wasn't saying any English words yet, she seemed to understand simple instructions – for example, put this piece of puzzle there.

One afternoon, while they were in the playroom, they heard English being spoken in the corridor outside without a heavy accent, which was unusual. Intrigued, Ian went out to investigate and saw two women in their early twenties. 'Are you from the UK?' he asked them.

'Yes. Are you?'

'Yes, pleased to meet you. I'm Ian.'

'Pam and Mel,' the girls said.

'My wife is in the playroom. Come through and say hi. What part of the UK are you from?'

'Bournemouth.' And so they got chatting.

It's always heartening to meet someone from your own

country when you're abroad, especially if the country you are in doesn't speak the same language. Friendships can develop and confidences can be swapped, when they might not at home.

'This is my wife, Elaine,' Ian said, introducing her. 'Pam and Mel. And this is Anastasia.'

'Ahh, she's cute,' Pam said. 'Is she your daughter?'

'We hope she will be soon,' Elaine said with a big smile. 'We're adopting her.'

'That's lovely,' Pam said. 'We met another couple adopting two boys, brothers. There seems to be a lot of adoption from this country.'

'Yes, there is,' Ian agreed.

'Why are you here?' Elaine asked, interested and making conversation.

'We're volunteers,' Mel said. 'We're students and we've come here on a project to help in the orphanages. We came at the end of June and fly back on 12 September, ready for the new term.'

'That's very good of you,' Elaine said. 'Are you going to be working in this orphanage?'

'We think so. We've been at another orphanage run by Dr Ciobanu about thirty kilometres from here, and he said we should come here as they needed the help more. He's supposed to be meeting us here.'

'They certainly could do with the help,' Ian said. 'They're very short-staffed.'

'We've only seen two care workers and there are thirty children,' Elaine added.

'That's a very low ratio,' Pam said. 'The orphanage we've been working in had two care workers for twenty children and that was nowhere near enough. The building there was much newer than this, though. This is very old.'

'I know,' Elaine agreed. 'And it has so little equipment. There's nothing for the children to do. Are you staying locally?'

'We might be sleeping here if they put us on the night shift. We're not sure yet. It depends what Dr Ciobanu says. Otherwise we'll get a room in town.'

The large front door of the orphanage could be heard opening and then clanging shut, the sound resonating down the empty and otherwise silent corridor.

'I wonder if that's him,' Mel said, and stepped into the corridor to look. 'Yes, it is,' she said. 'We'd better go.'

'Hopefully see you again,' Elaine called. 'Good luck, and well done for volunteering.'

'Thank you.'

'I'm going to catch Dr Ciobanu while he's here,' Ian said to Elaine and disappeared out of the playroom.

'Good afternoon, Mr Hudson, how are you?' Dr Ciobanu turned from the students as Ian approached.

'Well, thank you. Could I speak with you later?'

'Yes, of course. I was going to phone you. I have the news you've been waiting for. Come to my office before you leave.'

'Thank you,' Ian said, and returned to the playroom, greatly relieved. 'He says he has the news we've been waiting for,' he told Elaine.

'Fantastic.' They both assumed it was good news: that they'd been given a court date for the following week and would fly home with Anastasia as planned.

As they played with Anastasia, Dr Ciobanu's low voice could be heard outside showing the students around. It was reassuring to know there would be some extra help. They worried about Anastasia when they weren't there.

They kept to the hour and then began packing away the toys, telling Anastasia that they had to see Dr Ciobanu. She didn't say anything but recognized his name. She went with them to his office and as Ian knocked on the door she slipped her hand into Elaine's. It was the first time she'd wanted to hold hands and Elaine was delighted. As she felt her small, cool fingers tuck themselves inside hers, Elaine knew it was a big step forward and a moment she would treasure for a very long time.

'Come in,' the doctor welcomed, opening the door. 'She can come too,' he said, referring to Anastasia.

Ian and Elaine sat in the two chairs in front of the table as Dr Ciobanu took his place behind it. Anastasia stood between Elaine and Ian, close but not quite touching. Elaine would have loved to pick her up and sit her on her lap, but she knew she had to wait until Anastasia was ready for that.

'So you like your new mummy and daddy?' Dr Ciobanu asked Anastasia in his usual upbeat manner. It was unlikely she understood, but seeing the man in charge smiling and talking to her, she nodded. 'Good. And they obviously like you very much, so all is well.'

'Very much!' Ian and Elaine agreed.

He looked at them in the same positive manner. 'We have news of the court date at last. There is no free time before the judge goes on holiday, so the child's mother has returned to work abroad until the court hearing. She needs the money and Anastasia will stay here with us for that period.' He paused.

'I see,' Ian said, trying to understand what this meant. 'For how long?'

'Three months. As you know, unless the child is an orphan the mother has to be in court for the adoption hearing to give her consent, so I have booked the court date for the day after she returns – 23 November.' He looked at them as though they should be pleased.

It was a moment before either of them could speak. 'But I can't take another three months off work,' Ian said.

'No, of course not. You must fly home and return for the court hearing.'

'Oh. It can't be heard in another court with a different judge?' Ian asked.

He shook his head. 'Many staff are on holiday, there is no free time. And the child's mother has already left the country. It is nothing for you to worry about. Trust me. Anastasia will be looked after here.'

CHAPTER SEVEN

TIME APART

Ian and Elaine couldn't agree that the news Dr Ciobanu had given them was 'nothing to worry about'. In fact, they spent the rest of the day and most of the night worrying. They'd bonded with Anastasia and they were sure she was bonding with them. Three months was a long time in a young child's life, and wouldn't being apart for all that time undo most of their bonding, so they'd have to start all over again? Dr Ciobanu had been philosophical when he'd told them and said delays happened, it couldn't be helped, and he would explain to Anastasia that her new mummy and daddy were going home to get her room ready. He also said to keep their memory alive he'd show her the photographs he had of them on file that had accompanied their original application. He offered them the consolation that three months would pass quickly and that they needn't fly back until the day before the adoption hearing, as all the paperwork was now in court.

During the long hours of the night as they lay awake they tried to think of practical alternatives. Elaine said that possibly she could stay so at least Anastasia could see her each day, but they certainly couldn't afford for her to stay in the hotel.

'Perhaps I could find a cheap room in a lodging house like those students?' Elaine suggested doubtfully. For even as she said it her stomach churned. She wasn't an adventurous person, and, a little on the shy side, she relied heavily on Ian. The thought of spending three months separated from him in a foreign country among people she didn't know and where she didn't speak the language filled her with dread.

'Not unless I fly out each weekend,' Ian replied to her. 'But the cost of that would be prohibitive.'

Still awake at 2 a.m. they reached their lowest point. 'I'm beginning to regret ever starting international adoption,' Elaine said, close to tears. 'It's been one heartache after another. First Lana and now this.'

'Don't say that,' Ian chided, drawing her close. 'We've come this far. Let's try to focus on the positives. The court date is definitely set. All our paperwork is in and Anastasia's mother hasn't changed her mind.' Which they knew from other couples did happen – the parent(s) changed their minds or a relative came forward to look after the child at the last moment. 'And think about all those families we've been talking to online who have successfully adopted despite all the setbacks,' Ian added.

'Yes.' Elaine conceded he had a point. 'I wonder if anyone has experienced what we're going through,' she said.

'I'm sure they have,' Ian said. 'But once the adoption is granted you probably forget all the bad things.'

Finally, in the early hours, they fell into an exhausted sleep, but Ian was awake early. Leaving Elaine asleep, he quietly slipped into his clothes and went down into reception, which had the best phone signal, and from there he messaged Maggie, the founder of their online group for international adoption. She and her husband had adopted four children from two different countries and were happy to share their knowledge and encourage those going through the process for the first time. Ian messaged her that their court date had been postponed for three months and they had been told to return home, and they weren't sure what to do for the best. He then waited in reception to see if she would reply straight away, and five minutes later his phone bleeped with a message.

> Sorry to hear about the delay, Ian. A disappointment but I've heard of other cases. You can't do anything so fly home as Dr C said. We can chat when you get back. I am sure the adoption will go through. Don't lose heart. You'll have the rest of your lives with your child. M x

Which was exactly the message of hope Ian needed. He returned to their hotel room, and when Elaine woke he showed her the message and she, too, took comfort from it.

Nevertheless, it was with heavy hearts that they confirmed their flight home and then made the most of their last few days with Anastasia, but spending time with her now was bittersweet. While they wanted to make the most of every minute, they were acutely aware they wouldn't be seeing her for three long months and would miss her dreadfully. They tried to talk to her about what was going to happen and told her they loved her, but it was doubtful she understood. It was impossible to know what she was thinking or feeling, and if Dr Ciobanu had said anything to her to explain, it wasn't obvious from her behaviour.

On their penultimate day they bumped into Mel and Pam, who were working the night shift, and Elaine told them they were having to return home as their court date had been postponed for three months. The girls were very sympathetic and said they would keep an eye on Anastasia while they were here. But of course they were due to return home a week later and after that Ian and Elaine assumed the children would be left in the care of the two workers again. It was very worrying. They felt protective of Anastasia and wanted to keep her safe.

On the last day they took all the toys and clothes they'd brought for her that hadn't gone missing into the orphanage and left them in carrier bags marked with her name in Dr Ciobanu's office. Hopefully, at least some of them would be used by her. Then they had to say goodbye and it was heartbreaking. Anastasia walked between them down the path holding a hand each and the care worker unlocked the gate. As they bent to Anastasia's height they tried to hide their emotion, but their pain must have been obvious.

'Goodbye for now, love, don't forget us,' Elaine said, her eyes immediately filling. 'We won't forget you. We'll put your photograph in our living room so you are with us all the time. We love you so much.' She kissed Anastasia's cheek and straightened. She couldn't take much more.

Ian kissed Anastasia but couldn't say anything.

They left her at the gate with the care worker and climbed into the cab. Danny knew this was their last visit for three months and didn't immediately pull away. They both looked out of the side window. Usually, as soon as the care worker had locked the gate they returned inside, but now Anastasia clung to the wire netting, pressing her face against it and looking at them. It was one of the few occasions she made eye contact and it was pitiful. Elaine and Ian saw the pain and rejection in her eyes. She might not have been able to tell them in words what she was feeling, but her eyes said it all. Her mother had left her and now they were leaving too.

'We'll be back soon,' Elaine said through the window. But the image on Anastasia's little face imploring them not to go would haunt them in the months to come.

It was Danny who took them to the airport the next day and he seemed to appreciate that they didn't want to talk much. He had the radio on low, tuned to a local station, and wasn't his usual chatty self, only occasionally making a remark – about the weather or traffic. As they neared the airport he said, 'I'm sorry you have to go home without your child.'

'It's not your fault, Danny,' Ian said.

'But I have got to know you during our trips to the orphanage so I am sorry. Perhaps if I have time I can visit Anastasia and tell her you will be back soon.'

'That's very kind of you,' Ian said. Elaine kept quiet, struggling to hold back fresh tears.

At the airport Danny parked in the passenger drop-off area and took their cases from the boot. 'I see you here in three months' time,' he said more cheerfully. 'When you book the cab ask for Danny and I come to meet you.'

'We will. Thank you for everything,' Ian said, and they shook hands warmly. They felt they had at least one friend in the country who understood.

* * *

Elaine and Ian were emotionally exhausted from all they'd been through and slept for most of the flight, even though it was daytime. In England they had to take a train from the airport to their home town and then a cab to their house. It was late evening when they arrived at their modest three-bedroom house, but its neatly tended front garden seemed very bright and upmarket after the drabness of the orphanage. Their neighbour had been cutting their lawn, watering the plants and generally keeping an eye on the place while they'd been away. They'd messaged her with the date they'd be back, adding that the adoption had been postponed. They'd see her tomorrow to thank her and give her the gift they'd bought, but for now they just wanted to get inside.

As they set their cases down in the hall the comfortable, welcoming familiarity they usually felt on returning home was now tainted with the knowledge that they should have been returning as a family. Upstairs was the nursery, decorated and ready with a cot, changing station and first-year clothes and toys, all of which would need sorting out at some point, and the room would remain empty for now. They'd also have to telephone their friends and family and explain what was happening, as they'd told them only the minimum while they'd been away.

Elaine made them a cup of tea using the milk their neighbour had put in the fridge while Ian took their cases up to their room. Then, to try to relax ready for bed, they put the television on so they didn't have to talk and have yet another worrying conversation about Anastasia. They'd said it all. Ian was planning to return to work the following day, when he would talk to his boss about the two weeks' leave he'd need in November. He wasn't looking forward to the well-meant questions and comments from his boss and colleagues who knew the reason he'd been away but not the result. Elaine wasn't sure what she was going to do for the next three months, but thought she should find some temporary work. It would help pay the bills and would also stop her from sitting at home worrying. They opened their mail, of which there was a lot. It included an adoption congratulations card from Ian's brother and family – sent early and assuming all would go to plan. Ian said he'd phone him and deal with the mail tomorrow.

Over the next week, as Ian submerged himself in his work, Elaine grew more and more down. She telephoned her sister and told her what had happened, but didn't contact any of her friends or log into the online support group for international adoption. Her thoughts were permanently with Anastasia and the image of her little face at the gate as they'd said good-bye. What was the poor child thinking and feeling now? How was she coping? Had Dr Ciobanu and the care workers reassured her they would be back? Elaine doubted it – not in any depth, they were all too busy. Anastasia was one of many children, most of whom had multiple needs.

Elaine kept returning to the nursery even though it made her cry. She couldn't face sorting out Lana's possessions. She just sat on the pink velvet child's chair and looked around as her thoughts grew increasingly gloomy and morose. Not usually one to suffer from depression, she now found herself sliding down a long, dark tunnel with no way out and no light at the end. The walls closed in and she tormented herself with speculation that when they returned for Anastasia they would be told that she, too, was dead. The thought plagued her during the day and kept her awake at night, while Ian, tired from work, slept soundly beside her.

At the end of the second week, while Ian was at work, Elaine telephoned the orphanage and the phone was answered after many rings by a care worker.

'Is Dr Ciobanu there?' she asked, her voice faltering.

'He not here,' came the heavily accented reply.

'This is Mrs Hudson. Is Anastasia well?' She hoped the care worker understood enough to be able to reassure her.

'Yes. She's well. I tell Dr Ciobanu you phone.'

'Thank you. Will you tell Anastasia I phoned too?'

'Yes. I tell her. Goodbye.'

So at least Anastasia was alive.

Two days later Dr Ciobanu emailed to say Anastasia was doing well and looking forward to seeing them again, although Elaine doubted she had expressly said she was looking forward to seeing them again. She couldn't picture it and thought it was Dr Ciobanu again telling them what they wanted to hear, and it didn't really help. Ian, whose life had returned to some normality with work, was worried about Elaine, but also losing patience with her growing gloom and despondency. He suggested she made an appointment to see their doctor, or at least have a chat with Maggie, the founder of the support group for international adoption who Ian had messaged while away. Elaine did neither until the following week, after she and Ian had a blazing argument.

'You've got to snap out of it!' Ian cried, tired at the end of the day. 'Anastasia is going to need a lot of care when we

bring her back and you're in no fit state to help her. Get yourself sorted out now or we won't be going back!' He stormed
out of the room and went upstairs.

He apologized later and said he hadn't meant the threat of
not going back – he was as attached to Anastasia as Elaine
was. But it was the wake-up call Elaine needed. She
telephoned Maggie and cried as she confessed all her worries
and told her in detail what they'd been through. They were
on the phone for over an hour and Maggie was able to reassure
her so that when they finished Elaine felt far more positive.
Taking Maggie's advice, she sorted out the nursery, bagging
up what they didn't need and making a list of what she had to
buy for Anastasia. It would be winter when they went back so
she'd need warm clothes. While Elaine was in town she
registered with an employment agency that specialized in
temporary work and by the next morning had a position in a
local firm to cover staff sickness. It gave her a new focus, and
although she still thought of Anastasia and missed her, she
was in the real word again and far more positive. What
started off as one week's work stretched to five, so that by the
time the contract ended there were only three weeks before
they had to fly out for the adoption.

Dr Ciobanu emailed confirming all would be going ahead
for 11 a.m. on 23 November and they should arrive in the
country no later than twenty-four hours before. He added
that Anastasia was looking forward to seeing them and he
hoped they were both well. Ian emailed back saying they'd
arrive on 18 November so they could spend time with Anastasia in the days before the hearing. Then he booked the flight
tickets: two seats confirmed going out and three reserved
coming back. Aged two and a half, Anastasia would need a

seat of her own, but they couldn't confirm it until they had her passport number after the court hearing. They were very excited but also anxious that all would go to plan.

CHAPTER EIGHT

RETURN

I t was a clear but cold day, 3°C, the captain said over the
public address system as the plane began its descent, ready
for landing. Ian took Elaine's hand and smiled. 'Not long to
go now.' Their excitement had grown during the flight, but
so had their apprehension. Once they saw Anastasia and Dr
Ciobanu and knew all was well, they would feel more reassured, but for now they held hands and drew strength from
each other as they looked through the window and the land
below gradually rose up to greet them.

When they'd booked the cab they'd asked specifically for
Danny to collect them, but it was nearly an hour before their
cases arrived in the baggage hall. 'I hope Danny has waited,'
Elaine said nervously, imagining something else that could go
wrong.

'If not there'll be plenty of cabs waiting outside the airport,'
Ian reassured her.

But as they emerged through the arrivals door, pulling
their cases and with bags over their shoulders, they saw Danny
straight away. He was directly in front of them, holding up a
large piece of cardboard with Hudson written in black marker
pen. He spotted them and began waving frantically. Relieved,

they quickened their pace. 'Good to see you,' he said, greeting them with the warmth of an old friend or relative.

'And you,' Ian said, shaking his hand.

'So the time has come for you to return and you are happy!' he said, taking their cases.

'Yes, indeed,' Elaine replied, and they began towards the car park. 'How is Anastasia?' she asked. 'Did you have a chance to visit her?'

'I am sorry, I didn't have time. I have been very busy. But I took another couple to the orphanage and they saw her.'

'Really? Did they say how she was? What was she doing?'

'She is well. She was talking to the children in the cots.'

Elaine smiled, pleased and partly reassured. 'That sounds like her.'

Danny loaded their bags and cases into the boot of his cab and Elaine and Ian climbed into the back. He was then silent as he concentrated on navigating out of the busy airport car park, but once on the road he said, 'Dr Ciobanu told me you can go straight to see Anastasia if you wish. That good?'

'What, now?' Elaine asked.

'If you want to, then I take you to your hotel after.'

'Oh yes, please, that would be fantastic. We've missed her so much.'

'Thank you,' Ian said.

'The couple you took to the orphanage, are they adopting too?' Elaine asked out of interest.

'Yes, two boys, with disabilities,' Danny replied. 'The children are very lucky. They no longer have to live in cots.'

Immediately Elaine's eyes filled, for that was the truth of life in the orphanage for children with disabilities – they did live in cots.

Danny continued chatting as he drove and asked them about the weather in the UK, which although cold wasn't as cold as it was there now in November. Ian then asked him about his own family and how his children were.

'They are well, thank you,' he said. 'My daughter is studying hard at school but my son messes around sometimes and gets into trouble. I tell him off, and told him he needs to study hard and do well or he will end up driving a cab like me for a living.'

'He could do a lot worse,' Ian said. 'Cab drivers are always needed.'

'But I want him to use his brain, earn good money and be respected.' Which of course is what most parents want for their children, wherever they live in the world.

Half an hour later they turned into the lane that led to the orphanage. The trees were now bare in winter and the cold outside could be felt even in the heated cab. 'I hope the children are warm enough,' Elaine said.

'They have heating sometimes,' Danny replied, 'and wear woollens.'

He drew up outside the orphanage, parking in virtually the same spot he had on all their previous visits. Elaine's heart missed a beat as she looked at the decaying building, even more desolate now that the surrounding trees were barren. But one positive was that a children's slide had appeared in the strip of land at the front. 'That slide is new,' she said.

'Yes, it was donated two weeks ago,' Danny said. 'It was cemented into the ground so it can't be taken away.'

'Good,' Elaine said. Although of course it would only benefit the children if the care workers had enough time to help them play on it, which from what they'd seen before was highly doubtful.

'I wait here like before,' Danny confirmed as they opened their car doors.

'Yes, please,' Ian said.

They got out and went to the tall metal gate. As before the only way of attracting attention was to rattle it. Danny also gave a blast on the cab's horn. 'Not much has changed then,' Ian said.

'But that slide is nice,' Elaine said, wanting to stay positive.

A few moments later Dr Ciobanu appeared at the orphan-age door and with a wave came down the path. 'Hello Mr and Mrs Hudson. Good to see you again.'

'And you,' Ian said.

He unlocked the gate, waved an acknowledgement to Danny and then shook Ian's and Elaine's hands and relocked the gate behind them. 'So three months wasn't so long and passed quickly,' he said as they went up the path.

'It was long enough,' Elaine said.

'Some families have to wait much longer,' Dr Ciobanu said. 'The flight was comfortable?'

'Yes.'

Inside, Dr Ciobanu didn't show them into his office but stopped in the lobby, which was exactly as it had been on their last visit. 'There are no more forms for you to sign until after the court hearing,' he said. 'You have the time and date of the hearing in your diary?'

'Yes,' Ian said. 'And seared in our minds. Eleven o'clock on 23 November.'

Dr Ciobanu nodded. 'You need to book a cab to take you to the court and back to your hotel afterwards when you will have Anastasia with you. Arrive by 10.30. Use the same cab firm. They know where the court is and will wait for you.' Ian and Elaine nodded. 'Take your passports with you to court. Sometimes the judge wants to see them. Take a warm coat for the child. If you haven't brought one with you then you must buy one here.'

'We have one,' Elaine confirmed, 'and boots, gloves and a warm hat for her.'

'That is because you have come from the UK,' Dr Ciobanu said with a smile. 'Some families fly in from warmer countries and forget it is cold here. Also bring a drink for the child. She will have been waiting around for some time. Although the court hearing time is set for eleven o'clock, things in this country don't always happen on time.' They nodded again. 'And prepare yourselves for meeting the child's mother. You don't need to talk to her but the waiting room is small so she will be seated close by.' They'd already been warned this could happen, but even so Elaine felt her heart clench. She knew she was going to have to be very brave when she met Anastasia's mother, especially when the time came for her to say goodbye to her child.

'And remember,' Dr Ciobanu continued, 'you must not give the mother any money or gifts. It is illegal.'

'Yes,' Ian said. 'We know.'

'Once you are home you can send some photographs of Anastasia to show she is healthy and happy. I will give them to the mother.' Again, they knew this from the literature Dr Ciobanu had sent them when they'd first contacted him about adopting. 'Once the adoption is granted, I will apply for Anastasia's passport, visa and new birth certificate as quickly as possible so you can confirm your return flight, but it may take a week.'

'We understand,' Ian said.

'So now I fetch Anastasia for you.' The doctor smiled.

'Is her mother back in the country yet?' Elaine asked.

'No. Her flight is the day before the court hearing – the twenty-second. Don't worry, she won't forget.'

Elaine nodded, although she would rather have heard that she was already in the country, for if Anastasia's mother didn't return, the adoption would have to be postponed again.

'The mother knows we can't keep her child here at the orphanage any longer,' Dr Ciobanu added. 'So she will come. Any more questions?'

'I don't think so,' Ian said.

'You go to the playroom – you will see a difference – while I fetch Anastasia. Our new care worker is playing with her and trying to teach her some English.' Elaine's surprise showed on her face. 'We have another worker funded by the government and some more toys,' Dr Ciobanu said. 'You saw the slide at the front? Things are gradually improving.'

'That's good,' Elaine said.

Dr Ciobanu headed off to fetch Anastasia while Ian and Elaine went down the corridor towards the playroom. The orphanage was quiet, as it had been on their previous visits, and although the large old-style metal radiators were on, it wasn't warm. Stepping into the playroom, they saw straight away what Dr Ciobanu had meant. The room had been painted and on one wall was a large, brightly coloured mural showing happy, smiling children playing outside in the warm summer sun.

'Isn't that lovely?' Elaine said.

'It certainly brightens up the room,' Ian replied, going over for a closer look. He bent to read the signatures at the bottom.

'Guess who painted it?' Elaine shook her head. 'Pam and Mel, the students.'

'Wow, they certainly did a good job.'

Also in the room were a second beanbag and a toy box. Presently footsteps sounded in the corridor outside, and then the unmistakable voice of Anastasia. 'Mummy and Daddy,' she said evenly with a heavy accent. Elaine could have wept with joy. She appeared at the door wearing a thick grey woollen sweater rolled up at the wrists and jogging-style pants tucked into thick socks. 'Mummy and Daddy,' she said again, and looked at them.

Dr Ciobanu smiled, pleased. 'You see, she learns English.'

'Wonderful,' Elaine cried, and went to her. 'Hello, Anastasia. How are you, love?'

'Say, "I am well, thank you,"' Dr Ciobanu told her.

'I am well, thank you,' Anastasia repeated in cute broken English.

'That's very good,' Elaine said, blinking back tears.

Satisfied, Dr Ciobanu ruffled Anastasia's hair. 'I'll see you at court on Thursday then,' and he left.

'Yes, thank you,' Ian called after him.

Elaine knelt so she was at Anastasia's height. 'You've grown. You're a big girl.' Anastasia stared at her. 'We've come back for you just as we said.' Elaine felt her eyes fill again.

'We're going to be your mummy and daddy,' Ian said, joining them.

'Mummy and Daddy,' Anastasia repeated.

'Yes, love, that's right.' Unable to resist the urge to hug her any longer, Elaine wrapped Anastasia in her arms and held her close, but she felt rigid, unresponsive, which Elaine assumed was because she wasn't used to being held or cuddled. Not wanting her to feel uncomfortable, she kissed her forehead and let her go. 'Let's play with something in the toy box,' Elaine suggested, nodding towards the beanbags and toy box.

Anastasia stared at Elaine, then tapped her forearm. 'What is it, love?' Elaine asked. 'What do you want?'

Without language to explain, Anastasia tapped her arm again, this time more insistently, then looked at Ian.

'I think she's asking about the bag of toys we used to bring in with us,' he said.

'Oh, I see. We have brought new toys for you, but they are all packed in our cases in the car. We'll bring some in tomorrow when we've had a chance to unpack.'

Not understanding but appreciating there was no bag of toys, Anastasia pulled on Elaine's shoulder bag.

'Phone,' Ian said.

'I know,' she said, smiling, and took her mobile from her bag. 'Come and sit on the beanbags and we'll look at the photographs. We've got more photos of our house and your bedroom to show you.'

Ian joined them on the beanbags, he and Elaine sitting either side of Anastasia, as she scrolled through the photographs, while Elaine and Ian gave her a running commentary – bedroom, bed, garden and so on. Once Anastasia had exhausted Elaine's photographs, she looked pointedly at Ian. He laughed and, taking his phone from his pocket, passed it to her. They were pleased Anastasia had remembered the bags of toys they'd brought in before and their phones; it showed there was nothing wrong with her memory. She seemed bright and alert. She didn't try to repeat any of the words they said, except when they came to the photographs of themselves. 'Mummy and Daddy,' she said in her broken English.

'Yes!' Elaine cried, overjoyed.

'I think Mummy and Daddy are the only words they've taught her,' Ian said dryly. But it didn't matter, not one little bit. Anastasia was intelligent and would quickly pick up English once they were home, and of course Mummy and Daddy were the words they most wanted to hear. That Anastasia spoke them in a flat voice, as though simply repeating something she'd been told, didn't escape their notice. But she'd spent most of her life in the orphanage with only brief spells with her mother, a single parent, so had little experience of the love, warmth and nurturing that were normally associated with Mummy and Daddy. With time, she would come to know what these words really meant and her eyes would light up when she heard them. But for now Elaine and Ian were content and very happy that their long-awaited daughter sat between them saying 'Mummy and Daddy'.

Once Anastasia had finished with the photographs on Ian's phone, Elaine began going through the toy box. While the box was new, many of the toys it contained were old and broken. There was no sign of the toys they'd left for Anastasia. They hadn't really expected to see them again, and she wasn't wearing the clothes they'd left for her, but then they wouldn't have been warm enough now anyway.

Anastasia quickly exhausted what the toy box had to offer and, scrambling up from the beanbag, went over to the mural on the wall.

'It's a lovely picture,' Elaine said, joining her. Ian went too. 'Sun,' Elaine said, pointing to the big yellow sun.

'Sun,' Anastasia repeated.

'Yes, good girl!' Elaine was delighted. 'Swing,' she said.

'Swing,' Anastasia repeated, and Elaine and Ian clapped.

'Ball,' Ian said, pointing.

'Ball.' They clapped some more.

And so they went through all the images on the mural, with Anastasia repeating the words. They clapped after each one. When they came to the end they began again, but Anastasia had had enough – she was, after all, only two years and seven months old. With a quick glance around the room, she realized there was nothing else of interest and ran to the door.

'No. Not out there,' Ian called. But it was too late. She was that bit taller, stronger and possibly more strong-willed than before and easily opened the door and ran out. They quickly went after her in time to see her disappear into one of the nursery rooms further up. A care worker shouted at her from inside. They didn't know what she said, but it was obvious Anastasia shouldn't have been in there. She ran out, along the corridor and into the next room.

Elaine and Ian went in but she was nowhere to be seen. A dozen cots ran in rows with little room in between. They'd been in this room before on their very first visit when they'd arrived to be told that Lana was dead and the care worker had shown them other children they could adopt. What they saw now was no less disturbing and upsetting. Here lay some of the most disabled children, confined to cots and still without any stimulation, just staring into space, and thumb-sucking or rocking for comfort. The only improvement in the room seemed to be a single mobile hanging from the ceiling in one corner but visible to only a few infants in the cots beneath it.

'She must be in here somewhere,' Ian said quietly. 'There's no other way out.'

'Anastasia,' Elaine said, and bent down to look under the cots. 'There you are.' She was hiding under the cot furthest away, curled up and grinning. 'Come out of there.' Anastasia grinned some more.

Elaine made her way between the cots to where Anastasia was hiding and, getting onto her hands and knees, reached under the cot. 'Come on out. I'm sure you're not supposed to be here. You'll get into trouble.' The smell of urine was worse under the cots, and the floor needed a good scrub.

Anastasia finally came out and she and Elaine went to where Ian was waiting by the door. Anastasia seemed oblivious to the suffering of the children around them, probably because she saw them every day, but for Elaine and Ian it was a brutal reminder of the life these poor children had – existing rather than enjoying any quality of life. Like many couples who had adopted from this country, they made regular donations to charities set up to improve conditions in the orphanages, but change was painfully slow.

They returned to the playroom but Anastasia was restless and wouldn't settle to much for very long. Aware that this was their first meeting after a gap of three months and they had yet to check into their hotel and unpack, they stayed for just over an hour and then told Anastasia they would come tomorrow with toys, and went to find a care worker to see them out. The care worker was new, a bit more personable than the others, and willing to speak English. 'You come from England?' she asked as she opened the main door.

'Yes. This morning.'

'Anastasia is a very lucky girl to have a nice mummy and daddy,' she said.

'We're the lucky ones,' Elaine said, and Ian agreed.

She remained by the gate with Anastasia and encouraged her to wave goodbye as Ian and Elaine got into the cab.

'Goodbye, see you tomorrow,' Elaine called from her window.

'Yes, see you tomorrow,' the care worker replied.

'So, everything is good?' Danny asked, starting the engine.

'Yes, very good indeed,' Ian confirmed.

CHAPTER NINE

COURT HEARING

Ian and Elaine knew they'd made the right decision arriving a few days before the court hearing so they could spend time with Anastasia. Maggie had said she thought it was a good idea too. Although Anastasia clearly remembered them, there was a distance about her, a coolness towards them, which didn't immediately go over the following days and was probably a defence mechanism. They assumed it was the result of three months without seeing them, with little stimulation or interaction. Of course she was bound to feel rejected and cautious about showing affection in case she was abandoned again. It was only natural and to be expected, and they consoled themselves that once home any emotional damage she may have suffered would be quickly undone by their love, care and commitment. The new care worker was far more pleasant and approachable than the others had been and they asked her to take some photographs of Anastasia and them together.

Elaine and Ian were staying in the same hotel as before but hadn't seen Maria – the waitress they'd got to know – so after a couple of days they asked the new waitress where she was. 'Maria? Is she here?' Ian said.

'No. She leave.'

'Oh, where has she gone?' Elaine asked.

'To England to work. More money.'

Elaine nodded. Maria had told them that had been her plan. 'Did she take Lana with her?' Elaine asked.

'No. She stay with her mother.'

Although it was sad that Maria had to be parted from her daughter and would probably only be able to afford the fare home to see her once a year, it was common practice in this country. Wage earners went abroad to work where the wages were higher and then sent money home to the relative looking after their child.

'Do you know where she is living in England?' Elaine asked, thinking they might contact her.

'No. London, I think.' So it was unlikely they could trace her.

The days between their arrival and the court date flew by, with shopping in the morning and the afternoons spent at the orphanage with Anastasia. On the eve of the court hearing, having not seen or heard from Dr Ciobanu since the day they'd arrived, Ian and Elaine felt they would like to speak to him and have confirmation that Anastasia's mother had returned. They didn't want to antagonize him by suggesting they doubted his word, but it would be devastating if they arrived at court to find she wasn't there. After some deliberation, Ian telephoned Dr Ciobanu's mobile – he wouldn't be at the orphanage this late – and he answered with a rather curt 'Ciobanu'.

'Dr Ciobanu, Ian Hudson.'

'Yes, what can I do for you?'

'I'm sorry to disturb you but we just wanted to confirm that Anastasia's mother has returned ready for court tomorrow.'

'Yes, of course. Why shouldn't she?'

'No reason. Thank you. Sorry to trouble you.' Ian said a quick goodbye.

As they'd thought, Dr Ciobanu hadn't liked having his judgement questioned, but at least they had the reassurance they needed. Or did they? His response – 'Yes, of course. Why shouldn't she?' – almost sounded as though he hadn't checked, so Elaine and Ian weren't completely at ease. However, there was nothing further they could do but hope the doctor was right.

Good luck 4 tomorrow, Maggie texted as they were about to go to bed. *We're all thinking of you!*

Thank you! Elaine replied.

They didn't get much sleep that night and passed much of it by watching television programmes in a foreign language. Elaine kept getting out of bed to check that everything she needed for Anastasia was in the holdall they were taking to court: her coat, gloves, boots, drink and so forth.

They rose early and were the first down to breakfast, although neither of them had an appetite. Ian had fallen silent and kept checking his phone, while Elaine periodically raised the questions buzzing anxiously around her head: 'How long do you think the court hearing will last?' 'Will Anastasia's mother leave straight after?' 'Will she have someone with her for support?' 'Will she let us take a photograph of her?' And so on. They had photographs of the orphanage and their hotel room to include in Anastasia's Life Story Book, but they knew they wouldn't be allowed to take photographs inside the court, and Dr Ciobanu had made it clear that the mother had to be asked before one was taken of her. Elaine and Ian knew that some couples had photographs of their child's birth mother but others did not.

Once they finished breakfast, they returned to their hotel room to change into the suits they'd brought with them especially for their court appearance. With coats on over their suits, their passports in Ian's briefcase, Anastasia's belongings in a holdall and their anxiety rising, they went down to the lobby to wait for the cab they'd booked for 9.45. They'd used the same firm, as Dr Ciobanu had advised, but were disappointed when they saw a cab driver they didn't know come in and ask at reception for Mr and Mrs Hudson. It would have been comforting to see Danny's familiar face on such a momentous and nerve-racking day, and Danny had become part of their adoption journey. They even had a photograph of him standing by his cab to include in Anastasia's Life Story Book.

'No Danny?' Ian asked the driver once they were in the cab and on their way.

'He have day off. Visit his mother.'

'OK.'

'I take you to court building.'

'Yes, please.'

It was a twenty-minute journey to the court and Elaine and Ian passed the time by gazing out of their side windows at the unfamiliar streets. They hadn't ventured in this direction before. Houses gave way to a dual carriageway and then they were in the old part of the neighbouring town. The driver didn't try to make conversation – his English wasn't as good as Danny's – and he listened to the radio. When he parked outside a very old, grey stone building it took them a moment to realize it was the court house. It was tucked in one corner of a square of similar-aged buildings around a cobbled square that looked unchanged from a century or more ago.

'I wait here,' the driver said, and they got out.

'I'll need to use the bathroom,' Elaine said quietly to Ian as she followed him up the worn stone steps that led to the court house. A heavy wooden door with large wrought-iron hinges and a ring handle stood slightly ajar and Ian heaved it open. They entered a lobby with stone flagged flooring where a man – a court official – sat at a table with a printed sheet and a pen.

'Good morning. Mr and Mrs Hudson,' Ian said.

He ran his pen down the ten or so names on the list and ticked off their names, then gesticulated for them to put their bags onto the table. Giving the bags a perfunctory search, he waved Elaine and Ian through the door behind him. 'Waiting room – third door on your right,' he said.

'Thank you. Where is the ladies' bathroom?' Elaine asked.

'First door.'

Once inside it was obvious from the symbol on the door where the Ladies was. As Ian waited in the corridor outside, Anastasia and her mother arrived. Anastasia looked at him but didn't say anything and they went through a door further down.

'They're here,' Ian said as Elaine came out of the bath-room.

'Well, that's a relief,' she sighed, but her heart was racing. 'Was Dr Ciobanu with them?'

'No.'

'Where are they now?'

'In the waiting room, I think.'

They took a couple of steps and stopped, trying to prepare themselves for meeting Anastasia's mother. It would have been easier if Dr Ciobanu had been there to introduce them and possibly translate, but it seemed cowardly to wait in the corridor until he arrived. Anastasia's mother would be just as, if not more, nervous than they were. Although they'd known for a while that they'd meet Anastasia's mother, they had little idea of how to manage the situation – what to say or do.

Taking a deep breath, Ian opened the door and led the way into the waiting room. A dozen or so wooden chairs had been crammed in around the edges, and that was the only furniture in the room. A single light bulb hung from the centre of the ceiling, giving off a small glow in what was otherwise a dismal, dingy room. They looked at Anastasia and her mother sitting in one corner with spare chairs either side. Her mother had her head lowered and was looking down. Two men in their twenties, an elderly man and a middle-aged couple sat on the other side of the room.

Having seen them, Anastasia tugged at her mother's arm and then whispered something. Her mother looked up as Ian and Elaine crossed the room under the gaze of the others waiting. They both said hello to Anastasia's mother and she nodded in reply. They sat down, Elaine next to her and Ian beside her. Apparently she didn't have another adult with her for support. 'How are you?' Elaine asked awkwardly.

She shook her head and pointed to her lips, signalling she didn't have any English. Elaine threw her a reassuring smile, although she felt anything but confident herself. It was upsetting and surreal, sitting here in this foreign court waiting room beside the mother of the child who would shortly be theirs. It was like nothing she'd ever experienced before or would again. There was no point of reference, so she didn't know how to act. Elaine sat stiff and upright, struggling to contain her emotions under the inquisitive gaze of the others in the waiting room. It seemed Anastasia had been told to wait quietly, for there was none of her usual exuberance or inquisitiveness; she just sat beside her mother, looking around.

It was chilly; the only heat came from a small electric fire high up on one wall. Elaine and Ian, like the others waiting, had kept their coats on, but neither Anastasia nor her mother had coats. Anastasia was wearing the tracksuit bottoms and jumper they'd seen her in at the orphanage, her mother a long woollen dress with thick tights, a threadbare grey cardigan that could have been a man's and a headscarf. Elaine unzipped the holdall she'd placed at her feet and took out the coat they'd brought for Anastasia and passed it to her mother. She smiled and nodded, clearly pleased and impressed – it was probably the first new coat the child had ever possessed. She said something to Anastasia and then drew her from her chair and helped her into the coat. She turned to them and said, 'Thank you.' It was her only English and Elaine could have wept.

'Pity we didn't bring a coat for her mother too,' she said quietly to Ian. But that could have been construed as giving the mother a gift, which wasn't allowed.

The others in the court room had watched this and Elaine met their scrutinizing gaze and looked away, hoping they didn't have long to wait. If it was uncomfortable for them, it must have been torture for Anastasia's mother, although she seemed to be coping. Elaine tried to picture herself in her position, about to give up her child, and saw herself distraught and weeping uncontrollably. She assumed Anastasia's mother must have prepared herself for this moment over the previous year when it had became obvious, and she had accepted, that like other poor women in her position she couldn't look after her child and there was no alternative.

The door opened and another man came in, and then a few minutes later another couple, and the waiting room slowly filled. It was now 10.45. 'Where's Dr Ciobanu?' Ian said anxiously.

'How would I know?' Elaine returned tetchily, then apologized. Nerves were getting the better of her. 'I'm sure he knows what he's doing,' she said, and placed a reassuring hand on his.

Anastasia said something to her mother, who looked at Elaine, then she pointed to the holdall and gesticulated drinking. Elaine smiled and nodded. 'Yes, of course.'

Her mother must have been told they'd bring a drink for Anastasia. Elaine unzipped the holdall again and took out the selection of drinks she'd brought especially: small packets of apple and orange juice, strawberry and chocolate milkshakes and a bottle of water. Anastasia's eyes lit up and she took the chocolate milkshake.

'Thank you,' her mother said. She inserted the straw that was attached to the packet, then handed the drink back to Anastasia.

Five minutes later the door opened and Dr Ciobanu finally appeared. 'Thank goodness,' Ian said. He motioned for them all to go outside and they left the waiting room.

'Good, the child has a coat and a drink,' Dr Ciobanu said as they grouped around him. He exchanged a few words with Anastasia's mother in their own language and then turned to

them. 'Your hearing was set incorrectly for 2 p.m. this afternoon.' Elaine gasped. 'Don't worry, I have spoken to the judge
and it has been moved. We can't have the child waiting all
that time. You will go in second on the list.'

'Thank you,' Ian said gratefully.

'You have your passports with you?'

'Yes.' Ian took them out of his briefcase and passed them to
Dr Ciobanu, who tucked them into the folder he held. 'We
can wait outside the court room,' he said. 'The first case is
being heard now. It won't take long.' Elaine felt her heart
start to pound.

Anastasia's mother took her daughter's hand and walked
behind Dr Ciobanu. Ian and Elaine followed them down a
corridor where they stopped at the door at the end.

'We will be told when to go in,' Dr Ciobanu said, then
translated for Anastasia's mother. She nodded solemnly.

They stood in awkward silence, tense and sombre, and not
sure where to look. Even Dr Ciobanu had lost his usual
relaxed manner and kept opening and closing his folder –
more as a displacement for anxiety than checking the contents.
Elaine stole occasional glances at Anastasia and her mother,
who kept her gaze down. Then Dr Ciobanu said something
to her and she looked up and replied. Elaine glanced at him.
'I asked her when she was returning to work and she said
tomorrow.' Elaine nodded.

A few minutes later the court room door suddenly opened
and a man and a teenage boy came out. 'We're in next,' Dr
Ciobanu said, straightening. 'Wait here.' He disappeared
inside and the door closed behind him.

Elaine met Anastasia's mother's eyes and saw her anxiety,
and for a few seconds they were both united in the bond of

their ordeal. Ian cleared his throat nervously and no one spoke. Then the door to the court room opened again and Dr Ciobanu said, 'Come in. Only speak when the judge asks you to.'

Elaine swallowed hard. This was it. The time had finally come, and they followed Anastasia and her mother into the court room. Her gaze went to the judge, who sat behind a bench on a raised plinth at the front of the court, reading paperwork. Two rows of empty chairs were in front of him. He didn't immediately look up. A court official and a police officer sat behind a desk to the right of the podium.

'Wait there until you are told to approach the bench,' Dr Ciobanu said quietly, pointing to a place a few yards in front. He translated for Anastasia's mother and she joined them. Elaine saw she was chewing her lip anxiously as she held her daughter's hand; the empty drink packet dangled from Anastasia's other hand.

The room was quiet save for some distant street noise. They waited without moving as the judge continued to read their paperwork. In his fifties, he wore a dark suit and half-rimmed glasses. Elaine and Ian could see their passports on the bench beside their adoption application. The room was grey stone like the rest of the building and not much warmer. Elaine shivered, although more from nerves than cold.

Presently the judge looked up and said something to Dr Ciobanu, who replied. Then there appeared to be some more questions and answers between them. Elaine's and Ian's apprehension grew. Was there something wrong with their application that would stop the adoption going ahead? Anastasia's mother would understand what was being said but her face was expressionless. It fell quiet again as the judge turned the pages of their application, then he took a sip of water from the glass on the bench and nodded at Dr Ciobanu. He said something to Anastasia's mother who took her daughter's hand and stepped forward. The empty milkshake carton dropped and she quickly picked it up and stuffed it in her cardigan pocket.

The judge spoke to her and appeared to ask her some questions, his tone authoritative. She replied in a small, timid voice, head bent and only occasionally meeting his gaze. Then she must have been told to return to where she'd been standing, and it was their turn. 'Go forward,' Dr Ciobanu told them. 'Call the judge "Sir".'

They took the few steps to where Anastasia and her mother had stood. Elaine felt her legs tremble and hoped they wouldn't give way. 'You are Ian and Elaine Hudson?' the judge asked in very good English, addressing Ian.

'Yes, Sir.'

'You and your wife have applied to adopt this child Anastasia?'

'Yes, Sir,' Ian said again.

'You are from England. I studied there.' Ian nodded and then smiled, unsure if he should say something, but the judge was continuing. 'I have read the Home Study report from your social worker. You can't have children?'

'No, Sir.'

'And you can provide for the child? You know you are expected to open a bank account for her when you return and save for her each month.'

'Yes, Sir.'

He said something to Dr Ciobanu in their own language and then to Anastasia's mother, who gave a small nod.

Looking at them again, he said, 'I grant the adoption. The child is yours.'

It took them a few seconds to realize that it had happened, that the adoption had been granted and Anastasia was theirs. All those months of planning and waiting and it was over in ten minutes. But Anastasia's mother had clearly been expecting this moment and knew what to do. She brought her daughter to them, placed a small crucifix in her hand and, kissing her cheek, turned and hurried out of the court room. The door banged shut as Ian and Elaine stared after her.

'Wait outside the court room while I get the paperwork from the judge,' Dr Ciobanu told them. 'I will join you shortly.'

Numb and completely overwhelmed, they took Anastasia by the hand and began towards the door. It was then that Ian realized they didn't have a photograph of Anastasia's mother. 'Wait here,' Ian said as they emerged from the court room. 'I'll see if I can find her.' Dropping Anastasia's hand, he hurried down the corridor in search of her mother.

CHAPTER TEN

ALL NEW

No words can describe how Elaine felt at that moment as she stood in the corridor outside the courtroom holding her daughter's hand. Disbelief, euphoria, relief and panic combined as she stood immobile, staring after Ian. Then realization and responsibility kicked in. She was a parent and needed to behave like one. She looked at Anastasia, who returned her gaze, wide-eyed and confused. Did she understand what had just happened in the court room? Did she have any idea? She wasn't crying or upset, so perhaps like her mother this was simply the end of a long and inevitable journey. 'Are you all right, love?' Elaine asked quietly, and Anastasia stared back.

Ian reappeared, out of breath and clutching his phone. 'I got two photos of her,' he said.

'How was she?' Elaine asked.

'Upset, as you'd expect, but she wiped away her tears and put on a brave face for the photograph. I think she was pleased I'd asked her and that we are going to keep her memory alive for Anastasia.'

Ian showed her the two photographs he'd taken in the square outside the court house and Elaine's eyes immediately filled. The woman was looking directly into the lens and trying to smile so that her daughter would have a positive image to remember her by. It felt uncomfortable standing outside the court room, looking at photographs as if they were on holiday. But these two pictures would probably be the most important either of them ever took. Elaine was pleased they were nice photos. A copy would go in Anastasia's Life Story Book and another they'd frame and put on a shelf in her bedroom so she would grow up aware of her origins, just as the social worker had said.

Seeing Ian's mobile phone, Anastasia agitated to look and he showed her the photographs and then put it away. Phones and cameras weren't allowed in the court house.

'Well,' he said to Elaine with a big sigh, 'we've finally done it! Congratulations.' He kissed her cheek, then stooped to kiss Anastasia's. Her skin felt cold. 'I don't think she's warm enough,' he said to Elaine. 'Perhaps put on her hat, scarf and boots.'

'Oh dear, yes, of course,' Elaine said, immediately concerned for her daughter's welfare.

They tucked themselves in a corner of the corridor out of the way, and Elaine unzipped the holdall and took out the fleece-lined boots, then the matching scarf, mittens and hat. Anastasia's face lit up, clearly having never owned anything like this before.

'I hope the boots fit,' Elaine said, squatting beside her to put them on. She carefully slipped off the plimsolls she was wearing and, with Anastasia steadying herself against Ian's leg, she eased her feet into the boots. They were slightly too big but better that than too small. Anastasia looked down at them, delighted. Elaine tucked her jogging pants into the boots and then eased her little hands into the mittens. Anastasia was still holding the crucifix and later Elaine would put it somewhere safe. She tied the woollen scarf loosely around her neck and put on her hat. It felt strange dressing her, like dressing a doll, but she knew she'd soon get used to it.

'That looks snug and warm,' Ian said.

Elaine put the plimsolls into the holdall. They'd keep those and the clothes Anastasia had worn for the court hearing to show her when she was older. The crucifix she'd place in the Memory Box together with anything else significant that would help give Anastasia a better understanding of her past.

The court room door opened and Dr Ciobanu came out clutching a wodge of papers, his folder and their passports. 'You can have these back,' he said, handing the passports to Ian. 'I have the adoption certificate but I will need it to apply for Anastasia's new birth certificate, passport and visa. You can go to your hotel now and I'll be in touch just as soon as I've had these processed.' He clearly had a lot to do and wanted to get away.

'Thank you,' Ian said, shaking his hand.

'Thank you,' Elaine added.

'You have a cab waiting?'

'Yes.'

'OK. I'll be in touch.'

'Dr Ciobanu,' Elaine said quickly before he left, 'does Anastasia know what happened in court? That she has now been adopted?'

'Yes, I would think so,' he said. Then almost as an after-thought he said something to her in her own language.

'Mummy and Daddy,' she said, puzzled, then her brow knitted and her face clouded.

'She'll be fine,' he said, patting her woolly hat. 'Take her back to the hotel and give her a bath and something to eat.' He said a quick goodbye and hurried off. Months later, looking back, Ian and Elaine were sure that was the moment Anastasia had been told what had happened in court.

'Mummy and Daddy,' she repeated quietly.

'Yes, come on, love, let's go,' Elaine said.

They took a mittened hand each and Elaine felt Anastasia's fingers tighten around the crucifix, as they returned down the corridor. Outside the cab was waiting where they'd left it, the driver at the wheel. It seemed a lifetime ago that they'd arrived at the court house, although it was little more than an hour. Ian opened the rear door and helped Elaine and Anastasia in, then tucked the holdall in the footwell at Anastasia's feet and got into the passenger seat at the front.

The journey back to the hotel seemed quicker than going, for now they had Anastasia to tend to. To begin with she sat quietly beside Elaine under the adult seatbelt, looking at everything around her: the driver, the back of Ian, the seats, the hand brake, the windows, the door furniture and the view through her side window. Perhaps it was the first time she'd ever been in a car, they had no way of knowing, but clearly she was fascinated by what she saw. Then she grew restless. The car was much warmer than the court house and Anastasia pulled off her hat and threw it into the footwell at Elaine's feet. Elaine picked it up.

'Are you too hot, love?' she asked, taking off her scarf; she left on her mittens. A moment later Anastasia pulled off her mittens and threw them at Elaine's feet. She picked them up, took out the crucifix and tucked it into her pocket for safekeeping. Anastasia wriggled, tried to remove her seatbelt, which Elaine told her had to stay on, then she began straining forward, tugging on her belt to get at the holdall at her feet.

'Perhaps she wants another drink?' Ian suggested, turning round in his seat to look.

Elaine unfastened her own seatbelt so she could reach the holdall and took out the first carton of drink she came across – the apple juice. But it was obvious from Anastasia's scowl this wasn't the drink she wanted. Elaine rummaged some more and took out the other packets. Anastasia grabbed the strawberry milkshake.

'Do you want some help?' Elaine asked, refastening her belt, as Anastasia struggled to remove the straw from the side of the carton. But she wanted to do it herself and eventually managed to tear off the straw as she'd seen her mother do. She inserted it into the packet with too much force and strawberry milkshake shot everywhere – down the front of her coat, the car seat and her side window. Her expression immediately fell serious as if she expected to be told off.

'Don't worry,' Elaine said, taking tissues from her pocket. 'It was an accident.' She wiped the milk from her coat, the car seat and the window. The driver glanced in his mirror but didn't comment.

It was a relief when they pulled up outside their hotel. Ian paid and tipped the driver and then opened the back door and helped Anastasia out. As the three of them entered the hotel the staff at the reception desk stopped what they were doing to look. They knew they'd been to court that morning and were now interested to see the child they'd adopted. Ian gave them the thumbs up and Elaine smiled but they didn't go over. They wanted to go to their hotel room to get organized, give Anastasia a bath as Dr Ciobanu had suggested, dress her in fresh clothes and then use room service for something to eat. They knew they needed to take it slowly and give Anastasia time to adjust. To rush out to a restaurant or start meeting lots of new people straight away would have been too much for her to cope with. They'd learned from other couples that virtually every experience was likely to be new for the child, so they should take it very easy and not overload her – too many new experiences too soon would be confusing and distressing for her.

'This is a lift,' Elaine said to Anastasia as they got in. It was empty. 'Lift,' Elaine repeated as she did with all new words, hoping Anastasia would learn them.

Anastasia let out a startled cry as the lift began moving, then caught sight of her image in the mirror and stuck out her tongue. Ian and Elaine laughed. Anastasia gave another startled cry as the lift shuddered to a halt. 'It's OK,' Elaine reassured her. 'It's just the lift stopping.' The lift doors opened. 'We're going to our hotel room,' she told her.

Anastasia looked in awe at the patterned carpet in the corridor and bent down to touch it as though she'd never seen carpet before. Perhaps she hadn't. There was certainly none in the orphanage; all the floors were tiled.

Their room was meticulously tidy as always after the maid had been in. 'Let's take off your coat,' Elaine said, unzipping it. Anastasia stared around, amazed. She slipped it off but before Elaine had a chance to remove her boots, Anastasia had rushed over to the double bed, running her hands over the silky patterned bedspread. 'She's probably never seen anything like this before either.'

'They haven't put up the extra bed,' Ian said, slightly irritated. 'I told reception this morning we'd need it. I'll phone housekeeping now.'

As he did, Elaine took off Anastasia's boots and then watched her as she went around the room exploring, touching everything she could reach – the dark wood furniture, the velvet armchair, the glass-topped coffee table, their suitcases. Elaine told her the words for the objects, and when she went into the en suite Elaine followed. Anastasia looked incredulously at the gleaming white porcelain. They had showers and toilets at the orphanage but nothing like this, and it was likely that wherever she'd stayed with her mother was very basic too. Anastasia went over to the toilet, lifted the lid and, pulling down her pants, climbed on. 'Good girl,' Elaine said, pushing the door to. Ian was still on the phone trying to organize the bed.

While Anastasia wasn't at all self-conscious in going to the toilet and then wiping herself, Elaine felt a little awkward, not sure what her role was. Had Anastasia been a baby she would have changed her nappy, but she had obviously passed that stage and was now very self-sufficient. She flushed the toilet but was going to leave the bathroom without washing her hands.

'Come here, love,' Elaine said, steering her to the washbasin. 'You need to wash your hands.' Elaine ran the water to the right temperature and, placing the small tablet of hotel soap in Anastasia's hands, helped her wash them. They were grubby from the day's grime. 'We could give you a bath now,' Elaine suggested as the child dried her hands. It seemed as good a time as any. 'Then you can put on your new clothes.' She smiled.

Anastasia stared at her without the slightest idea what she was talking about. 'Bath,' Elaine repeated, touching the bath. Anastasia frowned, puzzled. They only had showers at the orphanage so it was possible she'd never seen a bath before. 'I'll show you,' Elaine said. She put in the plug, turned on the taps and ran the water, checking the temperature as the bath filled. She then helped Anastasia out of her clothes and lifted her in. As her feet touched the warm water she screamed with delight and screamed again even louder as she sat down and the water lapped around her waist. 'Shh,' Elaine said lightly, putting her finger to her lips. 'Daddy is on the phone.' Anastasia slapped the water at the side of her with the palm of her hand, creating a splash.

Elaine noticed her skin was very pale, as though she'd never been outside, and there were some red sores on her back, which she would get checked by the doctor when they took Anastasia for a medical once they were home. Anastasia loved her bath and it wasn't long before she was splashing and kicking. Water flew up the walls, in her face and all over Elaine. They both laughed and Elaine finally started to relax. This was an example of what motherhood was all about – enjoying bathtime with your child, and at home was a selection of bath toys and bubble bath to make the experience even more fun.

Ian finished on the phone and stuck his head round the door. 'They're bringing up a folding bed now,' he said. 'You're having fun.'

'We are!' Elaine cried. He left them to it.

The water turned grey, suggesting Anastasia hadn't had a

full body wash for some time. Elaine would have liked to wash her hair – it smelled of the orphanage – but decided to leave it for now. The water was cooling and they hadn't eaten since breakfast.

'Time to get out,' she said, and motioned for Anastasia to stand. Anastasia stayed where she was. 'Come on, love. We're getting something to eat. Food.' She pointed to her mouth and mimed eating.

Anastasia continued splashing, harder now, kicking her feet and soaking Elaine. Elaine laughed indulgently but she really did need Anastasia out now. When it became obvious she wasn't going to leave the bath, Elaine removed the plug and the water slowly drained away. Anastasia sat in the depleting water, watching it disappear until there was just a small puddle left. 'All gone,' Elaine said.

'Gone,' Anastasia repeated and Elaine clapped. She'd learned another new word!

Anastasia was now willing to be helped out and Elaine wrapped her in a bath towel and patted her dry. She guided her into the bedroom where she dressed her in the new clothes. Clean from the bath and wearing the clothes and pink furry slippers Elaine had chosen, Anastasia seemed to have become more their child. Once her hair was washed and styled, that would help too.

A knock sounded on the door and Ian answered it. Two chambermaids came in carrying a foldaway bed. They stared inquisitively at Anastasia and Elaine felt slightly uncomfortable.

'Over there, please,' Ian said, showing them where they wanted the bed. They unfolded it and put it into place, but there was just the bed and mattress, no bedding. 'Duvet?

Covers?' Ian asked. They looked back at him blankly. 'Bedding,' he said, showing them on the bed.

One of them nodded, said something to the other, and they headed out. As they passed Anastasia the same one muttered something to Anastasia in her own language. Anastasia clearly understood and, from her expression, whatever had been said wasn't positive, and could even have been nasty, for she looked at them anxiously. Clearly Ian and Elaine had no idea what had been said and Anastasia couldn't translate. They were aware that some of the population were opposed to international adoption, believing they'd be better off in the state-run orphanages – which clearly wasn't true. When the women returned with the bedding Ian thanked them but took it from them at the door and said they'd make up the bed, so they had no contact with Anastasia.

With little idea of the food Anastasia liked or was used to, Ian and Elaine ordered a selection of dishes from the room-service menu, including French fries. All children liked French fries, didn't they? When the food arrived Ian took it at the door, and they sat on the bed to eat with the trays of food between them and told Anastasia it was like having a picnic. She was fascinated by the plates of attractively presented food but ate virtually nothing. She took a tiny bite from everything but no more, which was worrying. She wouldn't have had anything since early that morning, apart from the two small cartons of milkshake. Elaine and Ian both tried to tempt her, offering little portions of the food to her mouth, but she refused, shaking her head and clamping her lips tightly shut.

'Perhaps she'll have something later,' Elaine said, and gave her the glass of orange juice they'd ordered. She didn't want that, or the cup of tea Elaine cooled with extra milk. Her gaze went to the holdall they'd taken to court but hadn't unpacked. Scrambling from the bed, she went over and began tugging at the zip, trying to undo it.

'Carton of drink,' Ian said as Elaine left the bed to help her.

Elaine took out the cartons of juice and the bottle of water, but these clearly weren't what Anastasia had in mind. 'There aren't any more milkshakes,' she said, shaking her head. 'All gone.' But Anastasia had to see for herself and emptied out the entire contents of the bag before she was satisfied, then grabbed the carton of apple juice. Elaine waited as she put in the straw and then mopped up the spillage with tissues. She finished the drink quickly and Elaine tried to tempt her to eat again, but she wasn't interested. Ian had nearly finished his meal.

'Tomorrow, we could all go to the supermarket we've been using,' he suggested. 'She could choose what she likes then.'

'Yes, good idea,' Elaine agreed.

Anastasia joined them on the bed as Elaine ate, then she began yawning and rubbing her eyes. 'You must be exhausted, pet,' Elaine said gently to her. 'Try to have a little sleep.' She helped Anastasia to snuggle down. Anastasia rubbed her face against the soft, luxurious feel of the duvet and began sucking her thumb. It wasn't long before her eyes closed and she fell into a deep sleep. Ian and Elaine gazed at her admiringly. Her little features relaxed in sleep, she was gorgeous and everything they could possibly have wished for. Her breath fell light and even and her thumb slipped from her mouth as she slept. If they'd known then what was to follow, they might have taken the opportunity to rest themselves while they had the chance. Anastasia slept for two hours and then woke with a start.

CHAPTER ELEVEN

EXHAUSTED

It was just after 4 p.m. when Anastasia's eyes shot open and she was immediately off the bed and at the door of their hotel room. It was such a sudden awakening that it made Ian and Elaine start and they wondered if she was fully awake, but any doubt quickly vanished as she began hammering on the door. Elaine went to her. 'No, love. Quietly,' she said, trying to draw her away. 'There are other people in this hotel. Don't bang the door.' Which of course was meaningless to Anastasia. She broke from Elaine's hold and ran around the room screaming – not crying or upset, just screaming.

'She's got a good set of lungs on her,' Ian quipped. They hadn't heard her scream before, but Elaine wasn't amused.

'Shhh, quietly,' she said, catching her by the arm. 'Shhh.' She put her finger to her lips. 'Too much noise. What's the matter?' Anastasia stared at her blankly. 'Let's get you some toys out to play with. Ian, can you help, please?'

He left the bed and, opening the suitcase containing Anastasia's belongings, took out some of the new toys they'd brought with them, including another activity centre. He set them beside Anastasia and then took the trays off the bed and put them outside the door for room service to collect later. Seeing the door open, Anastasia made a dash for it, but Ian quickly closed it. She banged on it with her fists, clearly wanting to be out.

'Come on, play with the toys,' Elaine encouraged, going to her. But Anastasia was more interested in the door.

'It's like that first day we were with her at the orphanage,' Ian said. 'Do you remember, she kept going to the window and then ran off?'

Elaine didn't find this reminder helpful and drew Anastasia away from the door towards the toys. They both tried to engage her in play, but a few moments later she was at the door again, hammering for all she was worth. Exasperated, not sure what to do for the best and feeling a little rejected, Elaine went to her. 'Anastasia, you can't go out, love. You're staying with us. We're your mummy and daddy.'

'Mummy and Daddy,' she repeated, and thumped the door harder.

'Perhaps we should go for a walk?' Ian suggested. 'I know we were planning on spending the rest of the day here to give her a chance to adjust but that's not working. We could go to the supermarket now rather than tomorrow?'

Elaine agreed, and with a plan of action felt more positive. 'We're going out,' she told Anastasia and picked up her coat and boots. As soon as Anastasia saw her outdoor wear she realized they were leaving, stopped banging on the door and went to Elaine.

Used to being self-sufficient and doing things for herself, Anastasia rejected Elaine's help and began struggling into her clothes herself. Putting on boots, a coat, mittens, hat and scarf is difficult for any two-year-old, even if they are independent, and it kept Anastasia quietly occupied for a good ten minutes. 'Perhaps give her clothes to play with in future,' Ian remarked dryly, and finally Elaine smiled. 'It will be OK,' he reassured her, kissing her cheek. 'Just give her time. It's all new for her as it is for us.'

With Anastasia finally dressed for going out, she allowed Elaine to do up the zipper on her coat and take her hand, and they left the room. Ian summoned the lift and the couple who were already in it moved aside to make space for them. However, the woman blocked Anastasia's view of herself in the mirror and she pushed her aside so she could see. The woman smiled indulgently but Elaine apologized and said firmly to Anastasia, 'No. It's rude to push.' She appreciated that until now Anastasia had probably had to push to fend for herself and take what she wanted, and was therefore more 'streetwise' than the average two-year-old. But that was behind her now and she'd have to slowly learn what was polite in order to fit in.

Reception was busy so Elaine and Ian were able to slip out without having to go to the desk and introduce Anastasia to the staff. They felt that once they knew Anastasia better and were used to her ways, they would be more confident parenting her, and would of course show her off. But for now there were so many unknowns, especially in her behaviour, that they didn't want any nasty surprises in public, which they might struggle to cope with.

Elaine had to insist that Anastasia held her hand while near the road. 'Cars hurt,' she told her. Ian took Anastasia's other hand and they crossed the busy main road.

Anastasia seemed less agitated now than she had done in the hotel and the walk to the supermarket was uneventful, although it was cold, and the light was failing early in winter. The supermarket wasn't much warmer and the two cashiers positioned near the doors were wearing their coats. They looked at Elaine, Ian and Anastasia as they entered, intrigued. Although the women didn't speak English they had got to know Ian and Elaine by sight from their daily visits and must have wondered who the child was. It was possible they'd surmised they had adopted her as this was the closest shop to the hotel where other couples who were in the country to adopt had stayed. Ian nodded politely and then the three of them began up and down the aisles, looking at the shelves crammed full of goods.

Anastasia was fascinated; perhaps she'd never been in a shop before – it was impossible to know. With a month to go before Christmas, new festive goods were being added daily, glittering and enticing. They had to stop Anastasia touching everything in case she dropped or damaged an item – the glass baubles were especially fragile. They'd really come here so she could choose some food she liked, and they gradually led her to the tins, packets, and fridge and freezer food. Anastasia was far more interested in baubles and tinsel. Elaine said that perhaps it was asking a bit much to expect a two-year-old – even one who knew her own mind – to choose food. Ian agreed and pointed out it was a pity they couldn't ask a member of staff what children in this country ate, as they didn't speak the language. Dr Ciobanu's guidance notes had advised adopters of babies which powdered milk to bring, and said that children on solids ate a variety of meat and vegetables, bread and thick soups. After spending half an hour in the shop they bought something that looked like a local variation on a Pot Noodle – it just needed boiling water to be added to it. They also bought bread rolls, apples, bananas, a milkshake and a fairy for the top of the Christmas tree that Anastasia wouldn't let go of.

The cashier smiled at Anastasia as she checked the items through and then gave her a lollipop from a box at the side of the till. Elaine thanked her. It was a nice gesture and her friendly manner towards Anastasia suggested that if she knew they'd adopted, she approved.

Outside, Anastasia enjoyed the lollipop as they headed back to their hotel. 'Well, at least that's one thing she'll eat,' Ian remarked. 'Perhaps we should go back and buy the whole jar?' Elaine smiled, aware he was joking.

It was dark now save for the street lamps and car headlights, and even colder as night fell. There was no way of knowing what Anastasia was thinking or feeling, or where she thought they were going. She seemed quite content sucking her lollipop until they approached the hotel, then she suddenly stopped dead and refused to move.

'What is it, love?' Elaine asked. She'd taken the lollipop from her mouth and looked frightened and confused. 'We're going to our hotel room,' Elaine gently reassured her. 'Come on, love. We can't stand out here. It's freezing.' But Anastasia refused to move.

Elaine tried persuading and coercing her, then tugged gently on her arm, but Anastasia stood her ground. Passers-by glanced at them. 'You'll have to pick her up and carry her,' Elaine said to Ian at last, trying again to move her forward. Anastasia resisted.

'OK, I'll give you a carry,' Ian said, and scooped her up. Anastasia opened her mouth and screamed for all she was worth. He quickly put her down again.

'You walk then,' Elaine said anxiously, starting to panic. 'Come on. We can't stay here.'

Anastasia stared at her but didn't move. Elaine tried again to persuade her, so did Ian, but the child's expression was set. It was clear she wasn't going anywhere of her own accord.

'You'll have to carry her,' Elaine said again in desperation.

Ian picked her up. Anastasia screamed but he continued into the hotel with Elaine following close behind. Reception was still busy but whereas before, on their way out, it had been an asset, now it was every parent's nightmare. Guests and staff turned to see where the noise was coming from, some with condemnatory expressions, wondering what the problem was, and why the parents couldn't control their child. Keeping their eyes averted, Elaine and Ian hurried across the lobby to the lift, which mercifully was waiting and empty. Stepping in, Elaine quickly pressed the button for their floor and the doors closed. Accepting defeat, Anastasia stopped screaming and struggled to be put down. A bit flushed but otherwise unfazed, she continued sucking her lollipop.

'First battle won,' Ian said perkily, but Elaine wasn't so sure.

Her confidence had taken a big hit. Not only had she no idea what had provoked Anastasia's tantrum, but she didn't know how they should have handled it. Supposing she did it again when they couldn't just pick her up and run to their hotel room? What would she do then? She suddenly felt great empathy for those parents she'd seen in the street or supermarket who gave in to their screaming toddler's demands. If held to ransom by her child in a public place, she was in no doubt she'd do the same.

Once in their hotel room, energized from the two-hour sleep that afternoon, Anastasia ran around opening drawers, pulling on cupboard doors, rummaging in their cases and generally exploring everything in sight. Although it was only natural for a child to be inquisitive, it was wearing. Elaine followed her around, returning items to their correct places and making sure she didn't do any damage or hurt herself. She picked up the discarded lollipop stick that Anastasia threw on the floor and put it in the waste-paper basket. A few times Anastasia babbled something in her own language, perhaps about the object she was investigating. Elaine told her the word in English but Anastasia didn't repeat it. When she ran into the bathroom Elaine followed her and had to stop her from repeatedly flushing the toilet and turning on the taps, which fascinated her. She tried to climb into the bath.

'You can have another bath tomorrow,' Elaine said. 'I'll wash your hair too.'

Not understanding, and preferring to have her own way, Anastasia kept trying to climb over the side of the bath and eventually slipped and bumped her head. Not a bad knock but enough to make her cry out, mutter something – that could have been a curse – and give the bath a good kick.

'Shall I make up that Pot Noodle or whatever it is?' Ian called from the bedroom. 'She may be hungry now.'

'Yes, please,' Elaine returned. The instructions on the side of the pot were diagrammatic, and simply involved pouring boiling water onto the contents of the pot and letting it stand for two minutes to hydrate. There was a kettle in the room for making tea and coffee.

Having heard Ian's voice, and sensing something was going on that needed her attention, Anastasia ran from the bathroom. Elaine then had to keep her away from the boiling kettle, which she wanted to touch. As they waited for the mixture to hydrate and then cool a little, Ian looked up the main ingredients listed on the pot in their phrase book. 'Mutton,' he translated. 'Flour, noodles, cabbage, onion, pepper …' and so on.

Once the food was ready, Ian tested it. 'Interesting,' he said, unsure.

Anastasia was also interested in what was in the pot as the aroma rose and spread around the room. Elaine guided her to the chair, spread a tissue on her lap and gave her the pot and spoon, but stayed close by to help her or mop up the mess. Anastasia peered in, stirred the mixture, jiggled the spoon up and down but didn't eat. 'Hmm, yummy. Eat it,' Elaine encouraged, smacking her lips.

Anastasia played with the food some more but didn't try to eat it. 'You must be hungry by now,' Elaine said. 'You've had nothing all day.' Taking the spoon, she ate a little herself in the hope Anastasia would copy, but she just pushed the pot away. Elaine tried again without success. It appeared that when Anastasia set her mind to something she was resolute.

'Perhaps we could try room service again?' Ian suggested when it was clear Anastasia wasn't going to eat the food in the pot. 'We'll have to order for us before long.'

'But what?' Elaine asked. 'She hardly ate anything of what we ordered last time.'

'I could ask someone in the kitchen for advice,' he said. 'Surely they will know what children here like to eat.' He went to the phone by the bed and pressed the key for room service. 'Speak English?' he asked when it was answered.

'A little.'

'What do children living here like to eat?'

'You want to eat?'

'Yes, but I need to know what a child living in this country likes to eat.'

'The room service menu is in your room by the phone,' came the reply.

'I know. Thank you. What do I order for a child?'

'You would like to order now?' So it appeared his English was very limited.

'We'll order later. Thank you,' Ian said, and ended the call. Elaine looked at him.

'I have another idea,' he said. 'At least one of the girls at the reception desk speaks good English. I'll take Anastasia down and ask her to find out what she likes to eat. Failing that, if she doesn't eat tomorrow we'll have to phone Dr Ciobanu for advice.'

'What if Anastasia throws a tantrum and starts screaming when you try to bring her back?' Elaine asked, worried.

'I'll carry her.'

'I'll come with you to help,' she said.

'No. You stay here and have a rest. We won't be long.'

'Are you sure?'

'Yes.'

Elaine smiled gratefully. A few minutes to herself would be very welcome right now. She took one of Anastasia's cardigans from her case as it was cooler in reception and helped her into it. 'See you soon. Be good,' she said, and kissed her cheek. Anastasia stared at her, uncomprehending.

Once they'd gone, Elaine had a quick tidy up – the room was in a mess – and then lay on the bed and tried to relax. Her eyes felt heavy and her forehead tight as if she had the beginning of a headache. Little wonder with everything they'd been through in the last twenty-four hours, and she reminded herself what a momentous, life-changing day it had been. They had woken as a childless couple, attended court, which had been emotionally exhausting in itself, and now they were parents, and Ian was out with their daughter. It didn't get more significant than that!

Ian was gone for over half an hour and Elaine was on the verge of going to find them when she heard thumping on the door – Anastasia – and then Ian inserting his key card into the lock. Anastasia rushed into the room, clearly very excited. Ian was smiling too. 'That girl on reception was so helpful,' he said. 'She was about to finish her shift but when I explained our problem she stayed and had a good chat with Anastasia. Then she helped me order from room service. I've ordered for us too. It should be here in about twenty minutes.'

'Fantastic,' Elaine said. She picked up Anastasia's cardigan, which she'd thrown on the floor. 'What else did she talk to her about? You were gone ages.'

'She told Anastasia we were nice people and she was lucky to have a mummy and daddy to look after her. I asked her to explain that we would be staying in the hotel for a week and then flying home, and I showed her the photos of where we lived on my phone. She also told me about a park not far from here. I thought we could try it tomorrow, although obviously it's cold so we wouldn't stay long.'

'Great. And Anastasia didn't scream when you tried to bring her up to the room?'

'No. She was fine. So hopefully she understands more now and will settle.'

'Wonderful. Thank you.' Buoyed up and feeling more positive, Elaine took out the crayons and colouring book she'd brought with them to keep Anastasia amused until their dinner arrived.

What she didn't know until months later, when Anastasia had learned sufficient English to tell her, was that she'd repeatedly told the receptionist she didn't want to stay with Mummy and Daddy, but to go back to the orphanage.

Despite ordering what Anastasia had told the receptionist she wanted, when the food arrived she ate very little. Ian said again that if it didn't change tomorrow they'd have to phone Dr Ciobanu for advice. He and Elaine ate and then it was time for Anastasia to go to bed. Elaine helped her change into her pyjamas without too much fuss, explaining what she was doing and why, although Anastasia didn't understand. Then she took her to the bathroom to brush her teeth. Anastasia seemed to know how to brush her teeth but didn't like the toothpaste, although it was one sold in England for toddlers. She pulled a face and spat it on the floor. Elaine tried her with their adult toothpaste but she didn't like that either. Perhaps she'd never used toothpaste before, but at least she had brushed her teeth, which was important.

Elaine and Ian knew it wasn't ideal all sleeping in one room, but there wasn't an alternative, and it was only for a week and then they'd be home and Anastasia would have her own room. Elaine also knew that establishing a good bedtime routine was important, so she read Anastasia a story, persuaded her into the foldaway bed, which was close to theirs, then they both kissed her goodnight and Ian dimmed the lights. As they were all in the same room Ian and Elaine lay on their bed and pretended to be asleep, with the intention that once Anastasia was in a deep sleep they could read for a while. But Anastasia had different ideas. She was in a strange room where everything was new and interesting. She certainly wasn't ready to sleep. And unlike at the orphanage where the bars on her cot had kept her in, as well as a good telling-off if she tried to climb out, there were no bars on her bed and she was able to slip out easily. She ran around the room, not upset but more hyperactive, opening and closing drawers, picking up anything she could reach and then banging on the door. Elaine and Ian repeatedly resettled her and told her it was bedtime.

By midnight, when she still hadn't settled, they were exhausted and craving sleep themselves, so they tried taking her into their bed, but she clambered out. Just before 2 a.m. their bedside phone rang and Ian answered it. It was reception. Someone had complained about the noise coming from their room and they were asked to keep it down for the convenience of other guests. Ian apologized and Elaine felt acutely embarrassed. They knew they were going to have to be firmer with Anastasia, so they took her into their bed again and this time stopped her from leaving. She screamed, kicked, tried to hit them but eventually fell asleep. When Elaine woke at 7.10 Anastasia was nowhere to be seen.

CHAPTER TWELVE

ANOTHER WORRY

'Where's Anastasia?' Elaine cried, sitting bolt upright and waking Ian. They were both immediately out of bed. She wasn't in the room and Elaine rushed into the bathroom, followed by Ian. She was sitting on the floor, surrounded by the contents of Elaine's handbag and playing with her mobile phone. 'That's naughty,' Elaine said, taking the phone from her. Anastasia looked hurt.

'She's only playing,' Ian said.

'It's not your phone,' Elaine said sharply, checking to see what damage had been done.

Ian began collecting together the contents of Elaine's hand-bag and returning them to the bag. Seeing her playthings disappear, Anastasia screamed.

'Stop it!' Elaine shouted, her nerves frayed from tiredness.

'Come on,' Ian said, taking Anastasia's hand. 'You can look at the photos on Daddy's phone while Mummy showers and dresses.'

He took Anastasia into the room, sat her on their bed and gave her his phone to play with while he made coffee. He had a coffee ready for Elaine when she came out of the shower. 'Thanks, love,' she said gratefully. 'Sorry I snapped.'

'It's OK.' He hugged her. 'We hardly got any sleep last night. It will get easier.'

Elaine nodded and, cupping the mug in her hands, sipped the coffee, thankful that Ian was understanding. It wasn't like her to be so short-tempered.

Showered and dressed and partially rejuvenated by coffee, Elaine chose some clothes for Anastasia to wear and helped her into them while Ian got ready. She praised Anastasia at every opportunity, told her she loved her, then found the words for restaurant and breakfast in their phrase book and tried to explain they were going to the restaurant for breakfast. Anastasia looked at her blankly. Elaine had big concerns about going to the restaurant but as Ian said, they couldn't stay holed up in their room all week, and Anastasia wasn't interested in what room service had to offer. He said that if she wouldn't sit at the table or caused any trouble, they'd come straight back to their room.

Ten minutes later they were ready and went down in the lift. There were two couples and three business people already in the restaurant and Ian and Elaine went to their usual table. Anastasia climbed onto a chair, but at her age she could barely see over the table. 'That's not going to work,' Elaine said, immediately growing anxious. The waitress came over, said something they didn't understand and returned with a child's bolster seat. 'Thank you so much,' Elaine said. Of course a hotel restaurant would have a child seat. She should have realized that.

The waitress left them to study the menu, which at breakfast was the same every morning. 'Something quick,' Elaine said, glancing at Ian. At present Anastasia was sitting still, watching the other guests and what was going on around her, but how long that would last was anyone's guess. When the waitress returned to take their orders Elaine asked for croissants, and Ian scrambled eggs on toast.

'What for the child?' Elaine asked, pointing to the menu and then at Anastasia. This waitress spoke some English but not as much as Maria had.

'She have breakfast?'

'Yes, please. What?'

The waitress understood and pointed to cornmeal porridge and orange juice on the menu.

'Thank you. Yes, please,' she said.

Relieved, Elaine took the crayons and small colouring pad she'd brought with her from her handbag and set them in front of Anastasia to keep her amused, although at present she was engrossed in all that was going on around her, doubtless having never been in a restaurant before. When the food arrived Elaine was feeling more confident and they were both hopeful Anastasia would eat the porridge the waitress had chosen. She looked at it, interested, picked up the glass of juice and drank some, then dipped her spoon into the porridge, took a mouthful and stopped. 'Eat up,' Elaine encouraged, taking a bite of her croissant.

Anastasia put the spoon down.

'Perhaps it wants some more milk and sugar on it,' Ian suggested, and added a little of each.

Anastasia watched him, intrigued, then reached for the sugar and added lots more herself. 'That's enough,' Elaine said, moving the sugar bowl out of reach.

Anastasia tipped on some more milk, then spent a while stirring the mixture before returning the spoon to the table. Ian and Elaine tried to encourage her to have some without success, then offered her bite-sized portions of what they were eating, but she shook her head. She drank some more juice but then lost interest in what the table had to offer and, slipping from her chair, made a run for the door. Ian went after her, brought her back, and gave her his phone to play with while they quickly finished their breakfast.

Although Anastasia's behaviour in the restaurant hadn't caused a huge problem, she'd eaten virtually nothing. It was at least twenty-four hours since her last meal – longer if she hadn't had breakfast before going to court the day before. Once in their hotel room Elaine gave her the milkshake they'd bought from the local supermarket and she drank half of it. Then, wrapping up warm, they went to the park the receptionist had recommended. Midweek in winter they were the only ones there, but Anastasia enjoyed herself running around and playing on the equipment. As Ian and Elaine helped her on or off the apparatus and pushed her on the swing, it gave them a glimpse of a positive side of parenting and the joy Anastasia would bring to them. This was what being a family was all about, although the fact that Anastasia wasn't eating hung over them.

'She must be hungry by now,' Ian said as they made their way back to the hotel, faces glowing from the cold.

'And tired,' Elaine said. 'Perhaps we can all have a nap after lunch.'

The hotel restaurant wasn't open at lunchtime, as most guests were out, so they ordered room service. While they waited, Anastasia finished the milkshake, but when the food arrived she took a bite from some of it and that was all.

'If she doesn't have anything tonight, I'll phone Dr Ciobanu,' Ian said.

With lack of sleep catching up on them, at mid-afternoon they drew the curtains in their hotel room, put the 'Do Not Disturb' sign on the door and lay on the bed with Anastasia between them and told her they were all going to have a sleep. Elaine was so tired she couldn't think straight and Ian looked pale, although he didn't complain. But Anastasia wasn't tired and as soon as they closed their eyes she was off the bed, running around and into everything. 'I swear that child runs on air,' Ian said, getting up to bring her back. 'She's had hardly any sleep and nothing to eat.'

They snuggled down again, but a few more attempts later they gave up, and Elaine ran a bath for Anastasia, which she liked, and washed her hair at the same time. Elaine praised her immensely. Anastasia sat still while Elaine dried her hair and brushed it into a pony tail. 'Good girl,' Elaine said again, and felt pleased that she'd been able to successfully do this for her daughter. She and Ian then spent the rest of the afternoon keeping Anastasia amused and as quiet as they could, which was exhausting. Shortly after 5 p.m., with the intention of having an early night, they ordered room service for dinner, including a milkshake for Anastasia. She drank it down, didn't want anything to eat, and was then sick everywhere.

'That's it, I'm going to phone Dr Ciobanu,' Ian said. 'Perhaps she's ill.'

He tried the orphanage but was told the doctor wasn't there, so he phoned his mobile. It went through to voicemail and Ian left a message asking him to phone as soon as possible, as they were concerned about Anastasia. Ian then put the tray and soiled bedspread outside the room for housekeeping to collect. Elaine cleaned up Anastasia and put her into her pyjamas. Five minutes later Dr Ciobanu returned Ian's call. 'What's the problem?' he asked evenly.

'Anastasia won't eat anything and has just vomited,' Ian said. 'She's very hyperactive and won't sleep or eat. We're wondering if she's ill.'

'I doubt she's ill,' Dr Ciobanu replied, an edge of forced patience to his voice. 'There's been a lot of changes for her in the last few days. It will take time for her to adjust as my notes on post-adoption explain. Not eating or sleeping properly is common in the first few weeks and is usually due to anxiety from all the changes. But as she has been sick, to be on the safe side, call a doctor to check her over.'

'You think that is necessary?'

'Yes.'

'And you can't see her?'

'No. I stopped practising general medicine some years ago. The hotel will give you the name and contact details of a doctor. He can visit you in your hotel room. You will obviously have to pay him, cash usually, but the charges are reasonable.'

'All right, we'll do that,' Ian said.

'If there is a problem the doctor may want you to take Anastasia to the hospital for tests, but I doubt that will be necessary. Some of our children need hospitalizing but Anastasia is healthy. I've filed your adoption papers and I'll be in contact when they have been returned.'

'Thank you,' Ian replied, and they said goodbye.

Elaine, who'd understood the essence of what had been said, was looking at Ian, concerned; Anastasia, who'd heard her name mentioned, was looking at him too. 'I'm sure it's nothing to worry about,' Ian said, 'but Dr Ciobanu is advising us to get her checked by a doctor. The hotel has the details of one.' He threw Anastasia a smile and, picking up the handset, pressed the button for reception. He explained that they needed to arrange for a doctor to visit their child.

'Is it an emergency?' the receptionist asked.

'No.'

'Just one moment and I'll find the doctor's details.' After a minute or so she came back on the line and gave Ian the name and phone number of a doctor, which Ian wrote on the pad by the phone. 'Would you like me to phone him and arrange the visit?' the receptionist asked helpfully.

'Yes, please.'

'I'll phone him now and call you back.'

'Thank you,' Ian said, and replaced the handset.

Half an hour passed before the phone rang and the receptionist said the doctor would visit them that evening as soon as he was free.

'Do you have a time?' Ian asked.

'No. He will visit when he has seen the patients at his clinic.'

Thanking her again, Ian said goodbye. Now there was nothing to do but wait and keep Anastasia amused as best they could. Despite Dr Ciobanu's assurance that Anastasia was healthy, they were worried. Supposing she did have something wrong? Would it delay them going home? They would feel far more confident if the doctors at home treated Anastasia, but that might not be an option if she was too ill to fly. She didn't appear to be ill, far from it, and she hadn't complained of feeling unwell, or perhaps she had and they hadn't understood her. They had cash with them and knew from Dr Ciobanu's guidance notes roughly what doctors charged, and that it was per visit plus any tests and medication required.

They put the television on to try to settle Anastasia, and she watched it for a short while, then they tried some of the games they'd brought with them, and finally Ian gave her his phone to play with. An hour passed and then two. Was it their imagination or was Anastasia less active now? Perhaps it was tiredness, or was she ill? Ian looked up 'ill' in their phrase book and repeated the word to Anastasia, but she stared at him blankly. He tried tummy ache and pain but with the same result.

Finally, around eight o'clock, a double knock sounded on their door and a deep male voice announced, 'Doctor.'

'Reception must have given him our room number,' Ian said, going to answer. Elaine got off the bed and straightened the covers. The room looked a mess again. They were living out of cases and their belongings were everywhere.

The doctor came in, middle-aged and of average build, and he shook Ian's hand and smiled politely at Elaine. 'So this is the child,' he said, going to her. 'What's she called?'

'Anastasia,' Elaine said.

'What is the matter with her?'

'She's been sick, won't sleep and hasn't eaten properly for at least two days,' Elaine said.

He nodded and spoke to Anastasia in their language as he took a stethoscope from his bag. He listened to her chest and her back and asked her some questions. She replied with a very serious expression. Elaine didn't like to ask him what he'd said. Returning the stethoscope to his bag, he took out an otoscope and looked in her ears, then took her temperature.

'That's all fine,' he said. 'How many times has she been sick?'

'Once,' Elaine replied.

He eased Anastasia down so she was flat on the bed and felt her stomach. 'You've adopted her?'

'Yes, two days ago.'

'A lot of change for her then.'

'Yes,' they agreed.

He finished examining her and helped her to sit upright. 'Has she been to the toilet?'

'Only for a wee.'

'Her stomach doesn't feel bloated and there is no soreness. Give her a choice of foods and I'm sure she will settle in time.'

'We've been doing that but she doesn't seem to want anything to eat. Also there are some sores on her back. I saw them when I bathed her.' Elaine eased up the back of Anastasia's top and the doctor took a closer look.

'I'll write a prescription for some cream to apply, and also some vitamin drops. The child will have a medical by your own doctor when you get home?'

'Yes,' Elaine confirmed. A medical was standard practice when adopting from abroad and had been mentioned in Dr Ciobanu's notes and by other couples in the online forum. Many of the infants, especially the older children, were found to have iron and vitamin deficiencies from very poor diets, so it was important that this and any other medical conditions were diagnosed early and treated.

'When you take her to see your doctor ask for a blood test,' he said. 'They should check her for HIV, syphilis and gonorrhoea.'

Elaine stared at him, horrified. 'Her mother wasn't a prostitute,' Ian said. They knew these tests were advised if the mother was working as a prostitute as some very poor women did, as she could have passed on the diseases to her unborn child.

'And the mother would tell you if she was?' the doctor asked, throwing Ian an old-fashioned look.

'We'll get the tests done,' Ian confirmed, and Elaine nodded.

The doctor wrote the prescription. 'I'll include a mild sedative to help her sleep at night,' he said. 'Give her one dose an hour before bed. You can give her a dose before you get on the plane too, to help keep her quiet. Flying will be a new experience for her – it upsets many children.'

'Thank you,' Elaine said.

The doctor handed her the prescription and picked up the notepad by their telephone and wrote again. 'All children like these to eat,' he said. Tearing off the sheet, he handed it to Elaine. 'Is she drinking?'

'Milkshakes,' Elaine said.

'Good. She'll be fine.' He patted Anastasia's head, said something to her in their own language and she nodded solemnly.

'Is she happy?' Elaine blurted.

'Yes, of course. She has you and your husband,' he said in a similar manner to Dr Ciobanu.

Ian paid the doctor and saw him to the door. Elaine took her daughter's hand. 'Don't worry, love, I promise you everything will be all right.'

Although the possibility that she might be HIV positive plagued her all night long.

CHAPTER THIRTEEN·

GOOD GIRL

Anastasia slept very little that night, although she wasn't sick again. The following morning, shattered from another broken night, Ian and Elaine drank coffee and took it in turns to shower and dress while the other one kept Anastasia amused. Once they were all ready they went down to breakfast. It was the same waitress as the day before, and being aware that Anastasia hadn't eaten the porridge then she now suggested something different, which Ian translated as a type of scrambled eggs. Elaine also ordered a milkshake for Anastasia, and croissants and coffee for herself, and Ian ordered a cooked breakfast. While they waited Ian gave Anastasia his phone to play with. The food arrived and they'd only just begun when Anastasia, having drunk the milkshake but left the food, made a dash for the door. Ian brought her back to her chair and tried to tempt her with bits from his own plate, sharing the same fork.

'Is that wise?' Elaine asked. 'I mean, if she has got something contagious you might catch it.'

'I suppose,' Ian said, and gave Anastasia his coffee spoon instead. She wasn't interested in using the spoon to eat but loved the noise it made when banged against the edge of his china plate. Ian finished his meal quickly, gulped down the last of his coffee and they left the dining room.

They returned briefly to their hotel room for their coats and then went down to reception and asked for directions to the nearest pharmacy. It was about a ten-minute walk so they didn't need a cab. Pleased to be outside, Anastasia walked nicely between them, holding a hand each. 'Good girl,' Elaine said, praising her at every opportunity.

In the pharmacy they had to wait for the prescription to be made up, and the woman who served them gave Anastasia a lollipop similar to the one she'd been given at the local supermarket. It seemed to be a custom for shopkeepers to keep a box of lollipops beside the till and give them to children who came in. As Ian paid he showed her the piece of paper with the name of the food the doctor had written down, and asked where they could buy it. To their surprise the cashier took a packet of what looked like biscuits from the shelf. 'You sell them here?' Ian asked. 'They are biscuits?'

She turned the packet over and pointed to the ingredients on the back, and they understood that the biscuits were fortified with iron, vitamins and minerals. They bought a packet, and on their way back to the hotel made a detour via the supermarket where they bought some more milkshakes, and bread and cold meats for their lunch. Anastasia was given another lollipop.

They ate lunch in their hotel room. Anastasia didn't want the food they'd bought but did drink a milkshake and ate three of the fortified biscuits, which was something. Obviously she couldn't live off these biscuits indefinitely, but at least they gave her some nutrition until she was more settled and began eating properly. Elaine decided that as the biscuits contained added vitamins and minerals it was wise not to give Anastasia the vitamin drops the doctor had prescribed, as too many could be harmful.

They spent the rest of the afternoon in their room keeping Anastasia amused, and then ordered room service for dinner at 6 p.m. Anastasia had only a few mouthfuls but ate another three fortified biscuits and drank another milkshake. Elaine gave her a bath, and an hour before her bedtime a spoonful of the sedative. They lay with her on their bed and looked at some children's books as she gradually grew drowsy and finally fell asleep. Ian carefully lifted her from their bed and tucked her into hers, where she remained asleep until nearly 7 a.m.

'I must be dreaming!' Ian said when they woke. And what a difference a good night's sleep made. Physically and emotionally refreshed, Elaine especially felt like a different person and was ready to face anything the day held. With more patience for Anastasia, her confidence in her role grew and she also made time for Ian, for out of necessity their relationship had taken second place.

During the next seven days, while they waited for their documents to be processed, their routine was largely unchanged. They went out each day to buy more fortified biscuits, milkshakes, lunch and whatever else they needed, and sometimes to the park, but it was too cold to stay long. Sometimes Ian said he had cabin fever and went for a walk around the block while Elaine stayed with Anastasia and had some mother-and-daughter time. Each evening, after Anastasia had her bath, Elaine gave her a dose of the sedative, and their sleeping routine returned to near normal. Although Elaine still woke at night worrying about Anastasia, especially her health. In addition to the massive concern that Anastasia might be HIV positive or have another disease passed on to her by her mother, she still wasn't eating, rarely spoke to them, even in her own language, and hadn't done a proper poo. The latter was doubtless due to her living on milkshakes and biscuits, but it was something else Elaine would need to see the doctor about on their return. She had a list and it was growing.

When Dr Ciobanu finally telephoned to say that Anastasia's passport, visa and new birth certificate were ready and they could confirm their flight home, they were ecstatic. Ian took a cab to the orphanage where Dr Ciobanu had his office and Elaine stayed with Anastasia. There was no need for them all to go and it could have been unsettling for Anastasia to revisit the orphanage. Ian was gone for an hour and returned clutching Anastasia's passport, which he proudly showed them. Elaine was delighted – they were finally going home.

They texted family, friends and their neighbour to let them know when they were returning, then the only things left to do were pack and book the cab to take them to the airport, which they did at reception. They said that if possible they'd like the cab driver Danny to take them. They hadn't seen him since he'd collected them from the airport and they wanted to say goodbye and thank him for all those trips to the orphanage when his happy, upbeat chat had been very welcome. The receptionist said she'd pass on their request to the cab firm.

Two days later they were up early with the intention of having a quick breakfast before they had to leave for the airport. It didn't happen. It took far longer than they'd anticipated to get Anastasia ready, as she'd become unsettled and hyperactive by all the activity going on around. They tried to explain, using words from their phrase book, that they were all going home, but to no avail. She ran around the room banging on doors and trying to take items out of their cases. Elaine's stress level rose, and she semi-jokingly suggested to Ian that perhaps they should give Anastasia a dose of the sedative now, rather than an hour before the flight as the doctor had said. Ian pointed out that if they did it would very likely wear off during the flight when it would be most needed. However, despite a stressful couple of hours and making do with coffee in their hotel room (Anastasia had a milkshake and fortified biscuits), they were down at reception with their luggage at 9.15 a.m. to check out and settle their bill, which was considerable because they'd used room service so much.

Ten minutes later, to their delight, Danny strolled into the lobby and greeted them warmly. 'The cab firm told me you were leaving. Hello, Anastasia.' He smiled at her and repeated hello in their own language. Anastasia eyed him cautiously, no doubt wondering how he fitted into everything that was going on. 'You won't remember me waiting outside the orphanage,' he said, then said it again in their language. Anastasia tried to hold his hand and Danny laughed, but Elaine thought it slightly odd that she would want to hold the hand of a stranger.

Danny picked up two of their suitcases and Ian took the third, and a little nostalgically they left the hotel, which had been their home for some weeks. Outside, Danny stowed their cases in the boot while Ian helped Anastasia into the rear seat, where Elaine joined her with her hand luggage. Ian got into the front passenger seat. Starting the engine, Danny immediately struck up conversation, his usual bright and chatty self. He asked them if everything had gone to plan, how they'd passed the time, what the weather was like in the UK, if it snowed at Christmas – just over three weeks away – and then told them about his own family.

Elaine saw Anastasia watching him intently and felt this was an opportunity too good to miss. So when he asked, 'How is your daughter?' and Ian replied, 'Good,' Elaine seized the moment.

'Danny,' she said, leaning slightly forward so she could see him round his seat. 'We're not always sure what Anastasia needs or is feeling because we don't speak her language. Could you ask her some questions for me, please?'

'Yes, sure,' he said amicably, and glanced at Anastasia in the rear-view mirror as he drove.

'Please ask her if she has everything she needs,' Elaine said.

Danny translated and Elaine saw the look of slight surprise on Anastasia's face that Danny was talking to her. She said just a couple of words in reply.

'She has what she needs,' Danny said.

'Can you ask her if she understands we are her mummy and daddy? If not, please explain about going to court and the adoption. I don't know how much she has been told or understands.'

Danny straightened in his seat a little and, concentrating on the road ahead, began talking to Anastasia, occasionally glancing at her in the mirror. Anastasia sat motionless, staring at him, but nothing could be read in her expression. Ian turned in his seat to glance at her. Danny stopped talking and Anastasia looked at her and Ian and then said a few words in her own language.

'She understands now,' Danny said.

'But she didn't understand before?' Elaine asked, immediately concerned. 'Dr Ciobanu was supposed to have explained.'

Danny shrugged, clearly uncomfortable about blaming the doctor. 'It's difficult for a small child to understand,' he said. 'I told her she is going to have a wonderful life with her new mummy and daddy in England.'

'Thank you,' Elaine said, sitting back.

'Don't worry,' Danny said a moment later. 'Everything will be good when you get home. You have medicine to make her sleep on the plane?'

'Yes,' Elaine said, surprised he knew.

'Good. Children can be frightened on the plane so the doctor gives the parents medicine to make them sleep.'

'So other couples who have adopted see a doctor here?' Elaine asked.

'Yes. Most do.' Which made Elaine feel a bit better; they weren't the only ones to have had concerns.

A few moments passed and then Anastasia said something very quietly to Danny in her own language and he replied.

'What did she say?' Elaine asked.

'I told her she doesn't have to go to the orphanage any more.' This wasn't exactly what Elaine had asked, but she didn't pursue it. Danny was a decent guy and wouldn't have said anything untoward. 'All will be good,' he said, then began chatting to them in English about Christmas and how his kids were already very excited.

There was no further conversation between Anastasia and Danny during the journey, although Elaine saw her watching him carefully. Fifteen minutes later they pulled into the airport and Danny parked in one of the drop-off bays and fetched a trolley. Ian drew Anastasia out of the car and took Elaine's hand luggage, which contained among other things a change of clothes for Anastasia, the small bottle of sedative and her biscuits. Danny loaded their cases onto the trolley and Ian paid him and included a good tip. They both thanked him for being their driver and wished him a Merry Christmas. He shook their hands and then said, 'Bye, Anastasia. You be a good girl.' She immediately threw her arms around him and hugged him.

He laughed good-humouredly but again Elaine felt it was slightly odd that Anastasia could spontaneously show affection to someone she barely knew, but not to them. Perhaps Danny reminded her of someone or perhaps it was simply because he spoke her language. It was impossible to know. With a parting goodbye, Danny returned to his cab, and Ian pushed the trolley towards the departure hall as Elaine walked beside him, holding Anastasia's hand.

'Airport,' Elaine told her as they went. 'We are going on an aeroplane.' She felt excited at the prospect, even if her daughter didn't. It would become so much easier once Anastasia learned English, which Elaine would concentrate on once home.

Their plane wasn't due to leave for another three hours, but the flight information board showed their check-in desk was open. 'Excellent,' Ian said. 'We can get rid of all our cases and then have breakfast. I might even have a beer.'

Anastasia was fascinated by all the people with their luggage and stood still watching them as they waited in line to check in. They had been warned to expect some questions about their child's status and Ian had the adoption papers ready in his briefcase to show if necessary. As it was, the check-in agent only asked, 'Is she your daughter?' as she looked at her passport. Ian said yes and Elaine nodded, then they were asked to load their cases onto the conveyor belt one at a time. The agent tagged them and sent them on their way, then handed Ian their passports and boarding cards, pointing out the gate number they would need later. The first stage of their journey home was completed.

They decided to go through security clearance first before they ate, as there would be a better selection of restaurants and cafés on the other side. Anastasia was mesmerized by security and the queue that slowly snaked its way forward through the scanner, having never seen metal detectors before. One small child, fractious from waiting, threw a tantrum, screaming and kicking his father as he tried to pick him up. Elaine was so pleased it wasn't them having to deal with it, as people were looking. Ian walked through the scanner first, followed by Elaine, holding Anastasia's hand, then they collected their hand luggage from being X-rayed. 'All done,' Ian said to Anastasia.

Having checked the flight information board, they used the toilets and then found a restaurant that served a full English breakfast. Elaine was hungry too, having only had a coffee at the hotel, and ordered the same as Ian. They also ordered a child's portion of the cooked breakfast in the hope that Anastasia, seeing them eating it, would follow suit, although it hadn't worked at the hotel.

'Good girl,' Elaine praised as Anastasia sat nicely at the table and they waited for their food to arrive. She was interested in everything going on around her, studying people and what they were doing.

'She's like you, a people watcher,' Ian said, and Elaine laughed.

When their food arrived Elaine cut up Anastasia's and then watched her out of the corner of her eye as she picked up her fork. They were delighted when she began eating and amazed when she finished most of her breakfast. It was the first proper meal she'd had since the adoption over a week before. 'Good girl!' Elaine exclaimed, kissing her cheek.

'Well done!' Ian said, and smiled at her across the table.

Although Anastasia might not have understood the words, surely their expressions conveyed how happy they were with her, so why didn't she return their smile or look pleased instead of just staring at them blankly?

'You don't think there could be something wrong with her, do you?' Elaine asked Ian, still watching Anastasia.

'Like what?'

'Autism?'

'Of course not!' Ian said sharply. 'She's just overawed by everything that has happened. It's been an incredible and stressful experience for us, and we were well prepared, so imagine what it must be like for her.' Which of course was perfectly true, and Elaine felt bad for even suggesting there was something wrong with Anastasia.

Having settled the bill, they wandered around the shops in the departure lounge, keeping an eye on the flight information board. They bought some small gifts for their family and friends – hand-painted coasters, fridge magnets and the like. Ian said he was going to have the beer he'd promised himself but he'd be quick. As he went to the bar, Elaine took Anastasia to watch the planes through the viewing gallery. Ian joined them when he'd finished. Forty-five minutes before take-off, the flight information board changed to show their gate number, and a message came over the public address system to say that all passengers on their flight should make their way to the boarding gate.

'Medicine!' Elaine exclaimed, having previously forgotten.

'Don't worry, there's still time for it to work,' Ian said, 'and if it doesn't, Anastasia will be interested in the take-off.'

'I'm not so sure. It could upset her.' Elaine delved frantically into her hand luggage and took out the small plastic bottle of medicine and spoon.

Anastasia didn't mind taking the syrup, it was very sweet. Elaine returned the bottle and spoon to her bag and they made their way to the waiting area by the departure gate, which was filling quickly. A couple moved along a seat so the three of them could sit together. Elaine took a book from her bag to keep Anastasia amused. It explained with large colourful pictures and short sentences what happened during a flight. Ian had read it to Anastasia in their hotel room to help prepare her and Elaine read it again now. But Anastasia was more interested in what was going on around her.

'She's being a good girl,' the woman next to them remarked.

'Long may it continue,' Elaine replied with a smile.

'Indeed, for there's nothing worse than a screaming child on a long flight,' the woman returned, stony-faced.

CHAPTER FOURTEEN

SETTLING IN

Anastasia didn't like having to stay in her seat on the plane.

'It's just until take-off,' Elaine said as the last few passengers boarded. 'Then you can sit on my lap.'

They had three seats together and Anastasia was by the window, but there wasn't much of interest to see at present, just tarmac and the wing of the plane. Elaine was sitting next to Anastasia and Ian was in the aisle seat. To keep Anastasia occupied they'd taken a selection of books and activities from their hand luggage, which was now stored in the overhead locker. Elaine couldn't get Anastasia interested in the books and toys. She squirmed and moaned, then got off her seat again and tried to squeeze past Elaine. Elaine was already flustered and it could be a while before the sedative took effect. Ian suggested they change seats so he was next to Anastasia and he lifted her into her seat, fastened her lap belt and gave her his phone to play with. This kept her reasonably occupied until they were ready for take-off, when the captain's voice came over the public address system and asked that all electronic devices be switched off and put away, ready for take-off.

'You can have it again later,' Ian said, trying to swap his phone for her toy one. It didn't work; Anastasia's grip tightened and, not wanting a scene, he let her keep it until the stewards approached making their last-minute checks, when he took the phone from her. This was a first for Anastasia; until now, Ian and Elaine had always given her what she wanted and, like many children her age, she wasn't happy about not getting her own way. She threw all the books and toys off her lap onto the floor, then struggled to get out from under her seatbelt again. Ian tried talking calmly to her, explaining that she had to sit in her seat for take-off. 'Look!' he said, pointing to the view through the window. 'The plane is starting to move.'

Anastasia gave it a cursory glance and then wriggled down under her lap belt as the plane began to taxi towards the runway. Ian sat her upright and tightened the belt. She pulled at the belt angrily, tried to unfasten it and when she couldn't, temper got the better of her and she began kicking the back of the seat in front. Ian put his hand on her legs to stop her but the man in front had already turned round and Elaine apologized. Her cheeks flushed. She could feel other passengers looking at the spectacle Anastasia was making, and the woman they'd sat next to earlier in the departure lounge was only a few rows in front.

'Look!' Ian said again, pointing to the window and trying to distract Anastasia. 'We're going to take off soon.'

The plane had taxied to the end of the runway and taken up its position. The engines revved and then they were moving faster and faster. Anastasia stared through the window, her face very serious as they hurtled down the runway. 'We're going up into the sky!' Ian said. But the sudden change in air pressure made their ears pop and Anastasia clamped her hands over her ears and screamed.

'Swallow, love,' Elaine said, leaning across Ian. 'Just keep swallowing. It won't last long.'

Anastasia wasn't the only infant upset by the change in air pressure; further behind them a baby had started to cry.

The plane continued its ascent and Anastasia screamed. Then she took her hands from her ears, babbled something in her own language and struggled frantically to get out of her seat, perhaps thinking she could leave the plane. Ian placed a restraining hand on her lap. 'When the seatbelt sign goes off you can sit on my lap,' he said, which was meaningless to her. She kicked the seat in front again, and again Elaine apologized and willed Anastasia to behave.

Finally the plane stopped climbing and the change in air pressure eased. Anastasia relaxed and, putting her thumb in her mouth, rested her head back and gazed out of the window. 'Look at all those fluffy white clouds. Aren't they beautiful?' Ian said. But Anastasia's eyes were heavy now as the medicine kicked in. She sucked her thumb and a few minutes later she was asleep.

'Thank goodness,' Elaine said, with a huge sigh of relief. 'Hopefully she'll sleep for most of the flight. Can you put the blanket over her? I can't reach.'

Ian took the blanket provided out of its sealed plastic bag and draped it over Anastasia. He held his wife's hand and they began to unwind. The seatbelt sign went off and the stewards came down the aisle with the drinks trolley. Ian suggested to Elaine that they buy a half bottle of champagne to celebrate. They hadn't actually toasted the adoption and what better time than on the plane going home with their daughter?

As they sipped champagne from plastic wine flutes Elaine turned to Ian. 'I've been thinking about Anastasia's name,' she said. 'It's quite a mouthful and rather unusual in England. What do you think about shortening it to Anna?'

Ian thought for a moment. 'Yes, good idea. I like that. Let's drink to our daughter Anna and her new life in England.'

Anastasia, or rather Anna as she was now to be called, remained asleep for most of the flight. She missed the in-flight meal but Ian and Elaine weren't worried. She'd had a good breakfast at the airport and could make up for it later at dinner after they'd landed. They gazed at her as she slept, her head relaxed back, lips slightly parted and so peaceful. Her thumb slipped from her mouth and Ian stroked a few wisps of hair away from her cheek. She was certainly a very beautiful child, but then they would have thought that about any child who was theirs.

When Anna woke it was with a start. She sat bolt upright, staring around, clearly wondering where she was. 'You're on a plane,' Ian said gently. 'We're nearly home, we'll be in England soon.'

She looked at him blankly as she usually did when they talked to her, probably because she didn't understand. Elaine offered her one of the juice drinks she'd bought at the airport. 'Thirsty? Drink?' she asked, and Anna nodded.

The captain's voice came over the public address system and announced they would be landing in thirty minutes. Elaine took Anna to the toilet before a queue formed. Then, still slightly drowsy from the medication, Anna was content to sit in her seat and gaze out of the window until the plane began its descent. As the air pressure dropped Anna covered her ears and began moaning loudly, then shook her head roughly from side to side as though trying to clear the popping. Ian soothed her and Elaine told her to swallow, but they were very relieved when the plane finally landed. 'Thank goodness we had the sedative to give her,' Elaine said quietly to Ian. 'Or it would have been a lot worse. I doubt she would have settled at all.'

'She did well – her first plane journey,' Ian said positively.

With the plane parked ready for disembarkation, Anna was content to sit in her seat and watch all the hustle and bustle going on around her, as passengers stood to retrieve their hand luggage and mobile phones bleeped. Ian suggested waiting until the crush had eased before they left, then they stood, retrieved their hand luggage and, with their coats on, followed the other passengers off the plane and into the much cooler air of the jet bridge. Elaine held Anna's hand and reassured her as they stepped onto the moving travelator. It was another new experience for her. As they waited for their luggage Anna grew restless again, so Elaine gave her the last of the fortified biscuits. 'Proper meals for you from now on,' she said. Anna stared at her blankly and munched.

Thankfully there wasn't much of a wait at passport control, and three-quarters of an hour after landing they were outside in the long-stay car park, looking for their car. It was dark now in early evening in winter and the lamps in the car park weren't that bright. A little disorientated from the flight, it took them some minutes to locate their car. While Ian stowed their luggage in the boot, Elaine helped Anna into her car seat. Brand new and now being used for the first time, Elaine adjusted the belts so they fitted snugly over Anna's shoulders and around her lap. 'We're going home,' she told her with a smile and kissed her cheek. Making sure her little hands were clear of the door, she closed it and joined Ian in the front.

As Ian drove Elaine fed a CD of popular children's songs into the player. The first song was 'The Wheels on the Bus', which was a long-time children's favourite that Elaine knew by heart from her own childhood. She turned in her seat so she could see Anna and gently sang along. The second song was another children's classic – 'If You're Happy and You Know it Clap Your Hands'. Elaine and Ian began singing, and Elaine clapped her hands. Yes, they were happy, very happy indeed, and as Anna joined in clapping Elaine's eyes filled. There'd been many times when she'd thought they'd never have a family and now here they were. She was so grateful, she said a silent prayer of thanks.

It was after 8 p.m. when they arrived home but their house wasn't cold, nor was their fridge empty, as their good neighbour had been in. She'd also left a present for Anna and a congratulations card. Anna unwrapped the present – a soft toy – and Elaine put the card on the mantelpiece with the one they'd already received from Ian's brother, sent at the time of their first trip to adopt. They were tired, needed to get organized, and didn't feel up to speaking at length to family and friends, so texted them to let them know they were all home safely and that they'd phone as soon as they'd recovered from their journey.

Ian showed Anna around the house, telling her the English name for the rooms, while Elaine made them something to eat. She was delighted when Anna finished most of her dinner; it seemed to bode well for her future eating. Elaine then took Anna upstairs to get ready for bed as Ian unpacked the essentials from their cases – they'd do the rest tomorrow. As it was getting late she just gave Anna a wash and brushed her teeth that night; she'd have a bath tomorrow. Then once she was in bed, Elaine and Ian sat beside her and read her some bedtime stories. It was a special moment and one they'd treasure forever: Anna's first night in her very own bedroom. They'd chosen the furnishings together, a white-and-pink colour scheme with a Cinderella patterned duvet cover and matching curtains and rug. The shelves contained an assortment of soft toys, books, games and toys, and brightly coloured mobiles hung from the ceiling, turning in the air. The wardrobe and drawers held a good selection of clothes and shoes, which would be added to as she grew. They took photographs of Anastasia in her bed on her first night, but they couldn't persuade her to smile. 'She must be very tired,' Ian said, feeling this was the reason.

They kissed her goodnight and came out, leaving the door slightly ajar, then waited on the landing to see if she would settle. A few moments later they heard her get out of bed and then her little face peered around the door.

'Come on, love, back to bed,' Elaine said gently.

They resettled her in bed and, giving her another kiss goodnight, came out and waited on the landing again. A minute or so passed and then she reappeared. They took her back to bed again and again. Eventually Ian said, 'I don't think she can be tired. Let's take her down with us for a while.'

Downstairs Anna quickly proved she was anything but tired, and now feeling more confident and perhaps realizing this was where she was going to live, she ran from room to room exploring, opening drawers and cupboards, peering under furniture and into corners, as she had in their hotel room. She picked up anything she liked the look of, including Elaine's glass and china ornaments, and clambered onto the furniture to get at objects she couldn't reach. There was so much more for her to see here than in the hotel room and the stark orphanage. To begin with Ian and Elaine laughed and indulged her. It was, after all, her first night. But by midnight they were both exhausted and needed to go to bed themselves. 'I've got to be up for work in the morning,' Ian said. He'd used up all his annual leave on the adoption trips and had also taken some unpaid leave.

'Anna, it's time for bed,' Elaine said more firmly. Catching up with her in the hall, she took her up to bed.

As Ian showered, Elaine tried to settle Anna, but each time she left her in her room she came out. When Ian had finished in the bathroom, wrapped in his dressing gown, he came to help. But half an hour later, when Anna still hadn't settled, they decided to take her into their bed so they could hopefully all get some sleep. Anna didn't sleep even there and at nearly 2 a.m., bone-weary, Elaine suggested they give her a spoonful of the sedative. 'Just to help her settle tonight,' she said, feeling guilty. It had been prescribed to help at the hotel and on the plane. There was a little left and they hadn't anticipated using it once home.

'Yes, just for tonight then,' Ian agreed, yawning. 'It won't harm her, it's twelve hours since she had the last dose.'

Elaine took Anna downstairs, gave her a spoonful of the medicine and then back up to their bed. It took nearly an hour for the medicine to work, during which time Anna bounced and wriggled, her little feet kicking their backs, and repeatedly tried to get out of bed. It was no longer endearing and they were exhausted. Finally, at around 3 a.m., she fell asleep, but at 6.45 the alarm went off and shocked them all awake.

'I'll get her into a better routine tonight,' Elaine promised as Ian struggled out of bed. She was the main caregiver so felt it was her responsibility. Ian was the breadwinner and had to be able to concentrate at work.

An hour later Elaine and Anna, still in their nightwear, saw Ian off at the door. 'Daddy's going to work,' Elaine told her. 'He'll be back this evening. Wave goodbye.' Elaine waved but Anna didn't. She stared after Ian, probably wondering where he was going and why. They knew it would take a few days of him going out to work and returning before Anna became familiar with their weekday routine.

Elaine had a long list of things she needed to do and people to contact. Apart from unpacking and speaking to family and friends, she had to register Anna with her doctor and book an appointment for a health check as a matter of urgency. She also had to notify the authorities that Anna was in the UK, put her name on the waiting list for a nursery place and so on. This was all in addition to spending time with Anna, playing with her and getting to know her better. For unlike a baby, Anna had come with her own character and it was important that mother and daughter familiarized themselves with each other and got along.

'I'll be a bit busy today,' Elaine told Anna, as the two of them ate breakfast together. Ian had made himself a coffee and a slice of toast before leaving for work.

She looked at Anna carefully. Thank goodness she was eating. It was a huge relief. If she'd just smile a bit more, make eye contact and want a hug occasionally, or even respond when Elaine hugged her instead of going stiff or drawing away, life would be perfect. Then she chided herself. The poor child hadn't been here for twenty-four hours, and prior to that there'd been so many changes that it would take time for her to adjust. Elaine would let Anna take it at her own pace. She knew from the posts on the online forum that the older the child was, the longer they needed to adjust. Children of eight or nine, for example, sometimes took months, even years, before they were fully integrated into their adoptive family. At Anna's age it would hopefully be a matter of weeks, although some children adjusted straight away. It depended on their past experience, how smoothly the transition to their adoptive family had been, and the child's resilience and acceptance of all the changes. Elaine thought that Anna seemed very resilient and the adoption had gone smoothly, apart from their three-month separation.

Elaine didn't achieve as much as she'd hoped that day. It flew by in phone calls, keeping Anna occupied and their neighbour popping in to say hello and staying for an hour. Elaine did manage to make an appointment for Anna to see their doctor the following morning but was told she'd have to register her as a temporary patient until her National Health Service number came through. Late in the afternoon, feeling she'd achieved little, Elaine tried sitting Anna in front of the children's television but she wasn't interested. When Ian came home at 7 p.m. their cases were still unpacked, there was no dinner and their usually tidy house looked like a whirlwind had torn through, and his wife was looking frazzled.

'I was going to be so organized and have Anna in her pyjamas, and dinner ready when you came home, but as you can see that hasn't happened,' Elaine said apologetically.

'Don't worry,' Ian laughed, and kissed her cheek. 'It's good to be home. Why don't you get Anna ready for bed while I do us some dinner? How does spag bol sound?'

'Wonderful,' Elaine said. 'I'll be better organized tomorrow.'

'Has Anna eaten?'

'Not dinner. Just a snack at four o'clock.'

'OK. We'll all eat together. That'll be nice. There are some presents and cards in my briefcase from the guys at work. We'll have a look at them later.'

'Some more cards came in the post today,' Elaine said. 'People are so kind and thoughtful. I've put them on the mantelpiece.'

Elaine felt reassured now Ian was home, and she bathed Anna and then had her in her pyjamas as Ian called that dinner was ready. As they ate she and Ian talked about their day, as they had done when Elaine had worked, only now her day was very different, and although she tried to make it sound interesting she wasn't sure it did. Anna ate well and when they'd finished Ian and Elaine took her up to bed, following a similar routine to the night before. They read her a bedtime story each, then kissed her goodnight and, dimming the light, came out. Elaine waited on the landing while Ian showered as he hadn't had a chance since returning from work. With no sleep during the day Anna was tired and settled reasonably quickly – only getting out of bed twice before falling asleep. However, when they came up to bed at eleven they found her wide awake and sitting at the top of the stairs. 'You gave me a fright!' Elaine said. 'What are you doing there? Goodness knows how long she's been here,' she said to Ian.

Elaine took her by the hand and led her back to bed, but two hours of sleep had rejuvenated Anna, and she was out of bed as soon as they left her room. Finally, to get some sleep, they took her into their bed again. 'I don't understand why she doesn't like her room,' Elaine sighed. 'It's a lovely room.'

'I'm sure she does like it, but it's all new to her.'

As most parents know, sleep takes on a whole new significance when deprived of it by a sleepless child and, exhausted, they will try anything to get some sleep. Ian and Elaine put up with Anna poking and kicking them, babbling, and the lack of intimacy her presence dictated, in the hope that she would fall asleep. Eventually she did and slept through till the alarm, so they felt some progress had been made. Anna climbed out of bed and ran round the landing to the toilet. Elaine followed her to make sure she washed her hands properly, but as she flushed the toilet, to her horror she saw something wriggling in the pan, and her stomach churned. 'She's got worms!' she cried, utterly repulsed.

CHAPTER FIFTEEN

BAD PARENTING?

'Did you bring a stool sample with you?' the doctor asked the following morning.

'No. I'm sorry. I didn't think,' Elaine said, flustered. Of course she should have thought of that.

'There are a number of different worms and we'll treat Anna for the most common. You and your husband will need treating too.'

'Really?'

'Oh yes, worms are highly contagious. One dose of the syrup at night. The reason you didn't see the worms before was because Anna wasn't eating properly so they were very small. Now she's eating well the worms have been feasting too so have grown.' Elaine swallowed the bile rising in her throat.

'Here is the prescription,' the doctor said, passing the printed sheet of paper to her, then recapping: 'The sores on her back are healing well so keep using the cream. Her heart and lungs sound fine. She's a bit underweight but that's only to be expected and should improve with time. Start the vitamin drops, and I've given you the form for her blood test?'

'Yes,' Elaine said, and held it up.

'Take it with you to the hospital. If you go this afternoon we should have the results back here in a week. From what you've told me there is nothing in her or her mother's history to suggest she might have contracted a sexually transmitted disease, so the test is precautionary. The clinic for the vaccination programme runs here tomorrow. I've booked her in. Is that everything?'

'Yes, I think so,' Elaine said, collecting together all the forms and putting them into her bag. They'd been in the surgery for ages and Elaine knew the doctor would be running late now.

'Well, good luck and congratulations,' she said. 'You have a lovely daughter.'

'Thank you.' Elaine felt very proud.

Outside, she retrieved Anna's pushchair from the pram park at the side of the surgery, but Anna refused to get in. 'It's a long walk to the pharmacy,' she said, and tried to lift her in. Anna went rigid so it was impossible. Elaine considered persisting but, not wanting a scene in public, gave in and let Anna walk, although it was awkward, manoeuvring the pushchair while holding on to her.

That evening, when Ian arrived home, Elaine felt she had plenty to share about her day, and dinner was at least in the oven, although not fully cooked. Anna ate with them and afterwards Elaine gave them all a dose of the worming medicine. It didn't taste too unpleasant. Come bedtime, Anna would only settle in their bed again with them either side of her, which meant she went to bed very late and they very early.

'She must find our presence comforting,' Elaine said, although Anna didn't want a cuddle, just the space between them in the bed. If Ian reached out to hold Elaine's hand, Anna roughly pushed it away, even smacking him.

They laughed and indulged Anna to begin with, but when these sleeping arrangements continued for another week Ian complained. 'When are we going to get back to normal?'

'I'm not sure you ever do when you have children,' Elaine said lightly. But she knew what he meant. They hadn't made love since the adoption – in the hotel they'd all been in the same room and now Anna shared their bed at night.

The following night Elaine made a big effort to settle Anna in her own room, but after a lot of screaming, which culminated in a tantrum, she gave up and let her go into their bed, by which time Ian was asleep.

The blood test results came back negative, a huge relief. Anna didn't have HIV or a sexually transmitted disease, but her iron levels were a bit low, so the doctor prescribed an iron supplement.

With less than two weeks to go before Christmas the shops were festively decorated and full of gifts. Anna was fascinated when they went into the High Street and wanted everything she saw, and then made a scene when she couldn't have them. Ian and Elaine had yet to decorate their house or buy a Christmas tree but intended to do so the following weekend when Ian was home. Elaine was viewing Christmas with mixed feelings. Anna's first Christmas with them would obviously be very special, but she was anxious about the inevitable socializing Christmas would bring and how Anna would cope with that. Ian had wanted to accept an invitation from his brother and family to stay with them over Christmas, but Elaine had persuaded him out of it, saying it would be nice if it was just the three of them on Christmas Day. In truth it was the thought of his brother's very well-behaved children, and she tortured herself with the look of horror on their faces if Anna played up and threw a tantrum, which Elaine would be helpless to control. When Ian came home with another invitation for them all to visit, this time from a work colleague, Elaine confided her concerns.

'Don't be silly, all kids play up sometimes,' he said, 'and we need to get out more. In fact, I was thinking that perhaps we could get a sitter and you and me could go out one evening. It will do us good.'

'But we can't leave Anna while she's so unsettled!' Elaine said, wondering why he needed to be told this.

'All right, so let's have someone round for supper like we used to.'

Which they did and it was a disaster. Anna refused to go to bed when their guests arrived and played to her new audience, interrupting, demanding attention and babbling in her own language.

'When will she start to learn English?' one of their friends asked delicately.

'She knows a few words already,' Elaine said a little defensively, aware she should have known more.

When the meal was ready Elaine tried to get Anna to bed again so the adults could eat in peace, but it proved impossible. Red-faced Elaine set another place at the table and then watched as Ian grew increasingly agitated that the adults couldn't have a proper conversation. She was embarrassed too; when they'd been to friends' homes for supper the children were either already in bed or went up soon after the guests arrived. When the main course was over Elaine left them with the dessert and took Anna up to their bed where she lay with her in the hope that she might fall asleep. Nearly an hour passed and Ian came up to find her and said their friends would be leaving shortly. Unable to face them, Elaine told him to say goodbye from her.

Later, he was annoyed. 'You're indulging that child too much,' he said. 'Anna has taken over and is ruling us. Children are supposed to fit in with their parents, not the other way round.'

Elaine knew he was right and felt responsible and even more of a failure.

Christmas came and went, and while it wasn't the disaster Elaine had thought it might be, neither was it a joyous first family Christmas. Anna had no sense of excited expectation, looking forward to Christmas as most children do, despite taking her to see Santa and a pantomime. On Christmas Day her face didn't light up as she opened her sack full of presents; indeed, they couldn't get her to smile for a single photograph. Her face remained expressionless, as it was most of the time, as if she was simply going through the motions. As she had so little English, it was difficult to know what she was thinking or feeling, although Elaine formed the impression she understood far more than she let on.

Anna stayed up to see in the New Year. Ian opened a bottle of sparkling wine and they let Anna have one sip. A new year brings new hope, the promise of change and a fresh start, but when, three months later, Anna had made no progress, hadn't slept in her own bed once, and screamed non-stop if they tried to make her do something she didn't want to, defeated, Elaine took her to the doctor.

'How can I help you today?' the doctor asked kindly, and Elaine burst into tears.

'I'm sorry,' she said, reaching for a tissue. 'It's all become too much.' The doctor waited patiently as Elaine wiped her eyes and composed herself before continuing. Anna watched her mother, emotionless. 'I don't know how we've come to this,' Elaine said, taking a deep breath. 'My husband and I wanted a family for so long, but I'm making a complete mess of it. We knew it wouldn't be easy, but something isn't right. We can't seem to reach her.' She glanced furtively at Anna. 'She doesn't want to be held or cuddled and barely even looks at us. When she does there is a blankness in her eyes. She never smiles or laughs. She does exactly what she wants when she wants, and if we try to stop her she just screams and throws a tantrum until we give in. I've stopped going out and I hardly see anyone. I don't know what to do.' Her eyes filled again.

The doctor looked at Anna thoughtfully. 'Has she learned English?'

'Only a few words. Not many. I think she understands but won't cooperate and speak the words. Sometimes she looks at me so coldly, like she hates me, and I don't know what to do to change it.' She wiped her eyes again.

'I'm sure she doesn't hate you,' the doctor reassured. 'She's only been with you four months. That's not long really. I'll examine her today and I can certainly refer her for speech therapy to help her language. But I think most of what you describe will sort itself out in time – when she's fully bonded with you and your husband. Will she be going to nursery when she's three?'

'We haven't decided yet.'

'I think it would be good for her. Mixing with other children her own age will help her language and social skills, and also give you a break.' She smiled kindly. Then to Anna she said, 'Come on, let's have a look at you, pet.'

The doctor listened to Anna's chest, looked in her ears, eyes and throat, and then, showing her a card with brightly coloured objects on it, asked her to point to the correct one. 'Dog,' the doctor said. Anna pointed to it. 'Ball.' Anna pointed. 'House,' the doctor said, and Anna pointed to the correct object again. 'Can you say "house"?' the doctor asked.

'House,' Anna repeated.

'She wouldn't do that for me!' Elaine said. 'I knew she understood more English than she lets on.'

'That's children for you,' the doctor said with a smile. The examination over, she returned to sit behind her desk. 'Anna is fine, but I'll make a referral for speech therapy to bring on her language skills. They are bound to be a bit behind those of children who have English as a first language. You'll receive an appointment in the post within a few weeks. Once she is talking more, I think life will become easier for you both. If you have any more concerns, see me again. If necessary, I can refer her to the child psychologist, but I'm sure that won't be necessary. Just give her time.'

'Thank you. There is one more thing,' Elaine said, embarrassed to ask.

'Yes?'

'I was wondering if you could prescribe a sedative for Anna to make her sleep at night?'

'Why? Isn't she sleeping?'

'Yes, but she will only sleep in our bed.'

The doctor smiled. 'Most children of her age would prefer to sleep in their parents' bed if allowed. You will have to be firm to get her back into sleeping in her own bed. Does she have her own bedroom?'

'Yes.'

'Good. Establish a bedtime routine with a bath and story, then settle her in her own bed. Say goodnight and come out. If she gets out of bed, which she will do to begin with, take her back. You may have to return her many times until she learns, but she will learn. I'm speaking from experience. My son went through a phase of wanting to sleep with us. It took my husband and me a full week of taking him back before he learned.' Elaine nodded politely, but didn't dare say Anna had never slept in her own bed, not once. 'Here are the names of some good websites that give parenting advice,' the doctor said, winding up and passing her a printed sheet. 'You use a computer?'

'Yes. Thank you,' Elaine said, tucking the paper into her bag.

'You're welcome.'

Elaine left the surgery, reassured by the referral for speech therapy, but aware that she and Ian were going to have to be firmer with Anna, although she wasn't sure how. Perhaps the websites would help.

Four months later she returned in tears and begged that Anna be referred to a child psychologist. The situation had deteriorated further and, now aged three, Anna had been excluded from nursery for repeatedly hitting and biting other children.

PART II

CHAPTER SIXTEEN

FOSTER CARE

'Cathy, she has had two foster carers since coming into care a week ago,' Jill said.

'You're joking!'

'I wish I was. She can't be moved again.'

'No, indeed.'

Jill was my supervising social worker, also known as a support or link worker, from the agency I fostered for. It was early afternoon and Jill had telephoned me with some details of a five-year-old girl the social services wanted me to foster. It was shocking that the poor child had had to move twice since coming into care. It's unsettling enough for a child to have to leave home to live with carers, without having to move carers – three times if she came to me.

'What went wrong?' I asked, aware that something must have happened to necessitate the moves.

'The first carers were very experienced and were already fostering a baby. Anna kept trying to tip the baby out of its pram and cot. They had to watch her continuously and felt the placement had become unmanageable, so they asked for her to be moved. Although the second carers didn't have young children, they were newly approved to foster and were horrified when Anna was cruel to their cat and kept throwing it downstairs. They tried sanctioning her but this morning, after another incident, they asked for her to be moved today.'

'Jill, we have a cat,' I said sombrely.

'I know.'

'At her age she should know it's wrong to treat a baby or cat like that,' I said, concerned. While a toddler might tip a baby out of a pram or throw a cat and not appreciate the significance or the harm they could do, a five-year-old certainly should know.

'Anna has been diagnosed with Reactive Attachment Disorder,' Jill said. 'As you know from your foster carer training, it is thought to be responsible for a lot of behavioural problems.'

'So she is seeing a child psychologist then?'

'She has been, but not at present, although the school want a referral again. They have raised concerns about Anna's behaviour since she started school, and she only attends part-time.'

'Why part-time?'

'She wasn't coping. There were a number of incidents, so rather than exclude her, they have reduced her hours.'

'Which school does she go to?' Jill told me and I knew where the school was – on the other side of town.

'We will need to move her later today,' Jill said. 'The only other carer we have free is newly approved. We can't send her there.'

'No, that's for sure.' Clearly Anna had very challenging behaviour so she needed to be placed with an experienced carer who would hopefully have the resources and strategies to manage and improve it. I was experienced but I was hesitating, because we'd just said goodbye the day before to a boy with very challenging behaviour. Was it fair on my children, Adrian, aged eight, and Paula, four, to look after another child straight away with similar or worse behaviour? Foster carers are expected to take the child referred to them unless there is a very good reason why they can't. That I had just fostered a child with behavioural difficulties wasn't sufficient reason to refuse; nor that I was a single parent and we had a cat.

'Has she been in care before?' I asked, hedging for time.

'No. The social worker will fill you in on the details once you agree to take her. I do know that Anna is an only child and has generally been well cared for, although the parents sought help for her behaviour when she was about three – that's when the psychologist was first involved. Ten days ago her mother telephoned the social services distraught and said she couldn't cope with her any longer. Apparently her husband left them just after Christmas and Anna's behaviour has deteriorated further since then.'

It was that piece of information that swayed me. I knew what it felt like to have your husband walk out, leaving you to face the future alone. The hurt and pain and crushing blow to your self-confidence. My husband had left me three years before (for another woman) and back then I had wondered how I would cope alone, then I found the resources. My children didn't have behaviour problems, but without doubt, for a mother who was already struggling with her child's behaviour, being left alone would be the final blow.

'OK, what time will Anna be here?' I asked. 'I'll need to collect Adrian and Paula from school later.'

'I'll find out and get back to you. Thanks, Cathy.'

Just to be clear, I could have refused to take Anna. Foster carers can't be forced into looking after a child, but there is the expectation that they will. If I hadn't taken her then very likely, rather than place her with inexperienced carers locally, the social services would have sent her out of the area for the care she needed. That would have created more disruption for the child, including a change of school or long car journeys to and from her present school. I hadn't asked about contact arrangements; the social worker would tell me later. Most children who come into care see their parents regularly. Neither had Jill told me what the care plan was – that is, the long-term plan for Anna – but from what I knew so far I assumed she would eventually be going home.

I went upstairs to check the spare bedroom, shortly to be Anna's room, mulling over what I knew about Reactive Attachment Disorder (RAD). It is a rare but serious condition found in children who have never bonded with their parents or main caregiver, usually as a result of severe neglect or abuse, although that didn't seem to be the case here – Jill had said Anna had been generally well looked after. RAD varies in severity and often becomes most noticeable around the ages of five and six, when the child's already worrying behaviour spirals out of control. They often appear cold, uncaring and without conscience, remorse, empathy or trust, and are unable to form normal, loving relationships. They are angry, destructive, defiant, manipulative and cruel, and can steal and lie for their own ends, and appear not to care about the consequences. Name a negative behaviour and it will come up under Reactive Attachment Disorder, although some of these behaviours can be found in other conditions too. However, so great is the RAD child's lack of emotion and conscience that on a brain scan there is a dark mass where their emotion should be. If left untreated, the condition can go with the child into adulthood, creating cold and calculating adults who show no remorse and are unable to form relationships.

The good news is that a child with RAD can improve dramatically with therapy, but in order to do so the child needs to be in a secure, stable and loving relationship with their parent (or main caregiver), which clearly Anna wasn't.

I checked the bedroom. It was fine. Aware that it probably wouldn't be long before it would be needed again, I'd changed the bedding and given it a good clean the day before, straight after the lad I'd been fostering had left. With 70,000 children in care in the UK and more coming in each day, there is a permanent shortage of foster carers and beds are never empty for long. As I neared the bottom of the stairs the phone rang. I answered it in the hall. It was Jill.

'I've spoken to Anna's social worker, Lori, and she will be going to collect Anna soon and will bring her to you. I've told her you need to pick up your children from school, so she will be with you when you get back around four o'clock. I'll arrive ten minutes before.'

'Thank you, Jill.'

'If Lori needs to talk to you without Anna present, I'll keep her amused in another room.'

'Thanks,' I said again. A good supervising social worker is invaluable in fostering. They know their carers and look out for them, offering support, advice and practical help when necessary. All I needed to do now was to tell Adrian and Paula that Anna would be coming to stay with us.

* * *

'Good, a girl my age,' Paula predictably said, viewing Anna as a playmate. She and her brother, Adrian, who was four years older, often played nicely together, but it's a bonus to have someone of a similar age to play with.

'OK,' Adrian said with a shrug. We were walking from school. 'But I need to watch something on television at five o'clock. Our teacher said we have to, it's about the Tudors.' This wasn't as random as it sounded. Our television is in the living room, where the adults would be while Lori, Anna's social worker, placed her, a process that Adrian knew would take an hour, or possibly longer.

'I'll set the recorder so you can watch it later,' I said.

'Why is she in care?' Adrian asked.

'I'm not sure of all the details but her mother was struggling with her behaviour and needed some help.' A direct question deserved an honest answer, but I didn't expand on this with talk about RAD and two carers unable to contain Anna's behaviour. It could have worried Adrian and also prejudiced him (and Paula) against Anna. I would deal with her behaviour as it arose, although to be honest I wasn't as confident as I might have sounded. Yes, I'd dealt with challenging behaviour before in children I'd fostered, but then it had been one of a number of concerns about the child; for example, a teenager who'd gone off the rails, experimenting with drink and drugs and getting into trouble with the police. To be fostering a child of five who'd had to leave her parents and two carers purely because of behaviour was a first for me.

Once home we just had time for a drink before Jill arrived. She said hello to Adrian and Paula and they disappeared up to their rooms to play. They'd come down when Anna and her social worker arrived. I made Jill a cup of coffee and we sat in the living room. As my supervising social worker, in addition to offering support and advice, she also attended meetings with me and was usually present when a child was placed.

'Do we know any more about Anna's background?' I asked as she sipped her coffee.

'No, because she's been moved as an emergency the referral was sparse.'

I nodded. Had Anna come to me with more notice, as a planned move, I would have had more details and very likely Anna would have been able to visit us before the move, so we weren't complete strangers to her. As it was, she'd meet us and see the house as she moved in, which wasn't ideal but couldn't be avoided. Jill and I chatted for a few minutes about another child I'd fostered a few years back and who was doing well. Foster carers are always pleased to hear news about the children they've looked after, even if it's a long time ago. We never forget them.

Just after four o'clock the doorbell rang and I felt my heart step up a beat as I stood to answer it. I'm often slightly anxious before a new child arrives, wondering if they will like us, and what I will be able to do to help them, but I now had the additional worry of Anna's behaviour.

Taking a deep breath, I opened the front door. 'Hello, love, you must be Anna,' I said with a smile, and wondered what all the fuss was about. Slightly built, with clear blue eyes and fair hair neatly trimmed to chin level, she looked as if butter wouldn't melt in her mouth. Her gaze went past me and down the hall.

'Hello, I'm Lori,' her social worker said, coming in. We shook hands. In her late thirties, she was dressed smart-casual in a jumper and trousers and a warm winter jacket. 'I'll need a hand bringing in her cases later,' she said.

'Sure.' It's usual to get all the paperwork done first and then bring in the child's belongs at the end, before the social worker says goodbye and leaves.

Lori automatically slipped off her jacket and hung it on the hall stand and left her shoes with ours.

'Shall we take off your coat and boots?' I said to Anna.

She looked at her boots as though considering this, then took off her coat, which I hung on the stand. 'They're nice warm boots,' I said. 'Leave them in the hall with ours.' Which she did. We always take off our outdoor shoes when coming in for good hygiene, and I encourage others to do the same.

'Jill's here,' I said to Lori. 'Come through.' I led the way down the hall and into the living room. 'This is my supervising social worker, Jill,' I explained to Anna.

'Hi, Anna,' Jill said with a smile. 'How are you?'

Anna glanced at Jill but didn't smile or acknowledge her in any way, just turned her head to look around the room. Jill and Lori said hello – they knew each other from working together before.

'Do you want to play with the toys while we talk?' Lori asked Anna, referring to the toy boxes I'd put out. Apparently she didn't, for Anna went to the sofa and sat down. Lori sat beside her while Jill and I took the easy chairs.

'Nice long garden to play in when it's warmer,' Lori said to Anna, glancing through the patio widows and trying to put her at ease.

'Or if it snows,' I said, hoping to capture Anna's interest. She glanced at me but her face was expressionless and cool. I formed the impression she kept her feelings very well hidden, which could be part of RAD.

Having heard the doorbell, Adrian and Paula now came downstairs and I introduced them. Paula looked hopefully at Anna, wondering if she wanted to play, while Adrian looked pointedly at the clock. 'I've set the recorder for your programme,' I told him.

Having said hi to Anna, he left – there was no need for him to stay; there'd be plenty of time for them to get to know each other later when the formalities were over. Paula was still looking hopefully towards Anna. Not only were they of a similar age, but a similar build too. 'Would you like to play with Paula?' I asked Anna.

'No,' Anna said. It was the first word she'd spoken.

'OK, maybe later then,' I said, and threw Paula an encouraging smile. She appreciated that when a child first arrived it could take a while for them to find the confidence to start playing and talking. Paula sat by the toy box and began taking out its contents as Anna watched. I didn't think it would be long before she joined in.

'Anna is in care under a Section 20,' Lori began, adjusting the paperwork on her lap. 'It was at her mother's request.' A Section 20 (of the Children's Act) is also known as Accommodated, and is when a parent or parents ask for or agree to their child going into care voluntarily. There is no court case and they retain parental rights. 'Anna has been diagnosed with an attachment disorder,' Lori continued. 'I haven't read the full report yet but it's thought it was a result of her early years' experience. She was in and out of a state orphanage in –' she named the country '– for the first two years of her life before she was adopted. We now know that the level of care in some of those orphanages was inadequate, and children were left for hours in their cots without any stimulation and their cries for help went unanswered. As a result, they can fail to trust adults or form loving relationships, and it comes out later in their behaviour.'

I saw Jill looking uncomfortably at Anna, as indeed I was. Lori was talking about her in quite personal detail in front of her. 'Lori,' Jill said, 'would it be helpful for you to talk to Cathy about the history in another room? I can stay here with Anna and Paula.'

'It's OK,' Lori said easily. 'Anna is aware of her history. She's grown up knowing the circumstances of her early years and that she has a birth mother and was adopted.'

Clearly it was Lori's decision. Anna remained expressionless, watching Paula.

'Anna goes to — school,' Lori continued, naming her school. 'But she is on reduced hours at present: ten o'clock till two. She is with her class in the morning for lessons with support, has lunch with the rest of the school, then has a small group activity with a teaching assistant in the afternoon. You are able to take her to and from school?' Lori now asked me.

'Yes.' Foster carers are expected to take the children they look after to and from school, contact and any appointments they may have. Sometimes it's quite a juggling act if you have school-aged children yourself, but Anna's reduced timetable would help. I would be able to take Adrian and Paula to school first and then Anna to hers, and do the reverse at the end of the day.

'The school arrangements will be reviewed but they seem to be working at present,' Lori continued. 'The school has asked for a referral to the child psychologist, although there is a waiting list. I'll have to arrange an LAC [Looked-after Children] review. I'll let you know the date. Here is the Essential Information Form Part One.' She handed Jill and me a copy. This form contained the basic information about the child I was fostering, which I needed to help me look after the child. As well as their name, home address, date of birth and names of their parents, it included any other family members, and I read that Anna had no siblings. Her ethnicity was given as British and her language English. The box for religion showed nominally Church of England.

'Does she go to church?' I asked.

'Not as far as I know,' Lori said.

I continued a quick read-through, as did Jill. The legal status showed Section 20, which Lori had already covered. There were no special dietary requirements and no known allergies. In the box asking if there was any challenging behaviour, 'Yes. Attachment Disorder' had been printed. Beside special educational needs were the hours she went to school and that she had support from a teaching assistant. The box for contact arrangements was blank.

'Do you know the contact arrangements now?' Jill asked, just as I was about to. I reached for a pen ready to make a note.

'There aren't any,' Lori said.

Jill and I looked at her. 'Why not?' Jill asked, as surprised as I was.

It wasn't Lori who answered but Anna. 'I don't want to see my mother and she doesn't want to see me,' she said, cold as ice.

CHAPTER SEVENTEEN

FIRST NIGHT

'Her mother is going through a difficult time at present,' Lori said, trying to smooth over Anna's harsh words. 'I'll be seeing her again shortly, so hopefully she will feel a bit stronger.'

'What about telephone contact?' Jill asked.

'Not at present, and I'm trying to trace Anna's father.'

'I don't want to see him either,' Anna said, her face hard.

Paula looked over, thinking she must have misheard. Although her father no longer lived with us, she and Adrian saw him regularly.

'What is the care plan?' Jill asked, moving on.

'I'll send you both a copy,' Lori said. 'We were hoping for rehabilitation home.' But I heard her doubt. Without regular contact there was little chance of Anna returning home.

Anna, who'd been eyeing Paula closely, suddenly stood and went to her. I assumed – as I think Jill and Lori did – that she was going to play with her, but instead she roughly snatched the toy Paula was holding and returned to her seat without saying a word.

'Paula was playing with that,' I said. 'There are plenty more farmyard animals in the toy box.' I went to Paula, who was looking shocked and rather hurt, and, taking a handful of toy animals from the toy box, placed them in her lap. 'You play with those,' I said. It wasn't the time to explain to Anna why you didn't snatch a toy from another child, and persuade her to hand it back; that would come later.

'You have to ask if you want a toy someone else has,' Jill said to Anna as I returned to my seat.

'She hasn't learned about sharing yet,' Lori said. 'The school has been working on it.'

I nodded. Paula had her head bowed, looking at the toys in her lap, but Anna was staring at her unabashed, gloating and victorious. Clearly she had a lot to learn when it came to sharing and mixing with other children.

Lori checked through her notes. 'Have I missed anything?' she asked, glancing at Jill and me. 'I've placed Anna three times in a week so I'm not sure who I've said what to.'

'Can you let us both know the date of the review when you've arranged it,' Jill asked, 'so I can put it in my diary and attend?'

'Yes, of course.' Lori made a note and then returned her papers to her bag-cum-briefcase. 'Shall we look around the house now and then we'll unpack the car?'

We all stood and Paula came to my side, not wanting to be left alone. 'This is the living room,' I said to Anna and Lori, beginning the tour. Jill knew my house well. 'We are usually in here in the evenings, playing a game, reading or watching television.'

'That's nice,' Lori said encouragingly. Anna looked back expressionless. I led the way into our kitchen-dining room. 'This is where we eat,' I said, pointing to the table in the dining area. Toscha, our cat, having heard people in the kitchen and aware it was nearly her dinnertime, came in through the cat flap. Paula went over and stroked her and was rewarded with a loud meow. Aware of the cat's fate in the last foster home Anna had lived in, I watched her carefully but her face was blank. She made no move towards Toscha to stroke or pet her as most children would.

'She's very friendly,' I said. 'Do you like cats?'

Anna shook her head. 'The one before scratched me so I threw it downstairs,' she said, unabashed.

'Toscha doesn't scratch or bite, but even if she did we wouldn't throw her. That would be unkind.' Paula joined me again as we went out, down the hall and into the front room. 'This is like a quiet room,' I said to Anna, 'if you want to be alone.' It held the computer, sound system, shelves of books, a cabinet with a lockable drawer where I kept important documents, and a small table and chairs. It tended to be used more by teenagers who wanted their own space rather than children of Anna's age.

'Very good,' Jill said, although she'd seen it all before.

Upstairs I showed Anna her room first, at the rear of the house and overlooking the garden. 'It'll feel more comfortable once you have your things in here,' I said encouragingly. Lori agreed but Anna met our comments and her new room with the same indifference, although I suspected there was plenty going on in her thoughts. You don't leave your mother and then have to change home three times in a week and come out unscathed.

I now led our little group into the bathroom. 'Anna has good self-care skills,' Lori said.

'Excellent,' I said, smiling at Anna. 'We usually have our baths in the evening before we go to bed.' She was unimpressed.

I briefly showed her my bedroom. 'This is where I sleep. If you need me in the night, call out and I'll come to you.' I then led the way along the landing to Paula's room. I opened the bedroom door just wide enough so Anna and Lori could look in and then closed it again. 'We all have our own bedrooms and they are private,' I told Anna, as I told all the children when they first arrived. 'We don't go into each other's bedrooms unless we are asked to, and we always knock first if we want the person.' To demonstrate, I now knocked on Adrian's bedroom door. 'Hi, can I show Anna and Lori your room, please?' I said.

'Yes, come in,' came his reply.

I opened the door so they could see in. Adrian was sitting on the floor, playing with some toys. 'Thank you, Adrian,' Lori said and closed the door as they came out. 'It might take Anna a while to get used to living here,' Lori commented as we returned downstairs. 'There was just her and her parents at home so they didn't need much privacy.'

'Don't worry, I know it takes time to settle in,' I said, 'but I think it helps if the ground rules are explained at the start.'

'Absolutely,' Jill agreed. 'Then everyone knows what's expected of them.'

'We'll bring your bags in now,' Lori said to Anna as we arrived in the hall.

'Can I help?' Paula asked, wanting to stay close to me.

'Yes, of course.' I took her coat from the hall stand and passed it to her.

'I'm not helping,' Anna said firmly.

'No, you can come with me. We'll play with some toys in the living room,' Jill said positively. Touching Anna's shoulder, she steered her down the hall.

'There are a lot of bags,' Lori warned me, as we slipped on our coats and shoes.

'No worries, I can store what Anna doesn't need.' Although it was unusual for a child who'd only been in care a week to come with a lot of luggage. More often the parents are reluctant to part with their child's belongings, as it's an upsetting confirmation that they are in care and no longer living with them. Then, usually after the social worker explains it's better for the child to have their own things rather than use the carer's, they gradually bag it up and pass it on a little at a time over months, often at contact.

Paula and I followed Lori out to her car. It was dark now in winter and the air cold. When Lori opened the car – an estate – and the interior lights went on I saw what she meant by 'a lot'. The boot, part of the back seat and the front passenger seat were full of cases, bags and boxes. 'I think her mother packed everything except her bike,' Lori said. 'Most of it hasn't been unpacked – she wasn't with the other carers long enough.'

I took a small child's handbag from the boot and gave it to Paula to take in while Lori and I loaded ourselves with as much as we could carry. We went back and forth, and as her car slowly emptied and my hall and front room filled, my concerns deepened. This wasn't the luggage of a child who was coming into care for a few weeks or months to give her mother a break, but one who was going away for good.

'What are the chances of Anna returning home?' I asked Lori quietly as we took in the last of the bags.

'Not good,' she said. 'We're looking for the father and if he can't look after her, then kinship carers [family members]. Anna's mother has a sister, and her father has a married brother who may be willing to offer Anna a home. Failing that, she will be in long-term foster care.'

I'd just shut the front door when I heard Paula cry out from the living room simultaneously with Jill's voice saying, 'No, Anna! That was naughty.'

Paula, visibly upset, ran into the hall and to me. Jill appeared behind her. 'Sorry, Cathy. Anna pushed her. She thought she'd taken her bag.'

'It's all right,' I said, consoling Paula. I went into the living room where Anna was standing clutching the bag. 'Anna, I gave Paula that bag to carry in. She was helping me, not taking it from you.'

'Don't care,' she said defiantly. 'It's mine!'

Again, I didn't say anything further for now as Lori was about to say goodbye and leave, but it was another small incident that showed how watchful I was going to have to be.

It was set to get much worse.

Uncooperative and confrontational aren't words I like to use about any child, but that's what Anna was that evening. Usually there is what foster carers refer to as a 'honeymoon period' when a child first moves in. Regardless of any negative behaviour that might have gone before, when they first arrive they are usually on their best behaviour. It can last for days, weeks, even months, then they relax, feel more secure and start to push the boundaries as a way of testing the carer's commitment to them. Anna clearly hadn't heard of the 'honeymoon period' and was determined to make herself as unpleasant as possible from the start, and who could blame her? In her eyes she'd been rejected three times in a week and must have felt unloved and very angry.

After Lori and Jill had left, Adrian came downstairs to see if he could watch the television programme about the Tudors I'd recorded.

'Yes, good idea,' I said. 'You can watch it while I make dinner.'

'I don't want to watch it,' Anna said, without even knowing what it was. Adrian hesitated.

'What do you normally do in the evenings?' I asked her, wanting to accommodate her wishes if possible.

'Watch television,' she said. 'But not the one you want.'

'So what do you like to watch?' I asked.

She shrugged.

As she had no preference, I didn't see why Adrian shouldn't watch the programme he needed to. I explained to Anna that it was for school and that if she didn't want to watch it she could play with some toys. The programme was only twenty minutes long. I set the recorder to play and waited until Anna was settled by the toy box. 'I'll be in the kitchen if anyone wants me,' I said. I went out with Paula, leaving the doors between the living room and kitchen open so I could hear what was going on. For a few minutes all that could be heard was the television, then Adrian came in.

'Mum, Anna keeps standing in front of the television so I can't see it.'

Leaving what I was doing, I went into the living room where Anna was now sitting by the toy box again. 'Try not to stand in front of the television,' I said.

'I didn't,' she replied confrontationally.

'Good. I'm pleased.' I waited until she was playing again and returned to the kitchen with Paula at my side.

A couple of minutes later Adrian appeared again with the same complaint. I went into the living room. 'Anna, I have asked you not to stand in front of the television, love. Adrian can't see it. It would be a great pity if I had to tell you off on your first night here.'

She shrugged. I waited until she was occupied again and returned to the kitchen. It was getting late and I needed to make us dinner. It wasn't long before Adrian appeared again. 'Mum, I'll watch the programme later. She keeps humming so I can't hear it properly.'

'I'm sorry, love.' He went up to his room while I went into the living room and switched off the television.

'I want to watch it!' Anna demanded.

'So did Adrian but you stopped him from doing so.'

'I want to watch something else.'

'No, love. That wouldn't be fair when you stopped Adrian from watching.' She looked mildly surprised, as though she really thought she would get her own way, but this was about fairness and if I didn't put in place what was acceptable now it would be more difficult later. The maxim 'start as you mean to go on' is very true.

'Hate you,' she said, then screwed up her face, opened her mouth wide and screamed for all she was worth. It was truly ear-piercing. Paula fled to her room, while I put my hands over my ears and waited for it to pass. Perhaps she thought screaming would change my mind, or possibly it was an expression of rage. Finally, red in the face, she ran out of breath and stopped. 'Hate you,' she said again, narrowing her eyes.

'I can understand why you might,' I said evenly, going to her. 'You must be feeling very hurt and alone from all the moves and not living with your mother. Would you like to tell me about how you are feeling and have a hug?'

'No!' She scowled.

'Sure?'

She stuck out her tongue.

'Another time then. You can play with the toys. I'll be in the kitchen if you want me.'

I returned to making the dinner, popping into the living room every so often to check on her. I heard Paula cross the landing and go into Adrian's room where they stayed playing until I called everyone for dinner. I fetched Anna, who hadn't immediately come, and showed her where her place was at the table – we tend to keep to the same places. She shook her head and said she didn't want to sit at the table but wanted her dinner on a tray in front of the television. I explained that we sat at the table to eat and anyway the television was staying off for now.

'My mummy lets me,' she said, jutting out her chin defiantly.

'That's her decision,' I said. 'Here we eat at the table.' Foster carers are expected to take meals at a table, as it encourages good eating habits, and the evening meal is often the only time the whole family sits down together. Adrian and Paula were looking at Anna anxiously, clearly wondering if this was going to develop into another screaming fit, but I think she was too hungry. She sat in the chair I showed her, and as soon as I set her plate in front of her she picked up her knife and fork and began eating.

'I don't like this,' she said partway through, but eating it nonetheless.

'What do you like?' I asked. 'I can get some in for another time.' Foster carers try to accommodate a child's food preferences and stick to their routines at home as much as possible, but that relies on the parent(s) passing these details to the carer, which hadn't happened here yet.

'Biscuits,' Anna said. 'I like biscuits.'

'OK. You can have a biscuit when you've finished your main course.'

'I don't want your biscuits. You won't have the ones I want.'

'I might,' I said. 'I'll show you what we have when we've finished.'

She looked a little confused but continued with her meal. Once we'd finished, I showed her our selection of biscuits, but she shook her head and looked genuinely disappointed. 'Do you know what the biscuits are called and I can buy some?' I said.

'You can't get them here. Mummy tried but they are too far away.'

It was my turn to look confused. 'So where did you have these biscuits?'

'In the hotel.'

'When you were on holiday?'

'No. In my country,' she said, as though I should have understood.

'Your country?'

She nodded. 'When I was adopted.'

'Oh, I see.' I smiled. 'You've got a good memory. You were only little then.'

'Mummy tells me and we have photos we look at.'

'That's nice.' I was pleased Anna had shared this with me but surprised the memory was so alive with so much going on at present.

It was getting late and I always like to round off the day with a story or game before I take the children up for their baths and bed, so leaving the washing up, I ushered everyone into the living room. Anna didn't want to listen to a story or play any game Adrian, Paula or I suggested, so I told her to fetch one of hers for us all to play. Her luggage was where I'd left it – I hadn't had a chance to unpack – but I'd seen plenty of toys and games in the boxes. I went with her and as she searched for what she wanted I saw that the bags had cardboard luggage tags attached to the handles (labelled either by Anna's mother or one of the carers) stating what the bag contained, which was helpful. I placed the bag marked 'Night-time clothes and school uniform' at the foot of the stairs ready to go up. The rest I would sort out tomorrow. Anna had now taken out a hand-held activity centre that only she could play with, thereby excluding us. We returned to the living room and while I read Paula and Adrian a story, Anna played independently until it was time to start their bath and bedtime routine.

I usually take the children up in age-ascending order – the youngest first and the oldest last, so it should have been Paula, Anna and Adrian, but I wasn't about to leave Anna downstairs unsupervised with Adrian. She was far too unpredictable and volatile at present. I took Paula and Anna up together, which gave Adrian the chance to watch the programme on the Tudors in peace. Upstairs, Anna told me bluntly she didn't want a bath.

'You can have one tomorrow then.' I would never insist that the child has a bath or shower on their first night. To have to undress and bathe in an unfamiliar house while the carer hovers is likely to make the child feel even more uncomfortable. So I left Anna in her bedroom to change while I gave

Paula a quick bath. Paula was exhausted. I tucked her into bed, then took Anna to the bathroom. 'Do you need any help washing or brushing your teeth?' I asked her, as I would ask any child of her age on their first night.

'No. I'm not a baby,' she snapped.

Nevertheless, I waited on the landing while she was in the bathroom, then when she came out I took the opportunity to praise her. 'Good girl. You did that nicely.'

'I'm not sleeping in that room,' she said, pointing down the landing to her bedroom, and began towards my bedroom.

'No, love, you can't sleep in there,' I said, drawing her out. 'That's where I sleep.'

'I'll sleep in your bed,' she said. Which I thought was an odd assumption for a child of her age to make.

'No. You've got a nice room of your own,' I said, closing my bedroom door. 'I'll leave your light on low and your bedroom door open if you like.' Many children prefer that.

'I sleep in my mum's bed at home,' she said, not moving from outside my bedroom.

'Not every night, surely?'

'Yes. With Mummy now, but with Daddy as well before he left.'

'But you're a big girl. You need your own bed.' I moved away and led the way along the landing to her room. She followed. I doubted she slept with her parents every night, not at her age.

'I sleep where I want,' she said defiantly as we went into her room.

'Not here, love. We all sleep in our own bedrooms. Would you like your curtains open or closed?' Small details like this can help a child settle.

'Don't care,' she said. 'I'm not staying here. You can't make me.'

'I'll close the curtains then and make it nice and cosy,' I said, ignoring her rudeness.

I then eased back the duvet and waited, wondering if we were going to have a standoff, but eventually she climbed in. 'Do you have a cuddly toy at night?' I asked. There hadn't been one in the bag containing her nightclothes. She turned away without answering. 'Would you like a goodnight kiss?' I asked, pretty sure of the answer.

'No. Go away.'

'OK, but don't be rude. It's bound to feel a bit strange for a while with everything new, but tomorrow you'll feel a bit better, and the next day and the next. Try not to worry. I'll look after you. Call out if you want me. Night then, love.' I waited but there was no response so I came out, leaving her bedroom door slightly ajar.

I checked on Paula, who was fast asleep, and then went downstairs to Adrian. As I entered the living room I heard movement on the landing and quickly returned upstairs. Anna's bedroom door was wide open and, when I looked in, her bed was empty. I found her in my bed.

'Anna, I've already told you, you can't sleep in here. Come back to your own bed. I'll stay with you until you're asleep if you like.' It's not acceptable for a child to sleep with their foster carer. Only babies in cots can share their carer's room. Apart from which, it wouldn't be fair on Adrian and Paula if she slept with me. I eased back the duvet for her to get out.

'No!' she said. 'Not going.'

'Why? What's the matter? Are you frightened of something?'

'No. I want to sleep here.' It seemed therefore it was more about Anna getting her own way than out of any fear or anxiety.

'Come on, I'll stay with you until you're asleep,' I said again, offering my hand.

'I'll scream if you try to move me,' she threatened.

'You're still going to have to sleep in your room.'

I waited and then took her arm and gently eased her from my bed. She screamed – all the way round the landing, waking Paula, and bringing Adrian running upstairs to see what was the matter. 'It's all right,' I reassured him. 'I'll be down in a few minutes.'

I returned Anna to her bed, asked her again if anything was worrying her, then once she'd settled I came out. I resettled Paula but as soon as I was downstairs I heard Anna's feet cross the landing as she returned to my bed. The pattern continued for most of the night. Each time she got up I took her back to bed with her screaming and waking Paula and then later Adrian. Goodness knows what the neighbours thought, but it wasn't the screaming of a frightened child but one used to getting her own way.

At 1 a.m. I stopped returning to my bed and sat on the landing ready to take Anna back to her room when she emerged. She was very angry at not being allowed to do as she wanted and tried to kick and pinch me. Eventually, at around 3 a.m., utterly exhausted, she fell asleep – in her own bed. I waited ten minutes and then returned to my room, shaken and drained. I couldn't ever remember having such a dreadful first night with any child I'd fostered before.

CHAPTER EIGHTEEN

I HAVEN'T GOT A HOME

The following morning we were all shattered and it took a lot of coaxing and cajoling to get everyone down to breakfast on time. Anna was so tired she didn't have the energy to object – to getting dressed (I'd set out her school uniform on her bed ready) or to eating the breakfast I'd prepared, which I think she might have done otherwise. Everyone was very quiet at the table as we ate. I saw Adrian and Paula stealing furtive glances at Anna, clearly concerned that the child they'd heard screaming 'I hate you' repeatedly during the night might reappear. Meanwhile Anna kept stealing glances at me, not quite sure what to make of me. Perhaps I was the only adult who'd made her do as they'd asked. I didn't know, but I behaved perfectly normally, and didn't refer to her tantrums of the night before. It had been dealt with and I hoped that Anna had begun to see that when I asked her to do something it was for a good reason and I wouldn't be bullied into submission. I'd explained at the time why she had to sleep in her own room, and sometimes children simply have to do as they're told. Whether there would be a repeat of last night remained to be seen. I hoped not. I wanted Anna to be happy while she was with us for however long that might be.

Despite our lack of sleep, we did manage to leave the house on time, and so began our new weekday routine. With the children under seatbelts in the back of my car, I drove first to Adrian's and Paula's schools, which were on the same site, saw them in and then went on to Anna's school. Hers was on the other side of town, about a thirty-minute drive in the traffic. We arrived with ten minutes to spare. I parked, released my seatbelt, then, turning in my seat, asked Anna if she'd like me to read her a story from the book she had in her school bag while we waited until ten o'clock when she went in.

'No,' she said sullenly, looking through her side window.

She'd been quiet in the car, and a few times during the journey I'd asked her if she was all right. She hadn't replied and at one point she'd looked as though she was about to nod off, so I thought she was probably just very tired. I switched the radio on low and tuned it to soothing classical music. Occasionally I turned in my seat to say something to Anna, trying to open up communication and establish a relationship. 'It's a nice school … I'm looking forward to meeting your teacher and TA (teaching assistant) … What do you like doing best? … You could invite a friend home for tea.' And so forth. She ignored me and continued to gaze out of her side window.

Just before ten o'clock I said it was time for us to go into school, so I got out and went round to open her door, which was child-locked. Now on familiar territory, Anna's assertiveness returned and she strutted up to the main gate and pressed the security button, then went ahead across the playground to the main door where she pressed the next security button. I joined her. The door clicked open and she went ahead into reception. Two office staff sat at their computers behind a counter to my right and one stood and came over. 'You must be the new foster carer?' she said.

'Yes.' Clearly Lori had updated them so they were aware of Anna's most recent move.

'Can you fill this in, please?' she said, passing me a form. 'Miss Rich, Anna's TA, will be down to collect her soon.'

I filled in the form: standard questions for when a child moved home, asking for the child's full name and date of birth, my name and contact details, and my relationship with the child – foster carer. I handed it back. 'I'd like to make an appointment to see Anna's teacher, please,' I said. I always like to meet the child's teacher to find out how they are doing and what I can do to help them.

'That's Mrs Taylor. She's left a note saying she'd like to see you. She's teaching now but if you can come in half an hour early at one-thirty today she will see you then.'

'Wonderful. Thank you. That's very efficient.'

'She is,' the secretary said.

The door behind me opened and a slender, fashionably dressed young lady I guessed to be in her late twenties came in and said hello to Anna. Then to me, 'Hi, I'm Lauren Rich, Anna's TA.'

'Nice to meet you,' I said, going over. But my gaze went to Anna. Having rejected any contact with me, she made a point of sidling right up to her TA and now had her arm around her waist. While this could simply have been because she knew her TA well and felt safe with her, her expression said otherwise. The smirk said, *See, I like her better than you*, which I ignored.

'I support Anna in the classroom, and also she is in a small group I take in the afternoon,' Miss Rich said. 'I know Mrs

Taylor, her class teacher, will tell you about Anna's progress when she sees you later, but do let me know if you have any concerns.'

'Thank you.'

'Her reading book and homework will be in her bag at the end of school each day. The homework is usually reading practice and a work sheet – maths or literacy. There is also a home school book in her bag where I write what they have to do, and also any comments about her day. Feel free to add anything that may help us here.'

I thanked her again. She seemed very pleasant, and as I was the third carer she must have explained this to in a week, very patient. I said goodbye to Anna and wished her a nice day, but she ignored me.

'Say goodbye to your carer,' Miss Rich encouraged. Anna shook her head.

'Don't worry,' I said. 'You both have a good day and I'll see you later.' Given all the issues I was having to deal with, the least of my concerns was Anna not saying a polite goodbye.

I arrived home at 10.30 so I had two and a half hours before I had to return to Anna's school to meet her teacher at 1.30. The hall and front room were still clogged with Anna's bags and boxes, but before I tackled those I needed to write up my log notes. I usually did them at the end of each day but I hadn't had a chance the evening before with constantly having to settle Anna. Foster carers are required to keep a daily record of the child or children they are looking after, which includes appointments, the child's health and wellbeing, education, significant events and any disclosures the child may make about their past. When the child leaves this record is placed on file at the social services. Over time the logs can show the improvement (or not) the child makes and also act as an aide-mémoire for the carer and social worker. With a mug of coffee, I took the folder I'd begun for Anna from the lockable drawer in the front room, and sitting at the table wrote a few paragraphs about Anna's arrival. It was objective and I hoped honest.

Returning the folder to the drawer, I then set about unpacking, taking up to her room the bags she needed now, and leaving in the front room the bags marked summer clothes, outgrown toys, Memory Box and Life Story Book, and so forth. Again I had that cold, sinking feeling. Why had Anna's mother packed all of this? It was Anna's history. Wasn't she going to try to bring Anna home ever again? The vast majority of parents whose children go into care would keep these things in the belief that their child would be returning home before too long, but it seemed Anna's mother had closed the door and said goodbye to her daughter for good.

I arranged Anna's winter clothes neatly in the wardrobe and drawers in her bedroom, and her books, small toys and other knick-knacks on the shelves. She had come with two framed photographs, which I also put on the shelves, pausing to look at them. One was of a couple in their forties whom I guessed to be Anna's parents, and the other was of a younger woman standing alone outside an old stone building in what looked like a cobbled market square. Who was she, I wondered? Then I saw the familial likeness to Anna and I guessed it was her birth mother.

With her room looking more homely and the hall (but not the front room) clear, I had a quick sandwich lunch before setting off to Anna's school. As I drove I thought about the photograph of Anna's birth mother and also Anna's comments the evening before about the biscuits from her 'own country'. Cleary her parents had worked very hard to make Anna aware of her roots and keep the memory of her birth mother alive. I knew this would be considered appropriate and PC (politically correct) by the social services, so when and why had it all gone so horribly wrong? As with many children I'd fostered, when they first arrived there was a lot I didn't know and I'd learn more as time went by. Sometimes the child's teacher was able to fill in some background details, and the more I knew about Anna the better, so I could understand and meet her needs.

I arrived at Anna's school five minutes early and signed in the Visitors' Book, then waited in reception where I looked at the children's artwork on the walls. Also on the wall was a laminate photo board with photographs of all the staff and their names beneath, including the caretaker and support staff. Mrs Taylor, Anna's teacher, I guessed to be in her early fifties, and she had short, neatly cut hair and looked confident and efficient, as the secretary had said. When she came into reception I recognized her immediately from her photograph. Wearing a tweed skirt, pale grey blouse and cardigan, she shook my hand warmly. 'Mrs Glass, lovely to meet you. Thank you for coming in.'

'Thank you for making the time to see me,' I said. She seemed efficient but also very personable and friendly.

'Have you been fostering long?' she asked, leading the way out of reception.

'Yes, about nine years now.'

'Good. So I take it Anna won't have to leave you as she did the others?'

'No. Not until everything is sorted out, and where she lives long-term is decided.'

Mrs Taylor opened a door on our right and I followed her into a small room containing filing cabinets, a small desk and a couple of chairs. 'Take a seat. We shouldn't be disturbed in here,' she said as we sat. 'I met Anna's first foster carers. They were very pleasant, but apparently unable to deal with Anna's behaviour. I didn't meet the second set. Anna was in and out so quickly, and in my view should never have been sent to them.'

'Unfortunately there is such a shortage of foster carers that often there isn't a choice of where to send a child,' I said.

She gave a little sniff. 'That's what her social worker said. Anyway, Anna is with you now, although probably more disturbed than ever by all the moves.'

What could I say? She was right. 'I will do all I can to help her.'

'Mmm,' Mrs Taylor said, as though that remained to be seen. 'What have you been told about Anna and her past?' She looked at me carefully.

'I know she was adopted at the age of two and a half from an orphanage overseas, and has since been diagnosed with an attachment disorder. Her father left home at Christmas and her mother wasn't able to cope with her behaviour alone.'

'That's about it in a nutshell. We've had Anna in the school since she was three, so we know her and her parents well. She came to our nursery after being excluded from another nursery. Have you met her parents?'

'Not yet. Hopefully I will before too long, or her mother at least. I don't think they know where the father is at present.'

Mrs Taylor suddenly looked very sad. 'I feel as if I have watched those poor parents unravel. They are a lovely couple whose hopes of a family have been dashed. It wasn't their fault. They were naïve and bit off more than they could chew with Anna. They never liked to say no to her.' I nodded. 'Anna is fiercely independent, probably from having to be as a small child. She rejects help, advice and comfort. Goodness knows what she went through in those early years, but problems began as soon as they returned home with her – even before, from what her mother, Elaine, told me. Elaine used to come in and see me and ask for advice. The school works very closely with parents, especially if their children are experiencing difficulties. They tried to deal with her as they thought fit, then someone put the idea in Elaine's mind that the child probably had a disorder. She took her to a round of specialist doctors until eventually Anna was diagnosed with an attachment disorder.'

'You seem to think that might not be correct,' I said.

'Oh, I don't doubt that Anna has failed to bond properly, presumably because of the neglect she suffered in those first few years. She displays all the symptoms of an attachment disorder, and we've asked for the education psychologist to be involved. But in my opinion what that child needs more than anything, and has done from the start, is tough love. By that I mean firm boundaries for good behaviour, and love and support to enable her to move on from the past, rather than all that stuff about keeping her in touch with her roots.'

'I see,' I said, taken aback by her directness.

'I know what I'm talking about,' Mrs Taylor continued. 'I've had first-hand experience. My sister has two adopted boys, brothers. They were six and eight when they went to live with her and her husband. The horrors those lads had been through were unbelievable. The parents were sent to prison for what they did. The boys were in care for a year with four different sets of carers, all unable to control their behaviour, before my sister and her husband adopted them. Feral was the word that came to mind. Their behaviour and problems were far worse than anything I've seen in Anna, but the difference is my sister had experience of working with disturbed children. Instead of feeling sorry for them and pandering to them, they were very firm from the start. They had to be – the boys were uncontrollable. They made sure they felt safe and set about changing their behaviour through a system of rewards and sanctions.' I nodded.

'The social worker kept pushing for the boys to keep in touch with their natural parents, even visit them in prison! My sister and her husband refused, saying it would undermine what they were doing and hamper the boys' chances of being able to move on from the past. They always answered their questions honestly and the lads knew that if they did want to see their natural parents they could, but their past wasn't kept alive like Anna's has been. Eight years on and both boys are doing well. The older one, who was more badly beaten, has learning difficulties, but they are both happy. As my sister said, the past is past and the kids have their whole future ahead of them. I see so many comparisons between my nephews and Anna.' Mrs Taylor's eyes filled and she reached for a tissue. 'You see, Anna is close to my heart,' she said, a little embarrassed. We were silent for a moment.

'Anna has come with a framed photograph of her birth mother, which I put on a shelf in her bedroom,' I said, now wondering if I'd done the right thing.

'She's brought photographs of her birth mother and what she refers to as "my own country" into school to show us. If you ask me I think her past is ruining the present and possibly her future, although I'm sure her social worker would disagree. But what can we do to help Anna? Her life is in even more turmoil now.'

'Does she have any friends?' I asked.

'Not really. We are trying to teach her to make friends, but Anna can be very bossy and manipulative. She wants it all her own way, which from my understanding is what has been happening at home. She screams when she doesn't get what she wants and it scares other children. She has also been quite cruel to some of the children. Her behaviour became so disruptive last term that we agreed with her mother to put her on a reduced timetable for now.'

I nodded. 'I've heard her scream,' I said, 'for most of last night, because I wouldn't let her sleep in my bed. Does she really still sleep with her parents every night?'

'I believe so,' Mrs Taylor said, raising an eyebrow. 'Her father had been sleeping in the spare room before he left. Anna was quite victorious when she told me. It's not good for a child to hold that sort of power. It's not good for the parents' relationship either.' She paused, collecting her thoughts. 'In respect of Anna's education, her learning is behind what it should be. I'll ask Lauren Rich, her TA, to give you a copy of Anna's Individual Education Plan.'

'Thank you. I'll help Anna with her school work. I have two school-aged children myself, so I always make time in the evening for homework.'

'Good. Although be prepared for a struggle. Her mother used to say that if Anna refused to do something, there was nothing she could do to change her mind. She often came in without her homework done. Is Anna going to see her mother?'

'Not at present.'

She looked at me thoughtfully. 'If Anna doesn't return home to live with her parents, will she be able to stay with you permanently?'

'I honestly don't know,' I said. 'It will depend on the social services.'

She gave a half-hearted nod. 'I need to go to my class now. It's after two o'clock. Anna can go straight home with you, but please feel free to see me when you want. Just let the office or Miss Rich know.'

'Thank you so much,' I said. 'You've been very helpful.' We stood and left the room.

'If you wait in reception, Miss Rich will bring Anna to you.'

I thanked Mrs Taylor again, said goodbye and returned to reception. Anna was already there with Miss Rich.

'You're late,' Anna said rudely. I was going to let it go but then she grabbed my arm, digging in her nails. 'You're late!' she said again.

'Don't do that, please,' I said, releasing my arm. 'It hurts. I've been to see your teacher.'

'Why?' she demanded.

'Anna!' Miss Rich cautioned.

'To hear how well you are doing,' I said, 'and how I can help you with your school work. Come on, say goodbye, it's time to go home.'

'I haven't got a home,' she said.

'Yes, you have. It's with me for now, and I've made your room look really nice.'

CHAPTER NINETEEN

MEMORIES

Despite all my best efforts in trying to make Anna's bedroom look comfortable and homely, she didn't like it. To be honest, given how objectionable she was making herself, I'd have been more surprised if she had liked it, but her only comment was quite telling. 'That's my real mother,' she said, picking up the framed photograph of her birth mother.

'She's your birth mother,' I said. 'But your real parents are your mummy and daddy, the ones who adopted you.'

She glared at me as if I'd just blasphemed. 'You don't know!'

'Anna, I know your mummy and daddy must love you a lot, as you do them, but something has gone wrong between you. How much do you remember of the time before you came to England?'

'Lots!' she said fiercely. 'I know my real mummy.'

'Do you really remember her or is it that your mummy and daddy have talked to you about her and showed you photographs?'

She looked confused, as well she might, and I was mindful of what Mrs Taylor had said about the past intruding into and damaging the present. 'None of your business,' Anna said at last.

'Don't be rude, love. It's not necessary.'

But Anna's past was my business. If I was going to be of any help to her, I needed to know and understand what her experiences and memories were. I had to try to break down the barriers that Anna had erected to protect herself; not all at once, but little by little over the coming weeks.

I hadn't seen Anna smile yet or allow herself to be pleased with something. I appreciated that she had a lot on her mind, but most children would have shown a glimmer of pleasure when something pleased them. A small example of this was the chocolate milkshake I made for her when we arrived home after collecting Adrian and Paula from school. She specifically asked for it when I offered everyone a drink, and clearly enjoyed it, but when I said, 'You liked that, didn't you?' she scowled and pushed the glass away.

'No!'

When she wasn't scowling or looking angry her face was blank and expressionless.

Anna had nothing to do with Adrian and Paula that evening and treated them as though they weren't there, although I saw her looking at them occasionally, and also at our cat, Toscha, whom I kept a close eye on. I didn't want her meeting the same fate as the last carer's cat. Children who are angry will grab and throw anything in sight, regardless of the harm they can do. A disturbed child in a temper is out of control and needs to be stopped for their own sake and for the safety of those around them.

Anna didn't have any homework that night and, knowing I wouldn't be receiving much cooperation from her, and that everyone was tired from the broken night before, I began the children's bath and bedtime routine early. However, Anna surprised me by actually getting into the bath I had run at the first time of asking. She liked her bath and I think she found the warm water soothing. It was getting her out at the end that proved the challenge. She refused and eventually I had to drain the water, which led to her shouting 'You can't do that!' and 'I hate you!' That's as maybe, I thought, but she did get out.

Similarly and predictably, Anna didn't want to sleep in her own bed, and I asked her again if there was a reason. She said, 'Because I always sleep in the big bed!'

'Not here you don't, love. We all have our own beds.'

Then followed a rerun of the night before, with me repeatedly taking her back to her own bed, in between seeing to Adrian and Paula. Anna grew increasingly angry with me as she couldn't get her own way and threatened to bite and kick me. When she tried to carry out her threat, advancing towards me, I folded her arms across her chest and faced her away so she couldn't kick or bite me, then I held her until her anger subsided. More like a hug than a restraint. She was only slight and I'd had training in holding a child who was going to harm themselves or someone else – an inexperienced carer might not. Possibly her parents didn't physically stop her either, as an angry child who is out of control is frightening, but the person who is most scared of their behaviour is the child themselves. Having someone control their anger is reassuring and helps them. Eventually she calmed down and I returned her to her bed again.

To my great relief, clearly exhausted, Anna didn't get out of bed again after 11.30, and when I checked on her she was fast asleep on her side with her thumb in her mouth. I viewed this as progress. If I could shave an hour off this performance every night, by the end of the week Anna should be asleep in her own bed at a reasonable time. Well, that was the theory at least.

I checked on Adrian and he'd gone off to sleep with his pillow over his head to block out the noise. I took it off, eased it under his head and kissed him goodnight. I went into Paula's room and she was just going off to sleep again after the last disturbance.

'I don't think I like that girl,' she muttered sleepily.

'Don't you worry. She'll get better with time,' I said, and stroked her forehead until she was fast asleep.

Anna slept through, and when I woke her the following morning and said it was time to get dressed ready for break-fast, she scowled at me but did as I asked. I viewed this as another small improvement.

The school run went reasonably smoothly. I tried to engage Anna in conversation as I drove to her school, but she ignored me so I switched on the radio. We waited in the car until it was time to go in, when Miss Rich met us in reception. We exchanged a polite good morning and I checked with her that Anna hadn't had any homework the night before. She looked surprised.

'I left it at school by mistake,' Anna said quickly. That wasn't what she'd told me, nor apparently Miss Rich.

'I asked you before you left yesterday if your homework was in your bag,' Miss Rich said to Anna, 'and you told me it was. Sorry,' she said to me. 'In future I'll check myself.'

'No worries,' I said. 'We'll do what she missed tonight.'

If Anna thought she was going to get the better of two

intelligent adults then she was wrong. She was behind with her learning and for her own good she needed to do her homework.

I drove home, where I had three hours before I had to leave again to collect Anna from school. Clearly, while she was on a reduced timetable my days were going to be very short. My priority today was to sort and clear Anna's bags from the front room. It's unsettling for a child to see their belongings in bags, as it suggests they might have to move again soon. However, before I had the chance to get started, Jill telephoned to see how Anna was settling in and also to make a date to visit me. As my supervising social worker she visited every month, when we discussed the child I was fostering and my training needs, and she checked my log notes and generally monitored my fostering. Lori telephoned straight after Jill, asking for an update on Anna and also giving me the date of Anna's first review. It was nearly an hour before I was able to tackle the bags in the front room. The first one I came across contained Anna's Life Story Book.

Children who are in long-term foster care or who are adopted often have a Life Story Book. It is considered good social-work and foster-carer practice and is a short record of the child's past for the child. It includes photographs, a brief narrative, and memorabilia that can be mounted in the book, such as examples of the child's drawings, school merit certificates and cinema tickets. Larger items that can't be included in the book are often put in a Memory Box. These photographs and keepsakes supplement the child's own memories so they can retain a sense of their past.

Anna's Life Story Book was subtitled 'Our Adoption Journey'. I was immediately transported back to a happier place and time: a photograph of Elaine standing in a child's bedroom and smiling as she packed children's clothes and toys into a suitcase. The caption read: *We are taking lots of warm winter clothes for our darling daughter, Anna. Mummy and Daddy are so excited!* The next photo was of Ian loading the boot of their car with the caption: *Will all our luggage fit in? On our way to the airport.* The next photo was a selfie of Elaine and Ian outside the airport with their luggage stacked high on a trolley. Then one of the departure board where they'd drawn an arrow marking their flight. Their boarding passes were mounted on the next page. Then a photograph through the plane window with the caption: *The sun rises on a beautiful day. One hour to landing!* I sensed their mounting anticipation and excitement.

Next was a photograph of a man called Danny standing beside a cab and I read that he was *the best driver ever.* Then a photograph of the orphanage Anna had come to know as home. Grim and uninviting at best, in winter it appeared cold and bleak and quite haunting, surrounded by bare trees. I looked at it for a few moments and then turned the page. I was greeted with a photograph of Anna, aged two and a half, sitting on a beanbag between Ian and Elaine. A younger, smaller version of Anna – and her hair was much shorter now – but her clear blue eyes were unmistakable. Below was written: *Mummy and Daddy visited you every afternoon. We always brought toys and activities but you preferred playing with our phones!* On the opposite page was a photo of Anna with a phone held high in each hand while her parents looked on, smiling indulgently. There were more photographs of *The playroom where we spent so much time*, including a close-up of a brightly coloured mural on one wall.

I turned the page again, to a photo of Elaine and Ian look-ing very smart in suits with the caption: *On our way to court. A very special day when Anna officially became our daughter.* The next photo was similar to the framed one of Anna's birth mother that I'd unpacked and put in Anna's bedroom. I now realized it had been taken outside the court. The caption read: *Anna's mother. A lovely lady, being very brave after the court hearing. We will never forget her.* A lump rose in my throat and I looked more closely at the photo. The same blue eyes as Anna but trying hard to smile. I could see how brave she was having to be as she struggled to maintain her composure. What had been going through her mind as she held it together long enough for the photograph to be taken? The last picture, the one Anna would remember her by. It was heartbreaking and I swallowed hard.

I turned the page: photographs of Anna in their hotel room. A foldaway bed was beside the double bed but Anna was in that instead and playing with a mobile phone. Then a picture of her watching television, and the three of them having breakfast in the hotel. This was followed by pages of photographs of the area in which they must have stayed with captions beneath explaining where it was. For example: *Daddy pushing Anna on the swing in R— Park,* and so on. The legal paperwork must then have been completed, for the next page contained a photograph of Anna's passport stamped with a visa, and one of her new birth certificate.

Then began their journey home – the three of them. A photo of Danny unloading their luggage at the airport, the departure board with an arrow marking their flight. Three boarding cards: Mr Ian Hudson, Mrs Elaine Hudson and Miss Anastasia Hudson. I knew from the Essential Information Form that Anna's name had been shortened from Anastasia. Then a picture of Anna asleep on the plane, and then they were home – *Tired but very happy*. There were photos of their first Christmas together, with Anna opening a sack full of presents, then beside a gaily decorated Christmas tree, although she wasn't smiling in any of the pictures. The three of them wearing party hats and having their Christmas dinner, followed by a photo dated 28 December and entitled *Anna's extended family*. It showed about a dozen or so people, including three children, posing in what must have been a relative's house decorated for Christmas.

The last photograph was headed *Happy New Year* and showed Anna with her parents beside a picture of Big Ben striking midnight. They were raising their glasses to see in the New Year. Beneath was the caption: *A New Year, a new start*. And that was it. Their adoption journey had ended and I assumed the photographs that followed in the last two years since the adoption were in their family album.

I flicked back through the Life Story Book, looking more carefully at some of the photographs. I suppose I was looking for any sign of where something might have gone wrong. But of course a photo is a small moment in time, a second, not the full picture. Mrs Taylor had said there'd been problems almost straight away. It was so very sad – from all that promise of happiness to the reality of now. I wondered how much Anna looked at her Life Story Book. I hoped it wasn't too much. A Life Story Book should be used with discretion to help answer any questions the child might have about their past, not as a constant reminder. Again, Mrs Taylor's words came back to me about her sister's adopted children needing to move on from their past.

I returned the book to the bag and took out the Memory Box, which had Anna's name on the front in fancy lettering. Inside it was a treasure trove of memorabilia from Anna's past. An empty milkshake carton that, the tag said, Anna had drunk in the car after leaving court. Then a wrapper from a packet of biscuits with the name and ingredients in a foreign language. The tag said, *Anna's favourite biscuits. Pity we can't get them in England*, so I guessed these were the biscuits Anna had mentioned to me. I took out the clothes she'd worn at court, and then a crucifix on a chain in a box with a note saying it had been given to Anna at court by her mother. 'Birth mother,' I found myself saying out loud. 'Elaine, you're her mother.' Little wonder Anna is angry: to lose one mother is traumatic, but to lose your adoptive mother too was painful beyond belief.

Aware that time was ticking by, I carefully returned the items to the Memory Box. I felt I had been party to their adoption journey and it helped me to understand, although clearly there was a lot I still didn't know. I continued sorting through the other bags and boxes and took them upstairs. The items Anna would need with her now I took into her bedroom, and the rest I stowed out of the way in the loft. Then it was time to collect Anna from school.

At two o'clock Miss Rich brought Anna to reception as arranged and told me she'd done a nice piece of literacy work, but unfortunately there'd been an incident with another child in the playground and as a sanction Anna had lost some of her playtime. 'Oh dear,' I said, frowning at Anna. It was important she knew I was disappointed with her behaviour, even though it had happened at school. Miss Rich said there was spelling homework in Anna's bag, and she'd checked it was still there.

'Also,' she said, looking a little uncomfortable, 'I need to tell you that Anna said your son has been bullying her.'

'What! Adrian?' I said, astonished. 'That's ridiculous. Anna hasn't had anything to do with him since she arrived. They're never alone together in the same room.'

'Anna said it just after she'd been told off in the playground for bullying the other child, so we thought it might be a reaction to that,' Miss Rich added.

I looked at Anna, who didn't meet my gaze. 'You mustn't make up things like that,' I said firmly. 'It's very wrong and could get people into trouble.'

'Well, he did!' she persisted.

'When? What did he do?'

'Can't remember,' she said with a shrug.

'No, because it didn't happen.'

She shrugged again. I didn't think Miss Rich believed her, but that wasn't the point. Incidents like this can have serious consequences for foster carers and their families. Any allegation made by a foster child is noted by the social services and investigated. If it is serious enough, the child can be removed from the carer and the carer even suspended from fostering pending an investigation. I'd make a note of what Anna had said and the circumstances in which it had been said in my log, and also inform Jill the next time we spoke.

Worried, I said goodbye to Miss Rich and left the building with Anna. 'You mustn't make up things,' I said to her again.

'Can if I want,' she returned.

'Anna, I know you're angry and upset, but trying to make trouble for others because you've been told off is not going to help. And it could lead to you having to move again to another carer.'

'Don't care,' she said, and that was part of Anna's problem. She didn't care. One of the symptoms of a Reactive Attachment Disorder is the child's apparent callous disregard for consequences, others and what others think of them. All children test the boundaries sometimes and say they don't care, but mostly children do care and want to do the right thing to please their parents (or main caregiver). But because Anna hadn't formed a secure and meaningful attachment in those crucial early years, she didn't feel she needed to do the right thing or please others. The damage could be undone but it would need the help of a therapist, so I hoped the referral Lori was making wouldn't take too long.

I watched Anna like a hawk once we were all home, and didn't let her out of my sight, but then I hadn't before. I also mentioned to Adrian that he wasn't to be alone with Anna even for a second. Sad though this was, I daren't risk her making more potentially harmful allegations; she wouldn't see the damage she could do. Adrian didn't ask why but knew enough of fostering to appreciate that sometimes these steps were necessary.

Aware that Anna was likely to be resistant to doing her homework, I created a small incentive and said we'd do homework before we had pudding. Anna liked her puddings. I fetched her school bag from where she'd left it in the hall and, returning to the table, took out the list of spellings she had to learn. Adrian had his homework and Paula was getting her reading book from her school bag. Anna spent a lot of time fiddling around, ignoring me and avoiding what needed to be done, then said her spellings were too hard. 'I'll help you,' I said.

'I don't need your help.'

'OK. I'll listen to Paula read then.'

'I want my pudding first,' Anna demanded.

'We'll have pudding after we've all done our homework.'

'Why not now?' she persisted. I heard Adrian sigh.

'Because we'll do the homework first.' I returned my attention to Paula and eventually, after more fiddling around and trying to distract Adrian, she began learning her spellings. There were only six but she did seem to find them difficult to remember. When I tested her on them she only knew three well, but at least she had done as I'd asked – eventually.

Because everything was such a struggle with Anna we didn't have time to sit down together and relax as a family in the evening. After homework and pudding I began their bedtime routine and steeled myself for more refusals and confrontations. It was 8.30 before Anna was out of the bath and in bed. Adrian and Paula were already in bed with their bedroom doors closed, so they would hopefully be able to get off to sleep. I took up my place on the landing ready to return Anna to bed with minimum disruption. She was persistent to say the least – old habits die hard. If she had been sleeping with her parents every night, it would take time to change that. There was less screaming and kicking tonight, and when she was in her bed asleep at ten o'clock I viewed it as a huge step forward. I still had time to go downstairs, make a cup of tea and write up my log notes before going to bed.

I'll admit that looking after Anna was stretching me to the limit. I went to bed exhausted and was continually on guard. I could understand why the previous carers had given up so quickly. Looking after Anna wasn't the joy of fostering a child who just wanted to be loved and cared for. It was part of

Anna's condition that she gave the impression she didn't need anyone. I knew from my training that managing her behaviour was paramount, but I could only do so much. Once in therapy she would hopefully be helped to understand her own emotions and taught to appreciate those of others too.

CHAPTER TWENTY

BAD AT HOME

The strain of having Anna live with us was taking its toll on Adrian and Paula. Since she'd arrived I had hardly spent a minute with them, and they were looking forward more than usual to spending the day with their father on Sunday, when he would take them out somewhere nice. He saw them every month and phoned in between. Regardless of what I thought of him leaving us, I didn't let it impact on Adrian and Paula's relationship with him. I told Anna they were seeing their father and I wondered if this would prompt a comment from her about seeing her own parents. She'd hardly mentioned them at all since she'd arrived, which was very unusual. Most children who come into care, even those who have been abused by their parents, pine for them, want to see them as soon as possible and often ask when they can return home. Anna had originally said she didn't want to see her mother. Had that changed? Apparently not. She didn't mention wanting to see her parents at all – not then, at least.

Once Adrian and Paula had left with their father, I asked Anna what she would like to do and suggested the cinema, a park (the weather was cold but dry) or an indoor activity centre. She didn't want to do any of these, so I said we could do something at home then. She shrugged and didn't offer a better suggestion, so I opened the toy cupboard in the conservatory and asked her to choose some games we could play together. The phone rang and I answered it in the living room. It was my mother; we usually spoke a couple of times a week, but now I said I'd have to call her back later for a chat. When I returned to the conservatory Anna was nowhere to be seen. I'd only been away from her for a couple of minutes. I went round the downstairs calling her name and then upstairs. My bedroom door was wide open and I went in to find her going through my wardrobe.

'Anna, whatever are you doing?' I asked, going over.

'Nothing,' she said. But she didn't immediately stop.

'That's private,' I said, and closed the wardrobe door. 'Do you remember when you first arrived, I explained our bedrooms were private and we didn't go into each other's rooms unless we were asked?'

'You go into mine,' she said.

I was taken aback. It wasn't the reaction of an average five-year-old, even one with behavioural issues. 'Yes, because I am your carer and I look after you. I go into your room to make your bed, put your clothes away and keep it clean and tidy. At your age it's part of my responsibility. When you are older you can do it yourself. Now come on, out of here, we're going downstairs to find a game to play.'

She didn't move, but stood with her back to the wardrobe. 'I go into my parents' bedroom whenever I want,' she said brazenly.

'That's up to them,' I said.

'No, it's up to me.'

I believed her, and not for the first time I saw that the distinction between adult and child in their house had become blurred. This, among other things, would make disciplining Anna very difficult. Children need to see the adult in the parent, set apart from them, in order to respect and be guided by them, until they become adults when (hopefully) they have learned what they need to be responsible for themselves.

'Well, in this house we don't go into each other's rooms unless asked,' I reiterated. 'Now, come on downstairs and I'll choose us a game to play.' This was enough for her to leave.

'I'm going to choose the game, not you!' And she rushed out.

I closed my bedroom door. I didn't want to have to start locking it as I had done with one young person I'd fostered, but I might have to if Anna kept going in. Apart from the privacy issue, I had items likes scissors and nail varnish remover in my room, which could be harmful in a young child's hands.

Downstairs Anna was already rummaging in the toy cupboard. Taking out a large, brightly coloured jigsaw puzzle suitable for quite young children, she took it to the table. I sat on the chair next to her but it soon became clear she didn't want me to join her, so I simply sat beside her. When the puzzle was only half complete she gave up, despite my offer to help her finish it, and chose another. The second didn't get completed either, but the third did. Then she wanted to crayon, then ten minutes later paint, then model with Play-Doh, and so the day continued with a break for lunch.

Usually when I have one-to-one time with the child I'm fostering I find our time together is enjoyable and it advances our relationship, with the opportunity to talk and break down barriers. But I didn't feel that with Anna, not at all. Although I stayed close by her as she played, she didn't want me to join in any of the activities and continued to reject me and shut me out of her world. Any questions or comments I made she answered with a shrug or 'don't know', or she just ignored me. It was hard work and the day disappointing. Also, not only had our one-to-one had no positive effect on Anna, I discovered later it had actually had a negative one. When Adrian and Paula returned Anna clearly resented them being back, as she was no longer the centre of attention. She told Adrian she didn't like him and that his father would die soon.

'Anna, that's a hurtful thing to say, and untrue,' I said.

She shrugged dismissively, then pushed Paula out of her way so hard she fell over. I told her off again and said she'd lost television time. It was an impotent sanction as Anna barely watched television, but I had to do something.

'Don't care,' she said, and clearly didn't.

The atmosphere was strained, with Adrian and Paula even more wary of Anna now, and at dinner they weren't their usual chatty selves after a day out with their father. Of course I felt guilty for allowing this to happen. After dinner I read to Adrian and Paula while Anna, who didn't want to listen, played with one of her toys. Then I began their bath and bedtime routine, taking Anna and Paula up first.

'Why do I always have to go up before Adrian?' Anna grumbled.

'Because you're younger than him.'

It was around ten o'clock again when Anna finally settled and stopped getting out of bed, and as usual once asleep she slept through until I woke her the following morning for school. I praised her, but not too much, for my amateur psychology said that if Anna thought she was starting to cooperate she would rebel and go back to square one. The following night, to my absolute delight and relief, after I'd said goodnight and come out of her room she didn't leave her bed, not once! Nor the night after, so I knew we had turned a corner with this issue at least. She might relapse, but it would be easier to correct the next time – the hard work was done here. And this wasn't just about us all having a good night's sleep, but about Anna doing what the adult looking after her had asked.

The next morning at eleven o'clock Jill visited as arranged. I made us coffee and we settled in the living room, with the heating turned up and Toscha asleep on her favourite chair. Her visits usually lasted about an hour, but she was with me for nearly two as there was so much to discuss – an indication of how complex Anna's needs were. By the time she left there was just an hour before I had to return to collect Anna from school. The next time I'd see Jill would be at Anna's review in three days' time.

As well as managing Anna's challenging behaviour I was trying to help her sort out the muddle of thoughts about past and present and who her 'real' parents were. The longer Anna was with me the more I appreciated what her teacher, Mrs Taylor, had said about Anna confusing the past and present. So successful had Anna's parents been in doing what is seen as the right thing and making Anna aware of her origins that it had created confusion, mixed loyalties, insecurity and uncertainty in her. If I asked her about home, she was unsure if I meant the orphanage, home with her birth mother or home with her adoptive parents. Similarly, if I mentioned her

mother she'd say, 'Which mother?' She told me her father
was dead. I didn't know if her natural father was dead or not,
the paperwork didn't say, but certainly her adoptive father –
the one she should have thought of as her father – was alive.
Lori was in the process of tracing him.

What I had also noticed was that if Anna mentioned a
memory from her early years, before the adoption, it was
always of a scene in one of the photographs in her Life Story
Book. Sometimes she repeated the caption her parents had
written beneath, for example: 'My mother is a lovely lady. She
was very brave outside the court.' Or, 'I went on a plane. An
hour to landing.' So that I thought most of her 'recollections'
were in fact false memories from the Life Story Book. If I
asked her anything outside of these, such as, 'Did you have
toys at the orphanage?' or, 'What did you have to eat there?'
she didn't know. I'm not saying she didn't have any memories
of her early years, just that most of what she believed she
remembered appeared to be from the photographs and what
her parents had told her. It was something I would bring up
with her social worker and possibly at the review.

All children in care have regular reviews. The child's
parent(s), social worker, teacher, foster carer, the foster carer's
supervising social worker and any other adults closely
connected with the child meet to ensure that everything is
being done to help the child, and that the care plan (drawn up
by the social services) is up to date. Very young children don't
usually attend their reviews, whereas older children do. I'd
received the review forms in the post, which Anna and I were
expected to fill in and I would take to the review. There'd
been a note enclosed from Lori saying she wouldn't be able to

see Anna before the review, but as her parents were being invited and there was no contact at present she didn't think it was appropriate for Anna to attend. At her age not many children did attend anyway, and their views were expressed through the review form and their foster carer.

Given Anna's general lack of cooperation, I wasn't expecting her to be at all interested in completing her review form, but the expectation is that the carer tries. It is a child-friendly booklet with colourful illustrations and questions designed to ascertain the child's feelings and wishes on being in care. After dinner that evening I asked Anna to remain at the table (while Adrian and Paula went into the living room) and, taking the booklet, I sat beside her and explained about the review and the questions. She *was* interested and grabbed the booklet from my hand. I knew she couldn't read the questions or write her responses, so I said, 'I'll read the questions to you and then you tell me what you want to say and I'll write it.' This was what I usually did. She nodded, which was a first.

'Great.' I picked up my pen, slid the booklet so it was between us and I could see the words, and read out the first question. 'Do you know why you are in care?'

'Yes,' she said.

'Can you tell me why,' I encouraged, 'so I can write it down?'

She thought for a moment. 'Because I've been very bad at home.'

I looked at her, taken aback. 'No, love, that's not the reason. You're not bad. Your mother was finding it difficult without your dad and needed time alone.' No child should ever believe themselves to be bad, and it wasn't Anna that was causing the problems but her behaviour.

'Mummy needed to be alone because of me,' Anna said quietly and without emotion.

'Who told you that?' I asked.

'No one. I just know.' I continued to look at her. 'Write it,' she said, nudging my arm. 'Why aren't you writing? You have to write because I have been bad at home.'

'You really want me to put that?'

'Yes.'

So I wrote it.

The next question asked if the child knew who their social worker was and Anna shook her head. I told her it was Lori and then I wrote *Anna didn't know her name so I reminded her.* I said the words out loud as I wrote them so Anna knew exactly what I was writing.

The next question asked: *Would you like to see more of your social worker?* Anna shook her head so I wrote *No.*

The next question asked what she liked about living with her foster carer.

'Nothing,' she said without any need to think.

'Nothing at all?' I asked, feeling a little hurt. She shook her head. 'What about the milkshakes and puddings I make you? You like those.'

'No, I don't.'

'Well, you eat them.'

She shrugged. 'Write nothing,' she said, nudging my arm again.

So I wrote *Nothing* and wondered what the review would make of this.

The next question asked what she didn't like about living with her foster family and Anna had plenty to say. 'I don't like you, I don't like Adrian and Paula, I don't like your cat, I don't like your house and I don't like having to stay in my bed.' There was so much it barely fitted in the space provided.

'Anything else?' I asked.

'Yes. I don't like you,' she said again.

'I think we've already covered that,' I said, pointing to the first line. I then turned the page and read out the next question. 'What has gone well for you since your last review? I'll write N/A, which stands for not applicable,' I said, 'as this is your first review.'

She eyed me suspiciously. Likewise the next question was: *What has gone badly since your last review?* I read it out and told her I was writing N/A again.

Who are your friends? was the next question. Anna said, 'Don't know.' Which was very sad. Most children of Anna's age can name a few good friends.

'Who do you play with at school?' I asked.

'Anyone.' She shrugged despondently but I could see the pain in her eyes. I didn't push it further as I knew from Mrs Taylor that Anna was struggling to make friends because she was very bossy and controlling. I wrote *Anna doesn't know who her friends are*. The next question asked if the child would like to see more of their friends and Anna shrugged, so I wrote *Anna wasn't sure*. The following question was *If you have a problem, who do you talk to?* She looked puzzled, so I rephrased it.

'If you have something worrying you, who would you tell?'

'Mrs Taylor,' she said.

I wrote *Mrs Taylor, Anna's teacher*. Interesting, as most children would have said Mummy. 'You know you can always talk to me and tell me your worries?' I said. Anna ignored me, so I moved to the final question. 'Is there anything you want to ask?'

She shrugged, then said, 'Will I go home?' A question asked by most children in care and I wrote it down, but Anna was looking at me for a reply.

'I don't know, love,' I said, 'but for now I will look after you. You won't have to move again until everything is sorted out.'

'Will I have to go on a plane again?'

'Not unless we all go on holiday.'

'When can I see my mummy?'

'Your adoptive mother?' I clarified.

Anna nodded.

'I'm not sure yet. Would you like to?'

'Yes,' she said quietly.

My heart clenched. 'I'll write that down too then: *Anna would like to know when she can see her mummy*,' I said as I wrote.

But would her mother want to see her? I had no idea, but I sincerely hoped so.

CHAPTER TWENTY-ONE

REVIEW

On Wednesday I met Jill in the reception of the council offices ten minutes before Anna's review was due to start. We signed in the Visitors' Book and then made our way up to the first floor. 'Hopefully we'll meet Anna's parents,' Jill said, voicing my thoughts.

'Yes, indeed.' Although I felt a familiar surge of nervousness at meeting the child's parents for the first time.

Lori was already in the meeting room, seated at the large oak table next to a man she introduced as the Independent Reviewing Officer (IRO). LAC reviews are chaired and minuted by an IRO who is a qualified social worker with extra training, and unconnected with the social services. Jill and I gave him our names and roles – supervising social worker and foster carer – as we sat and he noted these. I handed him the review forms Anna and I had completed and he thanked me.

The door opened and Miss Rich came in carrying a folder. The child's teacher or TA are usually invited to the review. Lori introduced her to the IRO and she sat on the other side of the table to Jill and me.

'Are we expecting anyone else?' the IRO asked Lori. She would have drawn up the list of those to invite and sent the invitations.

'No,' she said. 'The parents aren't coming.' I was disappointed and also knew this didn't bode well for any hope of Anna seeing them or returning home.

Sometimes there are many present at a review or, as with Anna's, just a few. Even so, the formality is maintained. The IRO opened the meeting, thanked us for coming and then asked us to introduce ourselves. We went round the table stating our names and roles. Introductions over, he began by saying this was the first review for Anna Hudson, aged five, although it was her third foster care placement since coming into care. Background information like this would have been sent to him prior to the review. Then, as often happened in reviews, the IRO asked me as the foster carer to speak first, simply because the carer usually has the latest information on how the child is doing. I glanced at the page of notes I'd brought with me and felt my pulse quicken. Although there were only five of us, all eyes were on me and I took a breath. I always start by saying something positive about the child, even if they have very challenging behaviour.

'Anna is eating well,' I said, 'has good self-care skills and is going to school each day. She is also sleeping well now and in her own bed.'

'Well done,' Lori said, appreciating the significance of this.

'Where was she sleeping before?' the IRO asked as he took notes.

'With her parents in their bed,' Lori said.

The IRO nodded and looked to me to continue.

'Anna has some very challenging behaviour,' I said, having exhausted the positives, 'and I am working on that. She is used to doing as she wants and being in control. It's taking time for her to learn that this isn't always in her best interest. She resists adult authority and struggles to show affection either verbally or physically. For example, she hasn't once said she misses her parents. She is also very confused about her past.'

'In what respect?' the IRO asked, looking up from writing. 'She was under three when she was adopted.'

'Yes, but the past is still very vivid for her and from what I have seen it has created a lot of confusion and insecurity in her. She's not sure who her parents really are and quite recently asked if she would have to go on a plane again, meaning to return to the orphanage.'

'Coming into care couldn't have helped her confusion and insecurity,' the IRO observed dryly as he made a note.

'She's been diagnosed with an attachment disorder,' Lori put in. 'We've made a referral to CAMHS [Children's and Adolescent Mental Health Service] and the educational psychologist, but there is a waiting list for both.'

The IRO nodded and looked at me. 'And presumably you reassure Anna and answer her questions as best you can?'

'Yes, although she doesn't really have many questions. She keeps it all bottled up.'

'Why aren't her parents here?' the IRO now asked Lori.

'Anna's mother didn't feel she could cope with it, and she wasn't sure what good it would do. I've only just traced the father and he said he didn't think he could contribute much to the meeting. Both parents are struggling with what has happened.'

The IRO made a note and looked to me to continue.

'I am helping Anna with her school work and am working closely with Miss Rich, her TA.' Miss Rich nodded. 'Sometimes Anna is very resistant to learning and finds it difficult. She's on a reduced timetable at school.' I didn't say any more about Anna's education as Miss Rich would give her report later. 'I try to involve Anna in my family's life, but often she prefers to play independently – in the same room. She finds it difficult to make friends.'

'You have children of your own?' the IRO asked.

'Yes, two.'

'How does she get on with them?'

'She doesn't really,' I had to say. 'I've tried, and it's early days yet, but she struggles to know how to make friends. It's the same at school and other children are wary of her angry outbursts.'

'Is she angry often?' the IRO asked.

'Yes.'

'How does she show it?'

'She screams, and tries to hit and kick people and throw objects.'

'What does she get angry about?' the IRO asked.

'Anything she doesn't want to do. I have to hold her sometimes when she is very angry to stop her from hurting herself or others. And you should know she can make things up. I've had a few incidents, which I've noted in my log, where Anna has said something that was blatantly untrue. Some of it she has repeated at school to her teacher and TA.'

'For example?' the IRO asked.

'She said my son was bullying her.'

'I take it he's not?'

'No, of course not,' I said, a little irritated. 'She doesn't want anything to do with my children and they are never alone. Anna was told off at school for bullying and retaliated by accusing my son of doing the same. My supervising social worker, Jill, is aware.'

As the IRO made a note Lori added, 'There was a similar incident at the previous carers'.' I looked at Jill; this was news to us.

'What happened?' the IRO asked.

'Anna threw their cat down the stairs and when I spoke to her about it she said she'd done it because she was angry with the carer for hitting her. The carer is adamant she didn't hit Anna.'

I held Jill's gaze. I should have been told at the start that Anna had made false allegations, instead of letting me find out the hard way.

'They were new carers and might not continue to foster now, which is a pity,' Lori added.

'Great pity,' Jill said pointedly under her breath.

'Thank you, Cathy,' the IRO said. 'Is there anything else you would like to add?'

I glanced at my notes. 'Not really. Hopefully the referral to CAMHS will help.'

'And Anna can stay with you until a decision is made on her future?' he asked. It was a standard question.

'Yes. She must. She can't have another move.'

He nodded and now looked at Lori. 'Would you like to give your report next?'

Lori sat upright in her seat as I sat back in mine and tried to relax. I was still smarting at the IRO's suggestion that Adrian might have bullied Anna. The worry with unfounded allegations, apart from them being hurtful and causing trouble, is that they can leave a stain, even though they're completely untrue. Anna's previous carers wouldn't be the first to stop fostering because of being wrongly accused.

'Anna is in care under a Section 20 at her mother's request,' Lori was saying. 'She was adopted from –' and she gave the name of the country. 'The parents, Elaine and Ian, couldn't have children of their own. They followed the correct procedures for international adoption and passed the assessment. It seems likely that Anna was badly neglected as an infant in the orphanage and during the brief spells she spent with her birth mother. As a result she failed to form positive attachments. She was diagnosed with Reactive Attachment Disorder prior to coming into care and I've asked for a copy of that report. The parents paid to see a psychologist privately, but I understand from Anna's mother that no treatment followed the diagnosis.' Lori paused to allow the IRO time to write.

'There is no contact at present,' Lori continued, 'and the care plan is that Anna should return home, but that is looking increasingly unlikely. The parents are separated now and neither feels they can offer Anna a permanent home, so I am looking into kinship carers, but that isn't hopeful. Both Elaine's parents are dead. Ian's parents are living but are in their seventies, and they had reservations about them adopting from abroad from the beginning. Ian has a brother but they already have three children. Elaine's sister has been supportive but she is single and has a career. She has said she will think about offering Anna a permanent home, but she hadn't planned to have children and would be reluctant to take a career break, which is what would be required for Anna's high level of needs. If she does put herself forward then we will assess her.' Relatives wanting to look after a child in care still have to be assessed and police checked, just as foster carers do, and they are not always accepted.

'Anna is in good physical health,' Lori continued, 'and she's up to date with her vaccinations, and dental and optician check-ups.'

'Any accidents or illnesses since coming into care?' the IRO asked. It was another standard question.

'No,' Lori confirmed. 'And no exclusions from school, although she is on a reduced timetable. I know Miss Rich will cover that later.'

'Any complaints about Anna's care from the parents?' he now asked. This question was usually put to the child's parents if they were present.

'Anna's mother was concerned that Anna has had to move twice since coming into care but appreciated why that was necessary.'

He made a note. 'What are the parents' long-term wishes for the child?'

'They don't know. The mother is very distressed. Putting Anna into care was a last resort. She was close to breaking point and I've advised her to see her doctor.'

The IRO nodded. 'And she doesn't want contact now?'

'No.'

'Will you be applying for a Full Care Order?' he now asked Lori.

'Not at present, but the department will have to consider it in the future.' A Full Care Order would transfer parental rights and responsibility to the local authority.

With Lori having finished her report, it was the turn of Miss Rich, and she looked slightly nervous and flushed as she started to speak. She had my sympathy. Speaking at a meeting is a bit of an ordeal if you aren't used to it. She began with some background information. 'Anna was in the school's nursery from the age of three and a half and then joined the reception class when she was four. I have been her TA since last September. I give her support in the classroom in the morning and take her with two others in a small group in the afternoon. She attends school from ten o'clock to two o'clock each day.'

'When were her hours reduced?' the IRO asked.

'At the beginning of December.'

'So three months ago. Whose decision was that?'

'It was a joint decision between the school and the parents – they were still together then. Anna's behaviour at home had deteriorated badly and she wasn't engaging at school, so it was thought reduced hours might help her cope. We were thinking she would return to a full timetable by the end of this term, but with all the recent disruption we don't think she is ready yet.'

'How is her behaviour at school now?' the IRO asked.

'Very difficult at times. She is behind with her learning and struggles to concentrate. She becomes easily frustrated and then disruptive. She's working at about a year behind her actual age. We've asked that the educational psychologist assess her. I've brought some recent test results with me. Would you like to hear them?'

'Yes, please,' the IRO said.

Miss Rich read out the test results, which showed Anna was working at reception level – about aged four. Then she went through Anna's Personal Education Plan, of which I had a copy on file at home.

The IRO thanked her and said he'd make a note that Anna was working towards rejoining school full-time.

He asked Jill if she would like to add anything and she said: 'My role is to supervise, support and monitor Cathy in all aspects of her fostering. We are in regular contact by phone and I also visit her every month when we discuss the child's progress. Cathy is an experienced and dedicated foster carer and I know she will ask for help and advice if necessary. Clearly Anna is presenting some very challenging behaviour, but I am satisfied that Cathy is doing all she can to meet Anna's needs. I have no concerns and am happy with the level of care Anna is receiving.'

'Thank you,' the IRO said, and smiled at me. 'I have the review forms here that Cathy and Anna have completed,' he continued, and opened Anna's. 'Thank you for helping Anna to complete it,' he said to me. He knew this from the line at the end of the form where the person giving help writes their name and relationship to the child. 'It's important the review hears the child's views, so I will read out the questions and Anna's replies. 'The first question asks, do you know why you are in care? And Anna replied, "Because I have been bad at home."'

I heard Lori draw a sharp breath, while Jill said, 'Oh dear,' and Miss Rich's face fell. Pitiful though Anna's words were, they didn't hold the same impact for me now as when I'd first heard them.

'I reassured her that wasn't so,' I told the review.

The IRO nodded and looked at Lori. 'Perhaps you could follow that up next time you see Anna and reinforce that she isn't to blame for coming into care.'

'Yes, of course,' Lori said.

'The next question,' the IRO continued, 'asks if the child knows who their social worker is, and Anna said she didn't so Cathy reminded her. The next asks if the child wants to see more of their social worker and her reply was, "No."'

'Show me a child who does,' Lori said stoically.

'What do you like about living with your foster carer?' the IRO continued reading from Anna's review form. 'Anna said, "Nothing." The next question asks what the child doesn't like about living with their carer and Anna said, "Cathy, Adrian and Paula" – they are your children?' he asked, glancing up at me.

'Yes.'

'Their cat, their house and having to stay in her own bed,' he continued.

'Don't take it to heart,' Jill said to me.

'The next two questions concern the child's last review so Cathy has written not applicable. The following is about her friends, and Anna said she doesn't know who her friends are, nor if she wants to see more of them.' He looked at Miss Rich. 'Doesn't she have friends at school? Most children her age do.'

'Anna finds it difficult to make friends,' Miss Rich replied. 'The children are wary of her controlling manner and outbursts of rage. We are teaching her to share and how to relate to her peers. She is joining in more with group activities within the class and team games in PE.'

'Thank you,' the IRO said, making a note. 'The next question asks who the child would tell if something was worrying her and Anna replied, "Mrs Taylor."'

'That's her class teacher,' Miss Rich qualified.

'Well, that's positive. Anna knows she has someone she can talk to,' the IRO said.

'Mrs Taylor is fantastic with Anna,' Miss Rich said passionately. 'She has two nephews who are adopted so knows some of the challenges and issues parents can face. She always makes time for Anna and was working closely with her parents. She was devastated when Anna had to go into care. Cathy has met her.' I nodded.

The IRO made a note and looked at Anna's review form again. I felt my pulse quicken. He had arrived at the last question and I thought of Anna's response. 'The final question asks if the child wants to ask anything,' the IRO read. 'Anna said she would like to know when she can see her mummy.'

There was silence. You could have heard a pin drop. Everyone in the room had heard what Lori had said and knew it wasn't possible, and it was heartbreaking. I looked at the sombre expressions of those gathered around the table, all of us wanting Anna to be happy. 'It's so very sad,' Miss Rich said, close to tears. 'I knew her parents well, especially her mother, Elaine. We worked together to try to help Anna. We did everything we could, so did Mrs Taylor. We never thought it would come to this.' I saw her bottom lip tremble.

'It's not your fault,' Lori said. 'I'll speak to the mother again to see if I can persuade her to change her mind and see her daughter. Even if a child isn't returning home, it's in their best interest to have some contact with the parents.'

'Thank you,' the IRO said. He set the date for the next review and closed the meeting.

I left the room with Miss Rich, as Jill was staying behind to talk to Lori. 'Is there really no hope of Anna going home?' she asked once outside, still visibly upset.

'I honestly don't know,' I said.

'If Anna can't go home, will she be able to stay with you?' she asked as Mrs Taylor had done.

'It will depend on the social services.'

She shook her head sadly. 'She's not a bad kid.'

'No,' I agreed.

CHAPTER TWENTY-TWO

FRIGHTENED OF
HER DAUGHTER

Anna wasn't a 'bad kid', to use Miss Rich's term, but she was putting my family and me under huge strain. I usually saw my parents every couple of weeks but with everything going on around Anna, time had slipped by. Also, I wasn't sure if I should subject my parents to the stress of spending a day with Anna, unkind though that may sound. But when Mum invited us again to their house for Sunday dinner we decided they'd come to us, as I thought Anna would feel more secure being on familiar territory, and also when she did kick off the damage would be done at my home and not at my parents'. They knew Anna had challenging behaviour because of what she'd been through as a child and were very understanding and sympathetic, but the day turned out to be a disaster.

Perhaps Anna thought she could get away with negative behaviour, as we had guests, possibly because she had done at home, or maybe she was jealous of Adrian and Paula. I don't know, but she made herself as objectionable as possible right from the start. My parents gave Anna as much attention as they did Adrian and Paula, but it wasn't enough for Anna. She wouldn't settle to anything and didn't want anyone else to either. She over-talked loudly if anyone tried to speak, to the point of shouting so no one could get a word in. She kept putting herself physically between my parents and Adrian and Paula to stop any interaction. She tormented Toscha by screaming at the poor cat until she fled outside, which upset Adrian and Paula and worried my parents. She pushed Paula off a chair simply because my mother was admiring the badge she was wearing, and kept 'bumping' into Adrian whenever he was close by. Mum told her off about it, but she put her hands over her ears and yelled rudely that she couldn't hear her, as she did sometimes with me.

Usually I kept a close eye on Anna and didn't let her out of my sight for long. Aware of this, she made a point of repeatedly disappearing upstairs so that I had to stop what I was doing to go up and bring her down, which of course took a while, as Anna never did anything the first time of asking. At the dinner table she tipped juice all over Adrian's new jersey and trousers that he was wearing for the first time especially for Nana and Grandpa's visit. I saw the look of satisfaction on her face as I mopped it up and then he left to change. The whole day was pitted with similar disruptive incidents and my parents understandably decided to leave early. Dad said he was concerned that Anna's behaviour was upsetting my mother.

'How long do you think she'll be staying with you?' he asked as they said goodbye, also worried at the effect it was having on us.

'I'm not sure yet,' I said. 'But don't worry. I can handle it.'

He looked doubtful.

'Let us know if there is anything we can do to help,' Mum said. 'I'm sure Anna will settle down soon.' Mum always looks on the positive side – a glass-half-full, not empty, type of person.

We said goodbye and I went upstairs to find Anna again. She was in Paula's room, trying to break the head off her best doll. I told her off and said she would have an early night, which of course led to a full-scale tantrum. As Paula was still downstairs, Anna didn't see why she shouldn't be too.

'But she's been good,' I said, loathing myself for having to say this, but Anna needed to learn.

'Hate you,' she said. 'Hate your parents. They're horrible.' She stuck out her tongue to emphasize this.

That evening as I wrote up my log notes, grateful at last for some peace, I thought of Mum's assertion that Anna would settle soon, just as the other children I'd fostered had. But I had doubts. Anna had been a very troubled child with a number of problems before coming into care. Now she'd been rejected by her parents, I feared it could be years before she 'settled down', if ever. The effect of trauma in infanthood, if not dealt with, can follow a child into their teenage years and beyond. Some adults never recover from the neglect or abuse they suffered as a child and turn to drink and drugs to try to block out and numb their pain.

On Wednesday Jill telephoned for an update as she did every week if we hadn't met. She knew that if I needed help or advice in the interim or if there was an emergency I would contact the agency straight away. When I'd finished updating her on Anna's progress, or rather lack of it, Jill said, 'You're doing everything you can, but there's been a development.'

'Oh, yes?' A development could mean anything – good or bad.

'You remember at the review Lori was going to speak to Anna's mother, Elaine, to see if it was possible to establish some contact?'

'Yes.' It was two weeks since the review and the last time Jill and I had spoken it hadn't been mentioned, so I'd rather assumed it wasn't going to happen.

'Lori has spoken to Elaine and she has agreed to see Anna for an hour a week.'

'Oh, I see,' I said, taken aback. 'Well, I suppose that's good.'

'Lori wants the contact to be at your house. She thinks it will be less disruptive for Anna, and there is no reason why contact should take place at a family centre as there are no safe-guarding concerns.' If a child is brought into care as a result of abuse or neglect then contact is usually supervised at a family centre for a set number of hours each week.

The expectation was that I would accept contact at my house. 'OK,' I said.

'It will just be Elaine, not Anna's father, and Elaine has only agreed to see Anna as long as you are present.'

'"Agreed"?' I said. That word again, implying reluctance on Elaine's part. Most parents of children in care would jump at the chance to see their child.

'Elaine is worried that Anna will be very angry with her,' Jill said. 'And of course she's feeling guilty for putting her into care.'

'I can appreciate that.'

'Lori suggested contact took place straight after school, as Anna is on a reduced timetable, but I said that probably wouldn't work for you.'

'No, it wouldn't. Although Anna finishes early her school is half an hour's drive away, so after I've collected her I go straight to collect Adrian and Paula.'

'That's what I thought so I suggested Saturday.'

'Yes, that would be better. What time?'

'Shall we say eleven?'

'All right.'

'I'll telephone Lori now and then get back to you to confirm. Lori's asked if you can prepare Anna for her mother's visit, as she won't be able to see her before Saturday.' Foster carers often have to explain and discuss contact arrangements with the child they are looking after.

'Yes, I'll do my best,' I said.

'Thank you.' We said goodbye.

I had concerns about Elaine suddenly 'agreeing' to see Anna. While it was generally considered positive for a child to be in touch with their parents, I'd have to make sure this didn't give Anna false hope. It wasn't about preparing Anna to go home, but just for her to see her estranged mother. And if Anna was going to remain in care, how much good would it do to re-establish their bond now? I wondered. Anna hadn't seen or heard from her mother since coming into care and she hadn't asked to see her as most children would. But then again, that could have been part of Anna's attachment disorder. I didn't necessarily mean she didn't miss or love her mother. She just didn't show it as other children might.

That evening after dinner I sat down with Anna, just the two of us, and explained what was going to happen on Saturday.

'She's coming on a plane?' she asked.

'No, love, in her car.'

'But it's over the water. I've seen a picture of the sea from the plane window.'

'Not your birth mother. She isn't coming.' It had never occurred to me she might think that. 'It's your adoptive mother who's coming to see you. The person you call Mummy. You've been living with her and your father for over two years.'

Finally she understood. 'Good. I don't want to go to that other home. I was poor there and no one loved me.'

'You won't have to go back there,' I reassured her. 'Your mummy and daddy adopted you so you are their daughter. They are your mummy and daddy, even though you are not living with them right now. Adrian and Paula's daddy doesn't live with us, but he is still their father.'

She looked as though she understood. 'Will you be my mummy too if I stay here?' How confusing this must be for her.

'I'm looking after you like a mummy,' I said with a smile, which was the best I could offer.

But of course suddenly being presented with the prospect of seeing her mother was very unsettling for Anna and doubtless reignited many old insecurities. That night and the following she had nightmares, crying out in her sleep. I was out of bed in a heartbeat, and round the landing to her room to settle her.

I told Miss Rich that Anna would be seeing her mother on Saturday and she was pleased and said she'd tell Mrs Taylor. She said she would help reassure Anna and answer any questions she might have. But Anna wasn't a child who confided her worries easily, even to Miss Rich or Mrs Taylor. It came out in her behaviour, which deteriorated badly at school and at home. On Friday Anna thumped a child in her class for asking who I was and pushed over another child for looking at her. That night she didn't get to sleep until after 3 a.m. I let her sleep in on Saturday and asked Adrian and Paula to play quietly, then at 9.30 a.m. I woke her.

'Time to get up and get ready,' I said.

'I'm not seeing my mother!' she yelled angrily as soon as she was fully awake. 'You tell her not to come here! Do as I say!' Anna still believed she was in charge.

'I can understand why you're angry and upset,' I said evenly, 'but your mother is coming here at eleven o'clock as arranged.'

'Why?' she demanded.

'Because she wants to see you and that's what your social worker and your mother have decided.'

'You don't have to do what they say!' she stormed, her eyes blazing.

'Yes, I do. We both do.'

'Why?'

'Because they are responsible for you.'

'I won't let her in,' she yelled, balling her fists. I felt my anxiety level rise.

'I will. Come on, up you get, time to get dressed.'

'I'll push her out of the door and shut it in her face,' she said, her cheeks flushed with rage.

'That would be very unkind. And you won't be doing that because I will be letting your mother in and making her feel welcome.' I hoped after all this that Elaine turned up. Some parents arrange contact and then don't show, which is very disappointing and distressing for the child and adds to their feelings of rejection.

'Hate you,' she said, but did get out of bed.

Anna never did anything the first or second time she was asked. So as a result of her lack of cooperation it was nearly eleven o'clock before she was finally ready, having washed, dressed and finished her breakfast. During this time Adrian and Paula had been left to get on with it yet again while I concentrated on Anna, and although I was grateful for their cooperation and praised them, I felt guilty. It was their week-end too.

I'd put a lot of thought into how to handle Anna's first contact with her mother. Sometimes, when I facilitated contact at home, I gave the child and their parents privacy, a room to themselves, and just popped in occasionally to see if everything was all right and if they needed anything, while keeping Adrian and Paula amused in another room. But Elaine had specifically asked that I be present when she saw Anna, so I took a selection of games, puzzles and toys into the living room for them to play with and told Adrian and Paula to carry on as normal. This would hopefully also feel less intimidating and more relaxing for Elaine, but Anna wasn't having any of it.

'You can put those away!' she stormed, and grabbed some of the boxes of games to take out. 'I'm not seeing her!'

I was about to return the games to the living room when the front doorbell rang, signalling Elaine's arrival. Startled, Anna threw the games onto the floor and fled upstairs to her bedroom, slamming the door behind her.

'It's OK, don't worry. She'll be down later,' I reassured Adrian and Paula, who were looking worried. I knew that Anna wouldn't stay up there for long if she thought her mother and me were downstairs; she'd want to know what was going on. However, I understood why she'd fled. An angry exit was her way of dealing with a difficult meeting. I was feeling nervous, and as I opened the front door it was obvious Elaine was too.

'Have I got the right house?' she asked in a small, quivering voice.

'If you're Elaine, then yes,' I said lightly. 'Come in. I'm Cathy.'

'Oh, thank you.'

She was older than in the photographs, of average height and build, but with blue eyes, pale skin and her hair cut in a neat bob like Anna's. They were so similar that Elaine could have been her birth mother. 'Shall I take your coat?' I asked.

'Yes, please.'

She began unbuttoning it, her nervous fingers struggling with the buttons. Under her coat she wore navy slacks and a beige jumper. 'You found our house OK then?' I asked, making conversation.

'I was early. I've been sitting in the car.'

She passed me her coat and I hung it up, then she nervously set down her handbag and picked it up again, unsure of where to put it. 'Bring it with you if you like,' I said. 'We're in the living room. Anna has just gone up to her room. I'll fetch her if she doesn't come down shortly.'

'Oh, so she isn't down here,' she said, apparently relieved she wasn't having to meet her daughter straight away. This was so different from other reunions I'd witnessed where the child or children I was fostering flew into their parents' arms and the parents cried with joy.

'This is my son, Adrian, and my daughter, Paula,' I said as we entered the living room.

'Hello,' Elaine said in a small voice. They smiled back shyly.

'Would you like a coffee or tea?' I offered her, but she didn't want anything to drink. 'Do sit down.'

Going to the sofa, she perched stiff and upright on the edge. I sat at the other end while Adrian and Paula continued playing on the floor. There was an awkward silence. 'I'll fetch Anna down if she doesn't appear soon,' I said again. Elaine nodded. Another silence. 'I've met Miss Rich and Mrs Taylor,' I said. 'They're very nice.'

'Yes, they are,' Elaine agreed, her gaze on Adrian and Paula. 'How do your children get on with Anna?' she asked. 'Your daughter is only small.'

'Paula is not much younger than Anna,' I said.

'Does Anna play with them?'

'We're working on it,' I said, throwing her a small smile.

She understood. There was another silence and then Adrian asked, 'Mum, can I go upstairs to play?'

'Yes, of course, love. Do what you would normally do.'

'Sorry, I've disrupted your morning,' Elaine said apologetically.

'You haven't,' I replied. 'We're used to having visitors.'

'Anna isn't,' Elaine said, and looked at Paula as she followed Adrian out of the living room.

'Are you sure you wouldn't like a drink?' I offered again.

'No, thank you. I'll see Anna and then I'll go. I won't stay for long.'

'Lori suggested an hour, but it's up to you.' I looked at her, so tense and uneasy I thought she could leave at any moment. 'Elaine, I know this must be very difficult for you, but Anna does need to see you.'

'Yes, that's what Lori said, but I'm not sure. She doesn't really like me.'

'No child likes their parents the whole time, it's part of the territory of being a parent, but I'm sure she loves you.'

'Thank you,' she said in the same slight voice, but didn't offer any more.

At that moment Anna's bedroom door opened with a loud thud, and footsteps stomped towards the top of the stairs. 'That sounds like Anna,' I said.

'You will stay with us, won't you?' Elaine asked anxiously.

'Yes, of course. Don't worry. Just enjoy your time together.' But even as I said it I knew that was going to be very difficult for Elaine.

Anna came heavily down the stairs, stomping as she did when she was annoyed. Elaine tensed even more, as if steeling herself to meet her daughter. 'Try to walk more quietly,' I called to Anna as she entered the hall. The stomping continued with marginally less force. 'Good girl, that's better.'

Elaine looked at me curiously. 'She does what you tell her?'

'Eventually, but we've had the stomping conversation before,' I replied with a smile.

Anna's heavy footsteps continued along the hall, into the living room, and then she stomped right up to her mother. I saw Elaine draw back. 'Why are you here?' Anna demanded, hands on hips.

Elaine didn't reply but her brow creased as if almost imploring Anna not to be cruel to her.

'She's come to see you,' I said, concerned by Elaine's reaction. She appeared to be frightened of her daughter.

'Why?' Anna demanded, glaring at her mother.

What I now wanted was for Elaine to say, 'Because I love and miss you.' And Anna would reply, 'I love and miss you too, Mummy.' Which would start the healing process and begin to build the bridge across the huge divide between them, but that wasn't going to happen. Elaine just sat looking at her daughter, so I stepped in.

'Anna,' I said firmly. 'Take your hands off your hips and don't glare at your mother like that, please. I told you she was coming to see you.'

'I want her to go!' she said, but did take her hands from her hips. Elaine made a move as though she was actually going to leave.

'Your mother is not going anywhere for now,' I said, touching Elaine's arm. 'She has come to see you. I think it would be a good idea if the three of us played one of those games together.' I'd found in the past that tension in first meetings was often eased if the parents and child were involved in a game, although those times had been a result of shyness and awkwardness, not intimidation, which is what I was witnessing. 'Would you like to choose a game or shall I?' I asked Anna, using the closed choice technique, and aware she'd want to.

'Me!' she said and stomped off to the toy box. Elaine breathed an audible sigh of relief.

CHAPTER TWENTY-THREE

SAVE A CHILD

Elaine managed to stay for the full hour, but her relationship with Anna didn't improve. Despite my arranging board games and cards to play, and illustrated books to look at, and giving lots of encouragement, mother and daughter went through the motions of playing without any real involvement or meaningful interaction passing between them. It was difficult to say the least. I was there to facilitate and support contact; I couldn't force them to get along. On the positive side Anna did at least join in when she might not have done, but she was rude and demanding throughout, barking instructions at her mother and generally demeaning her. Elaine took this and even apologized, instead of telling Anna not to speak to her like that. I corrected Anna a number of times when I couldn't ignore her rudeness any longer, but it should have come from her mother.

Adrian and Paula joined in the final game of Snakes and Ladders. It was the first time we'd all played together with Anna so I suppose that was a positive too, although the atmosphere was tense and not at all like when Adrian and Paula usually play, with squeals of delight at winning a point or sighs of frustration at losing. Anna didn't win, although I'm sure her mother would have let her just to keep the peace. Anna was furious and threw the board and counters all over the floor while shouting that it was a silly game, just like a spoilt child. It was left to me to tell Anna about her behaviour. Elaine just sat looking at her, anxious and ineffectual.

'It's not about winning but playing the game that counts,' I said to Anna.

When the hour was up I was as relieved as Elaine appeared to be. She immediately stood and said it was time for her to go, and Anna didn't protest either. I'd seen children cling desperately to their parents to try to stop them from leaving at the end of contact, with all of them in tears, which, while upsetting to watch, was far healthier than the cold and emotionless parting of Elaine and Anna.

'Goodbye,' Elaine said in the hall as she put on her coat. Anna stared at her blankly.

'Safe journey,' I said, opening the front door. 'We'll see you at the same time next week.'

She nodded without conviction and I wondered if she would come back. By the time I'd closed the door Anna had disappeared into the living room. It had been the strangest, most emotionless and joyless contact I'd ever seen.

Adrian and Paula, perhaps fearing another outburst from Anna, had gone upstairs. I went into the living room. Anna was sitting on the floor, uncharacteristically quiet and still. 'Are you OK?' I asked, going over.

'Is she coming back next week?' she asked blankly.

'Your mother? Yes, she should do. Would you like her to?'

'Not bothered,' she shrugged.

And that was all she said about her mother and her visit, not only for the rest of the day and weekend but for the whole of the following week, despite my bringing up the subject from time to time and asking her if she wanted to talk about it. 'No!' she replied or just ignored me.

I wrote up my log notes, and Jill and Lori telephoned for updates on how the contact had gone. They were disappointed when I told them, as was Miss Rich. On Wednesday morning, when I took Anna into school, Mrs Taylor made a point of coming to see me to try to find out more, but I could only tell her what I'd told Jill and Lori. She looked crestfallen.

'Do you think it would help if I spoke to Anna and Elaine?' she asked. 'Anna hasn't mentioned seeing her mother to me or Miss Rich.'

'I don't know. It's your decision. I'm sure it wouldn't do any harm.'

'I'll give it some thought,' she said.

I never found out if she did speak to them, but very soon it was Saturday again. I'd heard nothing to the contrary from Lori so I assumed that contact was going ahead. It was now the beginning of April and the garden was awash with brightly coloured spring flowers, bringing with them the promise of hope, new life and opportunity. Or that's how I saw it at least. I still had some doubts that Elaine would show, so I was relived when at exactly eleven o'clock the doorbell rang. She seemed slightly more at ease, if only from now being familiar with my home and us. She took off her jacket and hung it on the hall stand, left her shoes in the hall and then headed for our living room. 'Anna will be down soon,' I said, and offered her a drink, which she refused.

'You have a nice big garden,' she said, making conversation and glancing through the patio windows.

'We're out there as much as possible in the summer. Do you have a garden?'

'A small one.'

We sat on the sofa and continued making polite and somewhat stilted conversation – mainly about the weather – while we waited for Anna. Adrian and Paula were at the table in the kitchen, dough modelling. Anna hadn't wanted to join in. I could have gone up and fetched her down to see her mother, but it would be better if she came down of her own accord. She'd heard her mother arrive. As we waited I told Elaine about Anna's week at school, but the conversation we should have been having was about her relationship with her daughter, and whether there was any chance of them having a future together. I needed Elaine to broach the subject when she felt comfortable to do so, which clearly wasn't yet.

Eventually Anna's bedroom door crashed open and she stomped down the stairs. 'Tread more lightly, please!' I called. 'You are not the BFG.' Elaine almost smiled, but as soon as Anna appeared in the living room she tensed, as if bracing herself to meet her daughter again. It was ludicrous and very unhealthy. If Elaine could have taken the initiative and said, 'Hi, Anna, how are you?' standing up if necessary, it would have given her more presence. Instead she waited, almost cowering as Anna came right up to her, formidable and intimidating. Anna had quickly stopped approaching me like that, but she was doing it to her mother because she knew she could get away with it.

'Say hello to your mother nicely,' I said to Anna.

'Hello,' she said, and stomped over to the toy box.

Adrian and Paula appeared and, bless them, suggested that we play Snakes and Ladders as we had done last Saturday.

'Don't want to,' Anna scowled. 'It's a silly game.'

'It's a fun game,' I said, 'but you can choose something else to play if you like and we can play Snakes and Ladders another time.'

She picked up a pack of cards. 'Snap!' she said. 'I want to play Snap.'

'OK, but we'll need more than one pack if we're all going to play.'

'No, just her,' she said, pointing to her mother.

While it was positive that Anna wanted to play a game with her mother one-to-one, the way she'd referred to *her* and pointed was rude. I glanced at Elaine, wondering if she would correct her, but she stood and went over to play.

'She's your mother,' I said to Anna. 'Not *her*.'

I knew Anna had understood what I meant from her scowl. Elaine sat on the floor opposite her daughter while she divided up the pack of cards. The two of them began to play Snap while Adrian, Paula and I played Snakes and Ladders. Any cries of glee or groans of frustration as we played were smothered by Anna barking instructions at her mother and yelling 'Snap!' at the top of her voice every few seconds while grabbing the two stacks of cards. I was pretty sure she was cheating but Elaine didn't say anything; she just went through the motions of playing the game. When Anna inevitably won she gave herself a clap. 'I've won!' she shouted.

'Well done,' I said. 'I hope it was fairly.' She threw me a look – again, she had got the message. Anna then wanted to play Snakes and Ladders. 'Of course, love,' I said. 'Once we've finished this game we'll all play together.' She scowled. I really think she assumed we'd stop playing and start a fresh game straight away simply because she wanted to. It didn't take us long to finish the game and we then widened our circle to accommodate Anna and Elaine. Anna wanted the blue counter that Adrian was using and tried to take it from him.

'No,' I said, stopping her. 'Adrian is using the blue counter. There are plenty of others to choose from.' I pushed the other counters towards her so she could pick one.

She hesitated, a stand-off, and Elaine tensed. But Anna clearly thought better of it and took another counter. 'Good girl,' I said. Then to Elaine, 'It's OK to say no sometimes.' She gave a slight nod.

We played three games of Snakes and Ladders, of which Anna won one fairly. 'Well done,' I said with genuine feeling.

'Yes, well done,' Elaine repeated in a small, flat voice.

Years of looking after children has taught me that it is important to praise a child effusively when it's due. Not only does it build their confidence, but it makes correcting them when necessary more acceptable. Like many aspects of child rearing, it is a balancing act – praise and censure, talking and listening, encouraging a child to do something and warning them not to. Elaine's 'well done' was as passionless as all her interactions with Anna, and I thought it was probably a safety mechanism to protect herself – if she didn't give anything of herself to her daughter then her rejections were less painful.

The hour slid by and at exactly twelve noon Elaine said it was time for her to go. Anna didn't want to come with us to the door but said goodbye to her mother in the living room, again without any regret at her going. In the hall I took Elaine's jacket from the stand and helped her into it. 'Same time next week then?' I said. She nodded, said goodbye and left.

That evening I wrote up my log notes and the following week updated Jill and Lori when they telephoned.

Soon it was Saturday again and the third contact was the same as the previous two. I wondered how long it would be before one of them broke through the barrier and showed some real emotion. I realized that it was part of Anna's attachment disorder that she wasn't able to show love for her mother, and that Elaine was probably feeling a lot more than she showed. But this couldn't go on indefinitely. They would both need to change if there was any chance of them having a future together and I hoped therapeutic input would help, although no appointment had come through yet. At the end of Elaine's fourth visit, which had been no different to the previous three, she stopped as she was halfway out of the door and almost as an afterthought said, 'Cathy, can I talk to you alone one time? I think you may understand.'

'Yes, of course,' I said. 'We could talk on the phone or if you're not working you could come here during the day when everyone is at school.'

'I could come on Monday,' she said in the same small voice.

'Good. Eleven o'clock would suit me – give me time to get back from school.'

'Yes. I'll be here. And thank you for looking after Anna. You're doing a good job.' Her eyes filled and she hurried down the path to her car.

On Sunday Adrian and Paula went out with their father again, which gave me the opportunity to spend some one-to-one time with Anna. It was Anna who suggested we play some board games together, which was a first. As we played it struck me how much less rude and threatening her manner was towards me than her mother.

'Why do you speak to your mother so harshly?' I asked as we played. 'You're not very nice to her sometimes.' Actually it was all the time.

'Because I don't like her and she doesn't like me.'

'What makes you think she doesn't like you?'

'Because she was always telling me off.'

'Any other reason?'

She shook her head and rolled the dice.

'How did she tell you off?' I asked. Given the tension that must have existed at home, I wondered if Elaine had hit Anna. My gut feeling was that she hadn't, but then I couldn't visualize her shouting either; she always appeared so meek and self-effacing.

Anna finished counting her piece round the board before answering. 'She shouts and then she cries a lot and I don't like that.'

'Did she hit you?'

'No!' Anna said, jutting out her chin aggressively. 'I hit her.' Which I knew to be true.

'You mustn't hit your mother or anyone. You have to talk to the person about what is bothering you, not hit them.'

'I hit you,' she said defiantly.

'When you first arrived, but I stopped you.' I've found in the past that often young children open up and talk if they have the distraction of playing a game, more so than if you sit them down specifically to have a heart-to-heart.

'My other mummy used to hit me,' Anna added.

'You remember that?' I asked, surprised.

'She hit me a lot. She said I was bad like my father.' How much baggage from her past this poor child carried with her. I doubted she and her parents had ever stood a chance of a normal loving relationship.

'Did you ever see him?' I asked.

'No. He was so bad they locked him up.' So I assumed he was in prison for whatever crime he had committed. 'My mum hated him and she hated me too,' Anna said, staring at the board.

'Have you ever talked to your parents or anyone about this?'

She shook her head. 'Come on, your turn.'

I threw the dice and counted my piece round the board.

'Do you think you could talk to someone, like a doctor?'

'Don't know.'

We continued to play for a few moments and then I asked, 'Did your daddy ever tell you off or hit you? The one you lived with.'

'When he came home from work and Mummy was upset he'd shout at me. He said it was my fault she was crying.'

While I could see only too clearly why he would have felt that, for Anna it must have seemed that history was repeating itself – another nail in the coffin for her relationship with her parents.

I didn't know the reason why Elaine wanted to talk to me, other than she thought I would understand, so I assumed it was about why she had put Anna into care. I'd made a note of her request in my log and would update Jill and Lori on what Elaine said the next time we spoke, unless it was something urgent, in which case I would phone them straight away.

Monday was another fine, warm spring day, and Elaine arrived punctually at 11 a.m., dressed in a lightweight trouser suit and matching blouse.

'You always look so smart,' I said as I let her in.

'Thank you. It's a habit, from when I used to work as a legal secretary. We had to look smart for the clients.'

I smiled, waited while she hung up her jacket and then led the way into the living room where I offered her a drink. For the first time since she'd started visiting she accepted, and I made us both a coffee. Once settled, Elaine began making conversation by asking what work I used to do. 'Clerical and administration,' I said. 'I still do a little now, part-time, mainly from home to fit in around the children.' She sipped her coffee, admired the garden and appeared far more relaxed than she usually did when Anna was there.

'I hope I'm not stopping you from doing anything,' she said after a few moments, setting her cup in her saucer, 'but there isn't anyone else I know who would understand.'

'It's fine,' I said. 'I'm free until one-thirty when I have to leave to collect Anna from school.' This wasn't strictly true as I had a long list of jobs to do, but if Elaine needed to talk about Anna then I would listen.

She looked around the room as though gathering her thoughts, then took a small breath. 'It's difficult for me to talk about it all, even though you're in the same position.'

I didn't understand what she meant about being in the same position. Yes, I had children, but my children weren't in foster care. I waited. With another little sigh, summoning her courage to begin, she asked, 'When you and your husband separated did you try to get him back?'

I was completely thrown. It was the last question I'd expected. Surely this wasn't the reason she'd wanted to see me?

'Well, yes,' I said, 'I did, but it wasn't really an option. It was his decision to leave. He'd met another woman.' The words still choked me, although they weren't as raw now as when it had first happened.

'I'm sorry,' Elaine said. 'My husband didn't leave me for another woman but because of Anna and me. Me, really. It was my fault. I've changed so much since we had her. I was unrecognizable from the person he used to know. I should have seen it coming, there were enough warning signs, but I was so wound up in my own misery and failings as a mother that I had no time for what Ian was going through. Ian was my first love, we met ...' And Elaine began telling me how it all began.

'Ian and I met by chance in a coffee bar close to where we both worked,' she continued in a small voice as though viewing the scene from the distance of time. 'We kept bumping into each other as we collected our coffee and sandwiches to eat at our desks. His firm had offices not far from mine. He started smiling and saying hello, then one day, as we waited to be served, we found ourselves standing next to each other and he struck up conversation. After that we used to look out for each other and stand together in the queue and chat as we waited. I so looked forward to lunchtimes, the girls at work used to tease me. After a month or so Ian said, "We can't keep meeting like this," and he asked me on a date. That was the start of it. We began seeing each other regularly, and quickly fell in love. I met his family and he met mine. I was rather a shy, unadventurous young secretary, but he gave me confidence and brought me out of myself. After three years Ian asked me to marry him and I had no hesitation in saying yes. We got engaged, saved up and bought a home of our own. We had a beautiful romantic white wedding that my mother planned.' Elaine absently fiddled with the wedding and engagement rings on her finger. 'Tragically, within the year both my parents were dead. My mother died of cancer and my father of a heart attack. He never got over my mother's death.'

'I'm so sorry,' I said.

'Thank you. Ian was fantastic, so supportive. I don't know what I would have done without him.' She let out a heartfelt sigh.

'We always knew we wanted a family, but the months, then years, passed and nothing happened. Eventually we went to see our doctor, who sent us to the hospital for infertility tests. The results weren't a huge shock. After all those years of trying we guessed one of us couldn't have children and we were already talking about adopting by then. We had one go at IVF [in vitro fertilization] and then approached our social services about adopting. We soon learned that we were considered too old to adopt a baby or young child. Ian was thirty-nine then and I was thirty-five.

'Time passed and we'd almost resigned ourselves to not having a family, and then by chance I saw a story in the news about a couple who'd adopted from abroad. I started researching international adoption and found it had been going on for years all over the world. Orphaned and abandoned children who couldn't be looked after in their own country matched with couples abroad who wanted to adopt. You can imagine our joy. It seemed the answer to our prayers. Not only would we have the family we so dearly wanted, but we would be saving a young child from a life in an orphanage.' Elaine stopped and, overcome with emotion, wiped a tear from her eye.

CHAPTER TWENTY-FOUR

A FAMILY TORN APART

'The process to adopt from abroad is long and complicated,' Elaine continued when she felt able. 'We had to be passed to adopt in this country first, which involved many visits from a social worker who asked lots of searching and personal questions. She then wrote our Home Study report while we attended the training and preparation course. Then there were police checks, references – bank and personal – and we both had to have medicals. After that we had to go before a panel of ten people who asked us questions about our reasons for wanting to adopt and what we thought we could give a child. I was so nervous my hands were trembling, but we passed. Our papers were then sent to the Department for Education, and a Certificate of Eligibility was issued. That was the proof we were allowed to adopt – I still have it.' She paused and threw me a small, sad smile. 'How long ago that seems now.' I nodded thoughtfully.

'After we'd been accepted to adopt it was up to us to get in touch with an adoption facilitator in the country we wanted to adopt from. By then I'd done a lot of research on the internet and had joined an online support group for international adoption. The members were very helpful.

They had either adopted from abroad themselves so knew what to do, or were going through the process and were willing to share their experiences. If I had a question about procedure or the next step, one of them would help. Because our paperwork was going abroad it all had to be notarized by a solicitor here first and then legalized by our Foreign and Commonwealth Office. After that we had to send it to the facilitator in the country we were adopting from and pay to have it translated and legalized in that country. Weeks, sometimes months, passed in between, when all we could do was wait and hope. You try to think of other things and resist the temptation to keep phoning, but it's there with you the whole time. It's the biggest life-changing decision you ever make, but we were never in any doubt it was the right one for us.

'While we waited we got the nursery ready and bought baby clothes and toys. You can't leave it until the last minute, although it's a strange feeling shopping for baby things when there is no sign of a baby. If you're expecting you have the proof inside you, your stomach swells and you can feel it move, so you know that the nursery, clothes and toys will be used in time. But when you're adopting there is nothing but faith and hope. You are completely reliant on others. I tormented myself with the possibility it might not happen and the nursery would remain empty forever. Ian's parents weren't much good – they kept trying to put us off – but my sister was supportive and so were our online friends. Then, after all those months of waiting, we got the call. Dr Ciobanu, our adoption facilitator, phoned us at home one evening and said a baby girl had been left at the orphanage and was free for adoption. Can you imagine our joy? It was the best feeling ever. Our baby had arrived. He sent a photograph and we immediately fell in love with little Lana.'

'Lana?' I queried.

Elaine nodded sombrely and continued. 'We confirmed straight away we wanted to adopt her and the following week we were on the plane. I'd had our bags partially packed for some time, knowing that now all our paperwork was in we could get the call anytime, and would have to leave as soon as possible. On the plane I kept looking at the photo of Lana, the proof our baby was real, at the orphanage and waiting for us. We began bonding with her from the moment we received her details. Our happiness was indescribable.

'We took photographs of our adoption journey and I kept a journal so that our baby would know her roots, just as the social worker had said we should. It was late when the plane arrived, and we went straight to our hotel and to bed. Dr Ciobanu knew what time our flight was due in and had said we should go to the orphanage the following morning to meet him and our baby. Needless to say, we didn't sleep much that night – we were far too excited. We were up early but I couldn't eat breakfast. I just wanted to go to the orphanage and see my baby. We'd booked a cab through the hotel reception to take us to the orphanage. I can still remember that journey, our joy, our hopes and expectations that very soon we would be a family and our lives would be complete. We were let into the orphanage by a care worker who said Dr Ciobanu had been called away. She then told us our baby was dead and we should choose another one. Just like that.'

'Oh, no!' I gasped. 'That's dreadful. I'm so sorry. I had no idea.'

Elaine's eyes glistened with tears. 'It was awful. Bad enough our baby had died, but it was made worse by her heartless behaviour. Not, *I'm sorry to have to tell you your baby has passed*, just, *She's dead, you choose another one.* After, I wondered if her harshness might have been due to her limited English, but her manner was cold. I mean, you can show compassion in ways other than words.' I nodded. 'Anna doesn't know about Lana. We didn't want her thinking she was second best, so please don't tell her.'

'No, of course I won't.' There was no reason why I should tell Anna, as it didn't directly affect her. My thoughts flashed to Anna's Life Story Book and the Memory Box I'd unpacked and looked through before putting away. I now realized there was a far more painful back story, which for good reason Elaine and Ian had decided not to tell Anna.

Elaine then told me of the dreadful conditions they'd witnessed in the orphanage and my eyes welled. I'd read about those orphanages in newspapers and had seen pictures on the television, but hearing about them first hand moved me deeply.

'No words can describe our heartache and disappointment at losing Lana and we just wanted to go home. We wouldn't try to adopt again; clearly we weren't meant to have children. We were going to bring forward our flight home, but then late that evening Dr Ciobanu telephoned us at the hotel and apologized for what had happened. He asked us to go to the orphanage the following day as he had another child for us who was a bit older but very healthy. Ian and I spent the whole night talking about what we should do and decided to go the following day. We had nothing to lose, and of course this new child needed a home as much as Lana had done.

'It was obvious as soon as we met Anna, or Anastasia as she was then, that she was very different from Lana. At two and a quarter, she was very lively and robust, and obviously healthy. Dr Ciobanu wasn't a bad man, but with so few resources and only two care workers the level of care at the orphanage was very low and there was a limit to what he could do. We decided to go ahead and adopt Anna and we saw her at the orphanage every afternoon while Dr Ciobanu prepared our adoption application for the court there. We quickly bonded with Anna. She was feisty then and knew her own mind, but just when we thought everything was on track again there was a problem.'

'Oh, no. What happened?'

'Nothing to Anna, but it was the height of summer and with most judges on holiday we couldn't get a court date for three months. Anna's mother needed to work and took a job abroad for that period and we reluctantly returned home. The thought of Anna in the orphanage for all that time was very worrying but there was nothing we could do. Dr Ciobanu promised us she'd be well looked after. We flew back on 18 November, a few days before the court hearing, and went straight to the orphanage to see Anna. Dr Ciobanu was there and brought Anna to us. Her first words were "Mummy and Daddy". Can you imagine that! I hugged her, but even then I remember thinking how stiff and unresponsive she was. She clearly remembered us but didn't show any affection. She never has.

'We saw Anna every afternoon at the orphanage until the court date. Did we spoil her? Yes, definitely. Did she always have her own way? That was one of the questions the psychologist I eventually took her to asked. Yes, she did. We showered her with gifts and did exactly what she wanted. We'd waited so long for a child and Anna had led such a miserable life, why wouldn't we want to make her happy? Did we realize how badly damaged she was by her early years' experience? No, and we assumed that whatever had happened could be put right with our love and kindness.

'We met her mother for the first time in the court waiting room. She was a small woman dressed in thick woollens and a headscarf. She looked sad and we felt very sorry for her, naturally. We couldn't talk to her because of the language barrier, but we thought she was very brave and selfless to put her daughter first and want a better life for her. It was only later, when we were home and Anna had learned more English, that we discovered her mother had beaten her and locked her in a cellar at night. Little wonder Anna won't sleep in her own bed.'

'She does now,' I added.

'Does she? She wouldn't for us,' Elaine said quietly, and I could have kicked myself for being so thoughtless.

Elaine then told me of the very difficult first week they'd had with Anna in the hotel, when she wouldn't settle, eat or sleep properly.

'We thought she would settle once we were home and she did start eating, but the poor kid had worms and had to be treated for that. Otherwise she was physically healthy. It was her behaviour and attitude to us that caused the problems. Far from improving, it went from bad to worse. Every little thing was a challenge and she was so angry most of the time. She still is. To begin with she refused to learn English, and would never do anything we asked or wanted to do. It felt as though she was rejecting us and it hurt. We thought she'd be pleased to have parents, a nice home and room of her own. But when she started using English she said she liked the orphanage more than us, and other hurtful things. Then she'd watch for my reaction to see if I was upset.

'I couldn't take her anywhere for fear she'd have a tantrum, which I wouldn't be able to control. Eventually I stopped trying to go out. If Ian was with me it was a little easier, but he was embarrassed too. The children our friends had were usually well behaved if they were out or had visitors, so too were my nieces and nephew. Anna seemed to take delight in doing the wrong thing and would only ever do what she wanted. She was vicious at times – still is – hurting me and other children at nursery and then school. As she grew, her problems increased. She became sly, manipulative, defiant and always so angry. It sounds awful talking about her like this, but it's true. It was relentless and wore Ian and me down, and forced us apart. Anna came between us. We weren't even allowed to sleep in the same bed or have a minute to ourselves. Anna never smiled – she still doesn't – or wanted a cuddle. In fact, I'm sure she never wanted us. She seemed pleased when Ian left just after Christmas, as though she had won, but then of course all her rage was aimed at me.' Elaine stopped.

'Didn't you think to ask for help?' I asked.

'I did many times. I went to the doctor and we paid to see a psychologist privately – more than one. That's when Anna was diagnosed with Reactive Attachment Disorder. When the psychologist explained the causes and effects, it made perfect sense. It was Anna. The neglect and abuse she'd suffered as a baby and young child, and of course us having to leave her for three months added to this. We couldn't afford to pay for her to have therapy privately – it would have gone on for years – and there was a long waiting list for a referral under the National Health Service. Ironically, her being in care seems to have speeded up the process. As you know, she has been referred.'

I nodded. 'Where is Ian now?' I asked.

'Staying with his parents. I was already worn down with trying to look after Anna, and after Ian left her behaviour got worse. It came to a head one day when Anna had been particularly spiteful at school and I had to collect her early. I told her off and sent her to her room when we got home. I was surprised she went; she never normally did as I told her. I left her for a while and then went up. She wasn't in her room but in my bedroom. I had a drawer in there containing my parents' personal effects – their watches, spectacles, some costume jewellery of Mum's, a few ornaments they'd collected on their holidays. Personal things that reminded me of them, and a photograph album. I'd shown Anna them once when I'd tried to talk to her about losing your parents. She'd broken everything that was breakable and had ripped up the photographs of Mum and Dad. I was so angry and upset I nearly hit her. I'd never been that close to hitting her before. Then I began crying uncontrollably. I sat there among my parents' broken keepsakes and wept. Anna just looked at me without any compassion or sorrow and I knew then I'd reached the end. I telephoned the duty social worker. I'd had the number ready for a while, intending to phone to ask for help, but I broke down and sobbed, and said they needed to take her.' She paused. 'The rest you know.'

'Anna came into foster care.'

Elaine looked at me with guilt in her eyes. 'I know this sounds awful, but I was pleased when the first two foster carers couldn't cope with Anna's behaviour. It proved it wasn't just me, but you seem to be doing all right, so I suppose it must be me.'

'No. Absolutely not,' I said firmly. 'I've had many years' experience looking after children with challenging behaviour, but I can tell you that Anna's behaviour has stretched me to the limit.'

'Really?' Elaine asked, surprised. 'But she's improved so much since she's been here.'

It was my turn to look surprised. 'Has she?' I asked. 'You can see that?'

'Can't you?'

'Not really.' And for the first time we both allowed ourselves a smile. 'Well, that is reassuring,' I said.

But where to go from here? Elaine had told me so much and raised many issues that had combined to tear their family apart. She and Ian had been ill-equipped to look after a child like Anna, who'd had such a damaging start in life, and from the sound of it they'd had little or no professional help and support. Added to which, they'd lost their first child, Lana, and hadn't had a chance to grieve for her before going straight into Anna's adoption. Then there was the matter of how they'd set about managing Anna's behaviour. They'd felt sorry for her – who wouldn't? – so had spoilt her and given her everything she wanted to try to heal the wounds from her past, but in so doing had fuelled her challenging behaviour. I'd fostered children before who believed they were in charge (usually because they'd had to be at home with parents unable to function as a result of alcoholism or drug abuse). Part of changing that behaviour was to take away the responsibility and control they'd assumed, and place them in the role of a child again. That's what I'd been doing with Anna, as well as putting in place boundaries for good behaviour, reinforcing and repeating them endlessly. Even so, Anna had so many issues that would need professional help.

'Are you in touch with Ian?' I asked tentatively after a moment.

'I am now. I phone him after I've seen Anna here and tell him how she is. He's struggling. He's lost me, just as I have lost him.'

'And you've both lost Anna,' I pointed out.

Her eyes filled. 'I know, and I haven't a clue what to do about it and neither has Ian.'

CHAPTER TWENTY-FIVE

IAN

Elaine left shortly after; she thanked me for listening and said she'd see me as usual on Saturday. I didn't know if I'd been of any help. I hadn't said much, but hopefully just listening so that Elaine could tell her story had unburdened her and helped.

I collected Anna from school at two o'clock and the rest of the afternoon and evening passed as normal – or normal for us now, with me spending 90 per cent of my time making sure Anna did as she was supposed to and didn't get up to mischief. While I could view some of Anna's behaviour as 'mischief', there was other behaviour that was cruel and destructive. Trashing Elaine's treasured keepsakes of her parents, for example, was malicious – there's no other word for it – an act of mindless violence, unless you took into account Anna's past. Then you could see the logic of a five-year-old damaged child. Anna had suffered as a result of not having loving parents, so why shouldn't Elaine suffer too? If only Anna could be made to see that she was now loved and cared for, hopefully some of her anger and destructiveness would go.

Of some reassurance was that Elaine had seen improvement in Anna's behaviour, and I was very pleased that my relentless efforts not only to modify Anna's behaviour, but to try to make her feel wanted and cherished were having some success.

That evening, when I wrote up my log notes, I wrote only that Elaine had visited and talked about Anna's adoption. There was no need for me to go into all the detail, although I might when I next spoke to Jill or Lori. The week rushed by and on Thursday afternoon Mrs Taylor made a point of seeing me in reception while I waited for Miss Rich to bring Anna to me at two o'clock. I usually arrived a few minutes early as I allowed extra time for traffic. Mrs Taylor asked me how my family and I were and then said, 'I was wondering if Elaine had had a chance to speak to you in private?'

'Yes,' I said, slightly surprised she knew. 'She visited me on Monday.'

'Good. I told her to have a chat with you. I thought it might help. I've also given her the telephone number of my sister, Flo – the one with adopted boys.'

'OK. Good,' I said.

'How was Elaine when you saw her? I'm not asking you to break a confidence, but how was she in herself?'

'Struggling to see a way forward,' I replied honestly.

'She's in touch with her husband now, which gives me some hope.'

'Yes, she is.' Although I wasn't sure this was a sign of hope that the family could be reunited, which I assumed was what Mrs Taylor meant. She thanked me for all I was doing for Anna and told me to 'keep up the good work', then went to rejoin her class. Mrs Taylor's care and concern for her pupils' welfare went far beyond her role as a teacher.

* * *

I was expecting something different from Elaine on Saturday after she'd unburdened herself on Monday, thinking she might be more confident and positive in dealing with Anna, but to my disappointment she was exactly the same. Anna was her usual rude and demanding self and Elaine let her walk all over her, not once stopping or correcting her, even when she pinched her and shouted in her face. So it was left to me to tell Anna. Even Adrian and Paula were now standing up to her, for example by saying, 'No, Anna, don't snatch,' when she took something they were playing with. But Elaine didn't censure her once.

When the hour was up (Elaine never stayed longer) I saw her to the front door while Anna remained in the living room. 'You know, Elaine,' I said, 'our foster carer training teaches us that putting in place boundaries for good behaviour is a sign we care. That we want what's best for the child. Anna won't love you any less if you correct her sometimes.'

'She doesn't love me now,' Elaine said bluntly. 'She never has.'

'Of course she does, but part of her condition is that she can't show it. Therapy should help.' Elaine shrugged and, saying goodbye, left, clearly unconvinced.

I'd been trying to teach Anna kindness and affection, by stroking our cat gently, for example, rather than screaming in its face or trying to pull its ears and tail. I also hoped that by setting a good example – the way my family and I treated each other with respect and consideration – would help, but any advance I made was undone by Elaine allowing Anna to treat her so badly. Perhaps Elaine felt guilty and that she deserved to be treated this way, but it wasn't healthy and was creating double standards, which would be confusing for Anna.

On Sunday I invited my parents to dinner again and they, too, said they could see some improvement in Anna, although it seemed to me that I spent most of the day correcting her behaviour. I'd found before that when we had visitors she upped her negative behaviour, being demanding, attention seeking and in their faces, not doing what I'd asked and sometimes being overfamiliar with our guests. I knew that this overfamiliarity was part of Anna's attachment disorder, and I dealt with it quickly and quietly, moving her away from the guest, putting myself between them or taking her off their lap.

Jill visited on Tuesday for one of her supervisory meetings, during which time I told her some of what Elaine had said about Anna's adoption. She said she'd pass it on to Lori. As my supervising social worker, Jill was in direct and regular contact with the child's social worker.

'I spoke to Lori yesterday,' she said. 'She's been trying to contact Elaine but she's not returning her calls. She's left messages on her voicemail and answerphone. The social services won't leave Anna here indefinitely.' Which I knew. 'When you see Elaine can you tell her it's important she gets in contact with Lori?'

'Yes, I will.'

So on Saturday when Elaine visited I took her to one side, out of earshot of the children, while Anna was busy rummaging in the toy cupboard. 'Elaine, my supervising social worker, Jill, was here this week and said Lori has been trying to contact you.'

'I know, she keeps leaving messages.'

'You need to call her back as soon as possible.' I don't think she understood the importance.

'I don't want to talk to her right now.'

'Well, you have to. If you don't then decisions could be made without you being involved. Lori won't leave Anna here indefinitely; it's not fair on her. She needs to know where she is going to live permanently.' Elaine looked quite worried. 'Also, therapy is unlikely to start until Anna is settled in her permanent home, wherever that is.'

'I've had a letter from CAMHS,' she said. 'Anna has an appointment with the therapist next week.'

'Oh, that's come through quickly. Are you going to take her?'

'I thought you would.' I wondered when she was going to tell me.

'OK, but I'll need the details of where and when.'

'I'll phone you with them.'

'And you need to let Lori know. Promise me you'll phone her first thing on Monday.'

'I will.'

'Don't put it off any longer,' I emphasized. Elaine wouldn't be the first parent who had failed to engage with their social worker and found their child the subject of a court order. At present Anna was in care voluntarily so her parents retained full parental rights, which was probably why the letter for the appointment had been sent to her rather than to me or the social services. If the social services were granted a Full Care Order by the court, Elaine and Ian would lose their parental rights and have to go to court to try to win them back. Although, of course, they'd only do that if they were fighting to keep Anna, and at present I wasn't sure they would. I didn't like the fact that Elaine had asked me to take Anna to the appointment. It was as though she'd completely given up.

However, situations can and do change quickly in fostering. On Monday morning I let Jill know that Anna's appointment at CAMHS had come through and that Elaine had asked me to take her, and I was waiting to hear what day and time it was. Jill said she'd let Lori know. An hour or so later Elaine telephoned, I assumed to give me the details of the appointment. 'It's on Wednesday,' she said, 'but you needn't take her. Ian and I are going to.'

'Oh. Oh, good,' I said, surprised but pleased. That sounded positive. 'Have you told Lori?'

'Yes. The appointment is at three o'clock, so we are going to collect Anna from school at two and go straight there. We'll bring her back to you after – I'm guessing around five o'clock. Lori asked if you could explain to Anna what is happening as she won't see her before.'

'Yes, of course.' In Elaine's words I caught sight of a very different person, one who could organize and make requests, before her dreams had been shattered and she'd been beaten down by the relentless demands of a very challenging child. 'Excellent,' I said. 'Can I ask what made you change your mind about taking Anna to the appointment?'

'A couple of things, really. After you said the social services wouldn't leave Anna with you indefinitely and might apply for a court order, I phoned Ian and told him. He was worried too. I then returned Lori's calls and she sort of confirmed what you'd said, and said that if we are working towards Anna returning home in the future then we need to be part of

Anna's therapy. I also phoned Mrs Taylor's sister, Flo. She has two adopted sons. She was helpful.'

'Good. Although you know therapy can take months before you see any improvement.' I didn't want her and Ian thinking it was a quick fix.

'I know. We'll see how it goes, but can I ask you something?'

'Sure.'

'I sent Anna's Life Story Book and Memory Box in her belongings. What did you do with them? I've never seen them at your house.'

'I unpacked them and put them safely away.'

'So they are not on view in Anna's bedroom?'

'No, but if she asks for them I can easily get them out. Is that OK? She hasn't asked for them yet.'

Elaine was silent for some moments. 'Is that all right?' I asked again.

'Yes. Flo did similar with her lads. I should have, but I was so keen to follow the advice of the social worker about keeping the child's roots alive that I think I have caused some of Anna's problems. Flo said they'd been put under a lot of pressure to do the same and stay in touch with the boys' natural parents, even though her lads didn't want to. She and her husband refused. But I've been talking to Anna about her mother almost as if she was there. It was me who kept bringing up the subject of her past and suggested we kept looking at her Life Story Book and going through the Memory Box. Anna wasn't interested, but I thought I was doing the right thing. I always referred to Anna's birth mother as "her mummy" – little wonder she resented me and hasn't bonded with us.' I heard her voice break.

'Elaine, you can't blame yourself. Perhaps with hindsight you may have done things differently, but that's the nature of having children. We can only do our best and learn from our mistakes. Anna has other issues arising from being abused and neglected in her early years, which have never been properly addressed. Therapy should help.'

'I hope so. I was so pleased I talked to Flo. She spoke a lot of good sense. She invited us over to meet her family. She said her favourite saying, which she shared with her boys, is: "You can't start the next chapter of your life if you keep re-reading the last one." That's so true.'

'Yes, indeed it is,' I said. I remembered that quote and years later, when I fostered and then adopted Lucy (whose story I tell in *Will You Love Me?*), I used it with her. Those few words seemed to sum up so much for children and adults who are struggling to move on from a difficult past.

I made a note in my diary of the arrangements for Wednesday, and when I collected Anna from school that afternoon I took the opportunity of the two of us being alone in the car to tell her that her mummy and daddy would be collecting her on Wednesday and the three of them would go to see a therapist at the hospital. I explained that a therapist was a type of doctor who would talk to them, ask questions and probably play some games. Most therapy involving children includes therapeutic games. Anna was uncharacteristically quiet as I spoke and didn't keep interrupting or talking over me, or covering her ears so she couldn't hear – which she still often did. I glanced at her in the rear-view mirror. 'Are you OK? Any questions?'

'No.'

'Well, if you do think of any, ask me and I'll do my best to answer.'

Anna continued to be subdued for the rest of the afternoon and evening, so much so that I asked her a few times if she was all right and she nodded. On a lighter note, I overheard Adrian remark casually to Paula in his old-fashioned way, 'I think Anna may have turned a corner. We can only hope.' I smiled at Adrian's dry sense of humour.

At bedtime, having clearly been thinking about things, Anna finally had a question and it stopped me in my tracks. 'Are my mummy and daddy going to send me back?'

'To the orphanage?' I asked, horrified. She nodded. 'No, of course not. They adopted you, you are their daughter and they are your parents,' I said yet again. 'There is no changing that, even if you are not living with them.' Although I could see why she might think it.

'Are you sure?' she asked.

'Yes. Positive. Why?'

'I used to tell them I wanted to go back and they always do as I say, but I don't really.' Which was a very good example of why children shouldn't be given too much power. It's a frightening place to be, as they don't have the maturity to deal with it.

'Well, luckily for you, adults don't always do as you tell them,' I said, 'including me, Lori and your parents.' Anna looked at me carefully and then climbed into bed. I always tucked her in, even though she didn't want a hug or kiss goodnight.

'Do you think I'm wicked?' she asked, resting her head on the pillow.

'No. You are not wicked. You make the wrong choices sometimes. The therapist will help you learn how to make the right choices.'

'The kids at school think I'm horrible.'

'No, you're not horrible, Anna, but to make friends you have to be kind to other children, share and ask if you can join in, then play nicely. I'm sure you can do it if you try.'

'I don't know how to,' she said wistfully. 'Will the therapist teach me to be nice?' My heart went out to her. It was part of her attachment disorder that she didn't know how to treat other children (or adults). This was the longest, most meaningful conversation we'd had since she'd arrived and I caught a glimpse of a very isolated, fragile and hurting child.

'Yes, I'm sure the therapist will be able to help you,' I said with a reassuring smile. 'But in the meantime, you could think how you like to be treated and do the same to others. That would be a good start.' I wanted to give her a hug, but when I took her hand in mine she pulled it away. 'Is there anything else you want to ask then?'

'Can I sleep in your bed?' she asked, perhaps thinking our heart-to-heart had lessened my resolve.

'No, love. We've been through that.' Which she accepted. She snuggled down and I tucked in the covers, remembering only too clearly all those nights I'd been up repeatedly returning her to her bed, but it was an investment that had paid off.

'Night, love, see you in the morning,' I said. As usual Anna didn't reply so I came out, drawing the door to behind me.

The following morning, Tuesday, when I took Anna into school, I checked with Miss Rich that she knew of the change in arrangements for Wednesday – that Anna was being collected by her parents. She did. Elaine had telephoned the school and spoken to Mrs Taylor. Miss Rich also said that the educational psychologist would begin an assessment of Anna the following week. That was positive, although I knew it could take many months before her report would be complete and available. However, not only would her recommendations help to identity Anna's learning difficulties, but they would also give directions on what further support was needed for her in the classroom so she could return to school full-time.

Anna didn't mention the therapist or her parents again, so on Wednesday morning I reminded her of what was happening that afternoon.

'Don't care,' she said, but deep down I knew she did. It was another symptom of her condition that she couldn't show love or concern, and appeared cold and uncaring. I was hoping the therapist would address that too.

Wednesday was also 1 June, signalling the start of the summer months, and the weather obliged by turning very warm – a heat wave, the like of which surprises us in the UK every year. The children went to school in their summer uniforms and I was pleased to be able to wear a cotton dress and sandals. The birds were singing and the flowers blooming, and everyone I met was in a very good mood. What a difference clear blue skies and sunshine make! Some days there is precious little of them.

I took Anna into school and confirmed with Miss Rich that her parents would be collecting her and bringing her back to me later, then I said goodbye and returned home. After a cup of coffee I set about the list of jobs I had to do and made good progress. Not having to leave at 1.30 to collect Anna gave me nearly an extra two hours, although Anna was never far from my mind. I wondered what sort of day she was having at school and if the change in her routine and the prospect of seeing her parents and the therapist had unsettled her. It was nearly six months since she'd last seen her father.

At 4.45 Adrian, Paula and I were sitting on the patio in the shade and enjoying a cool drink when through the open patio doors we heard the front doorbell ring. They knew that Anna had a hospital appointment and her parents would be bringing her home. I'd also told them that her parents might come in, so we needed to keep the living room reasonably tidy. Adrian and Paula stayed where they were as I went to answer the front door. A man I recognized from the photo in Anna's room stood alone in the porch. 'Cathy Glass?'

'Yes. Hello, you must be Ian.'

He shook my hand, but it seemed more out of politeness than warmth.

'Where's Anna and Elaine?' I asked, looking past him.

'They're waiting in the car, just up there,' he said, pointing to the road behind my neighbour's hedge. Tall, with broad shoulders, he was wearing grey trousers and a white shirt, left open at the neck. The heat of the day beat down into the porch and his expression was serious.

'Are they coming in now?' I asked, but even as I spoke fear gripped me.

'No. Anna's not coming in,' he said. 'We're taking her home with us.'

CHAPTER TWENTY-SIX

MISSING HER

I stared at Ian and he looked back. 'What do you mean?' I asked.

'I'm sorry this has come as a shock for you, but we're taking Anna home. I've just phoned the social worker and told her, and that we've come here to collect some of her clothes.'

'But Lori hasn't phoned me,' I said.

'She won't have had time. Can you pack what Anna needs, please, so we can get her home?'

I hesitated. I'm not good at making snap decisions; I need time to weigh up the pros and cons, but I didn't have the luxury of time now. Had Anna been the subject of a care order then I would have called the police, as Ian and Elaine would have had no legal right to remove her from my care, but that wasn't so with a Section 20.

'You'd better come in,' I said to Ian, opening the door wider, 'but I'll need to speak to Lori first.'

'I understand,' he said.

He stood in the hall, clearly as uncomfortable as I was by what was happening. I picked up the phone on the hall table. With unsteady fingers I keyed in Lori's number and thankfully she answered straight away. 'It's Cathy.'

'Are they there now?' she asked tightly.

'Ian is with me in the hall. Anna and Elaine are outside in the car. They want to take Anna home now. Ian said he'd spoken to you. He's asking me to pack some of Anna's belongings.' Ian was staring at the floor.

'I told them I wanted Anna left with you for now but they're insisting on taking her,' Lori said. 'I'm leaving the office now to go to their house. Hopefully I can talk some sense into them, and then return Anna to you later.'

'Do you want me to pack a bag for her?'

'Easier to, but just a small one. I'll call you later.'

As I replaced the handset Adrian and Paula came into the hall looking concerned, having heard Ian's voice.

'Hello,' Ian said awkwardly to them.

'This is Anna's father,' I said. 'Could you two go and play outside for a while?'

Appreciating that there was something serious going on that required my full attention and their cooperation, they did as I asked.

'I'm sorry,' Ian said to me.

I looked at him. 'Ian, it would be so much better for Anna if she stayed here for now – as Lori suggested. Then, if it's decided she should return to you, we can do a planned move. It would be far less unsettling for her.'

He shook his head, a bit like Anna did. 'We've spent enough time apart. I don't know what I was thinking of going off like that after Christmas. I want us to be together again as a family. I've told Lori we can deal with whatever comes.' I'm sure he genuinely believed that to be so, but they hadn't been able to 'deal' with Anna before.

'Did you see the therapist this afternoon?' I asked. He nodded. 'What did she say about Anna going home?'

'We didn't discuss it. It was a decision Elaine and I made afterwards.'

'Ian, it's all too quick. Believe me, this isn't the best way forward for Anna or any of you. She will be even more troubled than before.'

'Please, just do as I ask and pack a bag with what she needs,' he nearly begged. 'I'll collect the rest another time.' He was very close to tears.

'All right. It'll take me a few minutes. Do you want to sit down?' I meant the living room but he sat on the chair in the hall, by the telephone table. 'Would you like a glass of water?' He'd gone very pale.

'Yes, please.'

I quickly fetched him a glass of water from the kitchen and handed it to him. 'Are you OK?'

He nodded and rubbed his hand over his forehead. 'I'm sorry, it's been a very difficult day. I'll be better once we're home and settled.'

Leaving him in the hall, I went upstairs, took the smallest of Anna's bags from the top of the wardrobe and set about packing the essentials: her toothbrush, flannel and so forth from the bathroom; her pyjamas, dressing gown, underwear, socks, and a set of casual clothes from her bedroom. She didn't have a favourite soft toy that she took to bed so I packed one of the teddy bears from her shelf, although I was expecting her to be returned later by Lori. She was wearing her school uniform and I packed another set, then I returned downstairs and passed the bag to Ian.

'Thank you,' he said, getting up from the chair. 'I am sorry I've caused you so much trouble.'

'It's not me I'm worried about,' I said.

He turned towards the door to let himself out, then as an afterthought said, 'Do you want to say goodbye to Anna?'

'Yes, please.' I was sure it wouldn't be goodbye, but I wanted to see Anna to check she was all right and let her know I wasn't abandoning her. Leaving the front door on the latch, I followed Ian out to his car. He opened the rear door, pavement side. Elaine and Anna were sitting together in the back, still under their seatbelts. Elaine had obviously been crying, her eyes were red, but Anna stared at me, blank and confused.

'Hello, love. Are you OK?' I asked gently.

'I'm not living here any more,' she said. I glanced at Elaine, who had the decency to look embarrassed.

'I've told the social worker,' Elaine said. 'She's coming to see us later.'

'I know, I've just spoken to her. But Elaine, this is not ...' I didn't get any further.

'Don't say anything,' she said, holding up her hand, her eyes filling. 'It's difficult enough as it is. I don't need a lecture.'

'I wasn't going to lecture you. I just want what's best for Anna.'

'So do we,' she said sharply.

The boot closed with a thud; Ian had stowed away Anna's bag. He went to the driver's door. What could I say to Anna? It wasn't goodbye, but I couldn't say see you later, as that was likely to confuse her more and antagonize Elaine and Ian.

'Take care, love,' I said. Instinctively I reached in and put my arms around her. To my amazement she didn't pull back but hugged me – our very first hug as she was being taken away – and a lump rose in my throat.

'Bye, Cathy,' she said in a small voice, relaxing her arms. 'Say goodbye to Adrian and Paula. I'll miss them.' Another first and an indication of just how upset and vulnerable she must have been feeling. It broke my heart.

'Time to go,' Ian said from the front.

'Take care,' I said to Anna. Straightening, I closed the car door.

Ian started the engine but then had to reverse before he had enough room to pull out. As he did I looked at Anna through the glass in her side window and a tear rolled down her cheek. The first tears of sorrow she'd ever shown me as the enormity of what was happening hit her. Before, her tears had been from rage at not getting her own way. Elaine and Ian had acted on impulse, believing they were doing the right thing, but had caused their daughter more upset and turmoil, although I'm sure they didn't see it that way.

The car pulled away. I returned indoors and straight away telephoned Jill. She was on another call and a colleague said she'd ask her to phone back as soon as she'd finished. Adrian and Paula, having heard the front door shut, appeared in the hall again, looking even more worried.

'Where's Anna?' Adrian asked.

'Her parents have taken her home with them for now. Don't worry, the social worker will sort it out, although I might be on the phone for a while.' I glanced at my watch. 'I'll put some dinner in the oven, and I'd like you two to be really big and amuse yourselves quietly.'

'Did Anna want to go with them?' Adrian asked.

'I don't know, but it wasn't the right thing to do – to just take her. Her social worker will bring her back later.' Anna wasn't the only one to be unsettled by suddenly being removed. Adrian and Paula had experienced many changes during our years of fostering but none as abrupt as this.

I didn't get as far as the kitchen before the telephone rang. It was Jill returning my call.

'Anna's parents have taken Anna home,' I said. 'Lori is going there now to talk to them and then return Anna later.'

'When did this happen?'

'Just now. Her parents collected her from school and took her to therapy as arranged, but then suddenly decided that they wanted to be together as a family. Ian phoned Lori and then they stopped by here to collect her things.'

'Have you spoken to Lori?'

'Yes. I phoned her straight away. She said to just pack a small bag. Elaine and Anna didn't come in, but I saw them in the car.'

'The poor kid. She didn't need this right now. She was just starting to settle with you.'

'I know, but there was nothing I could do.'

'I'm not blaming you. So Lori is going to contact you once she's seen the parents?'

'Yes. That's what she said.'

'OK. I'm on call tonight so will you phone me when you hear from Lori? I'll need to speak to her too.' The agency provided emergency out-of-hours cover every day of the year. A child being taken from a foster carer without notice was an emergency.

I made a quick dinner with enough for Anna, and once it was ready I called Adrian and Paula to the table. Everyone was very subdued and I didn't have much of an appetite, although Adrian and Paula ate. Chicken nuggets and chips was an occasional treat when I didn't have time to cook a proper meal. After we'd finished they returned to the garden while, with one eye on the clock, I cleared away. I was on tenterhooks waiting for the phone to ring or even the front doorbell to go if Lori didn't phone before bringing Anna home. Social workers have so much on their minds sometimes they forget to call the foster carer to say they're on their way with an approximate time of arrival. Then at 6.30 Jill telephoned to see if I'd heard anything, which I hadn't.

'Me neither,' she said. 'I've left Lori a voicemail message asking her to phone me as soon as she is able. If she calls you first can you let me know?'

'Yes.'

The phone didn't ring again until nearly 7.30, when I was in Paula's room reading her a bedtime story. I left her and took the call on the extension in my bedroom. It was Lori.

'I'm still with the family,' she said. 'I've agreed that Anna can stay here tonight. It will be less unsettling for her than coming back to you now it's getting late.'

'Oh, OK.' Clearly it was Lori's decision. 'Is Anna all right?'

'She's the quietest I've ever seen her.' Which wasn't the same thing and did nothing for my concerns. 'I'll be in touch with you and Jill tomorrow,' Lori said. 'Can you tell Jill what's happening? She left a message.'

'Yes. I will. Is Anna with you now?'

'No, she's upstairs with Elaine, unpacking her bag.'

'Can you say goodnight to her from me, please?'

'Yes, of course. I'll speak to you and Jill tomorrow.'

We said goodbye and I slowly replaced the handset, all manner of thoughts going through my head. I had no idea what had happened to lead to Lori's decision, although I appreciated that it would have been very late if Lori had returned Anna tonight, especially if she had needed persuading. But on the other hand, surely leaving her there was going to make it more difficult to bring her back to me tomorrow? I tried to picture Anna and Elaine unpacking Anna's bag, and Elaine seeing her into bed. What would Elaine do when Anna kicked off and refused to stay in her bedroom? Would she be firm or would she and Ian let Anna into their bed and go right back to square one? It was behaviour like this that had led to Anna going into care in the first place.

I now telephoned my fostering agency and after a few rings Jill answered. 'Jill, it's Cathy. Lori has just called and has decided to leave Anna with her parents for tonight as it is getting late.'

'I see. Is she going to return her to you tomorrow then?'

'I assume so, although she didn't say when. Just that she'd phone.'

'Well, there's nothing else you can do now so I'll speak to Lori as soon as I can tomorrow. I'm dealing with two runaways right now, one of whom is only ten. Speak soon.'

We said a quick goodbye and I returned to Paula's room to find her fast asleep.

Downstairs I told Adrian that Anna was spending the night at her home with her parents and would be back tomorrow, which he accepted. Without Anna to see to I had extra time to spend with him and I made the most of it; we chatted and played a board game, although Anna was never far from our thoughts. Adrian mentioned her a few times, clearly concerned for her. That night, when I went up to bed, I stopped off in Anna's room to close her bedroom window as a storm was brewing after the heat of the day. It was strange and slightly unnerving, standing there surrounded by her belongings with no Anna tucked up in bed, and again my

thoughts went to her house and how they were all faring
there. Doubtless Lori would tell me when she returned Anna
tomorrow. I looked at the framed photographs on the book-
shelf of Anna's parents and her birth mother and then,
straightening the duvet, came out.

It was even stranger the following morning without Anna
when I woke Adrian and Paula. There was an unnatural
calm and I found I had extra time, as I didn't have to keep
telling Anna what she needed to do or not do. Our routine
ran very smoothly, but we missed her. I told Paula as she
dressed that Anna had spent the night at her house with her
parents.

'I thought I couldn't hear her,' she said.

'No, the house is quiet.'

'I can change that!' Adrian called, having overheard. He
then yelled nonsense at the top of his voice for a good minute
until I told him enough was enough.

Anna's empty chair at the breakfast table was disconcert-
ing, and although there wasn't the usual constant pressure to
make sure she did as I asked, we would much rather have had
her there.

'When's Anna going to come home?' Paula asked.

'Later today, I think,' I said.

'I'll let her play with my doll,' she offered. I knew which
doll Paula was referring to and that this was a very generous
gesture. The week before Anna had purposely pulled the
arms off the doll and I'd repaired it as best I could. I was
aware that when Anna did return it was likely her behaviour
would have deteriorated from the upset of all the recent
changes.

It was another fine, sunny day, the storm that had been forecast the night before hadn't materialized, so, not needing to take Anna to school in the car, Adrian, Paula and I walked to school. Having seen them in, I returned home and began tidying up, all the while listening out for the phone. At 10.15 it rang. 'Mrs Glass?' A woman's voice I didn't recognize.

'Yes. Speaking.'

'It's the school secretary. Miss Rich is with me. Is Anna not coming into school today?'

'Oh. Isn't she there then?'

'No, didn't you know?' I heard her concern.

'I'm sure she's all right. Anna stayed with her parents last night. They must have decided not to bring her into school today. You'd better phone them for confirmation.'

'I'll tell Miss Rich,' she said. 'And just a reminder that if a child is absent we expect the parent or carer to phone in and let us know before the start of school.'

'Sorry,' I said. Although of course I didn't know Anna hadn't gone to school; it had been her parents' responsibility to notify the school.

'Will Anna be in tomorrow? Miss Rich is asking,' the secretary said.

'Yes, I would think so. I should be bringing her.'

'Thank you. I'll let Miss Rich know.' We said goodbye.

But why wasn't Anna in school? I wondered. Had she been too upset, or refused to go? Or was there another, more sinister reason? It wasn't for me to telephone the parents to find out, but I would tell Lori when she phoned. With one eye on the clock, I continued with various jobs and the morning ticked by. Just after twelve the phone rang and I quickly answered it, hoping it was Lori or Jill with news of Anna. It was Anna's teacher, Mrs Taylor.

'Whatever is going on?' she asked, concerned. 'Lauren Rich tells me that Anna didn't return to you last night and is staying with her parents.'

'Only for last night,' I said.

I then went over what had happened since Anna had been collected from school by her parents the afternoon before to go to therapy.

When I'd finished Mrs Taylor let out a heartfelt sigh. 'What a mess! I'm sure her parents don't realize the harm they are doing. I always hoped Anna would go home eventually, but this is not the way to do it.'

I agreed.

CHAPTER TWENTY-SEVEN

BAD ENDING

By 1.30 p.m., when I still hadn't heard from Jill or Lori, I telephoned my fostering agency and then waited for Jill to finish the call she was on. 'Sorry,' she said as she came on the line. 'It's manic here. I haven't had a chance to speak to Lori. Do you know the arrangements for bringing Anna back?'

'No, I haven't heard from Lori. That's why I'm phoning.'

'OK. I'll call her now and get back to you.'

'Jill, can you tell her Anna isn't in school today? I'm not sure if she knows. Also, remind her I shall be out between 3.15 and 3.45 collecting Adrian and Paula from school. I don't want her and Anna arriving to an empty house.'

'Will do.'

Another nail-biting wait followed and it was nearly an hour before the phone rang again. I answered in the living room – it was Jill. 'I've only just managed to speak to Lori. Anna isn't coming back to you today.'

'Why not?' I exclaimed.

'The parents are adamant that Anna should stay with them. Ian has moved back in and now they are in therapy they say they can cope with her.'

'But therapy won't change things that quickly!' I said with dismay.

'I know. Lori has concerns so she is arranging a case conference, hopefully tomorrow, to decide what to do. You don't have to go. They could return Anna to you straight after, but you need to prepare yourself for the other decision too.'

'What? That Anna might not come back.'

'Yes. Given that there is no suggestion the parents have abused or neglected Anna, it's possible the social services might decide to leave her at home and monitor them.' I was silent, my thoughts whirling. 'I'm not saying that will be their decision,' Jill said, 'but prepare yourself and the kids too. I'll phone you as soon as I hear.' Jill was obviously still very busy and, quickly winding up the conversation, she said goodbye.

I replaced the handset and gazed through the open patio doors to the garden beyond. A small brave bird was at the feeder while our cat watched from beneath. If a child comes into care or has to move carers then whenever possible it is a 'planned move' with introductions and a visit to their new home first, so it's not completely strange when they move in. While Anna obviously knew her parents and was familiar with her house, she hadn't been there for nearly six months, and had only seen her father once in all that time. Also, the very reasons that had brought her into care in the first place were still ongoing. As far as I knew the parents were no more prepared now for dealing with Anna than they had been before. In an ideal world Anna would have spent time with her parents over the course of a few weeks, including overnight stays, leading up to a move home. During that period they would all be getting to know each other again, with the benefit of therapy, and her parents would feel more confident in dealing with her. What would happen if she stayed at home now and it didn't work out? She'd come into care again, even more disturbed. I'd seen it happen – a child in and out of care – their behaviour deteriorating with each move. But social services budgets are tight and foster placements are in short supply. Anna hadn't been abused or neglected, so any free carer would very likely be needed by a child who had been. While this wouldn't be an overriding factor, it would be a consideration. Thankfully, it wasn't my decision, so all I could do was wait and prepare myself and my children for the possibility that Anna might not be returning to us.

I raised the matter with Adrian and Paula at dinner.

'The social workers are going to have a meeting soon, probably tomorrow, to decide where Anna should live.'

'She lives here for now,' Adrian said, puzzled.

'Anna's parents want her home and are working very hard to make that happen, so she might stay there.'

'And not come back at all?' Adrian asked, surprised.

'Possibly. I don't know yet.'

'But all her things are here,' he said, looking worried.

'Yes, I know. If they do decide she is staying there, I'll have to pack up all her belongings, then work out a way to get them to her.'

'Oh,' Adrian said. 'So we don't get to say goodbye.'

'I don't know yet, love.'

'Doesn't Anna like us?' Paula asked.

'Yes, of course, but her parents love her and want her home.' I changed the subject for fear of emotion getting the better of me. It was so difficult. This wasn't the way for a child we'd loved and cared for to leave.

* * *

On Friday I took Adrian and Paula to school and returned home but couldn't settle to anything. Jill had said she'd phone as soon as she heard the outcome of the case conference, but hadn't known when that meeting would be, or even if it would definitely be today. I thought it was likely, as if the meeting didn't go ahead today it wouldn't happen until Monday, as social services offices are closed at the weekend, and this wasn't a decision that could be left. Anna was supposed to be in foster care and officially living with me; if anything went wrong over the weekend it would reflect badly on the social services as well as possibly putting Anna's safety in jeopardy.

The day passed without any news and at 3.15 I left to collect Adrian and Paula from school. When they came out I could tell from their expressions that they were disappointed Anna wasn't with me. She'd always been in the playground to meet them, and despite all the aggravation she'd caused us, she'd been part of our lives for all this time, another sibling, so of course they missed her. 'I don't know what's happening yet,' I said. 'I'm still waiting to hear.'

It was nearly five o'clock before I got the call and I took it in the kitchen, where I was making dinner. Jill began with a big sigh. 'The meeting went ahead this afternoon and hasn't long finished. They made the decision to allow Anna to stay with her parents and the family will be monitored.'

'Oh.'

'Sorry, Cathy. I know it's not what either of us wanted to hear. The parents have given an undertaking that they will continue in family therapy and also take parenting classes. Lori's manager raised concerns that the parents' actions have had a detrimental effect on Anna. But it was felt that to insist she return to you and then start a planned move home was likely to make her more unsettled and upset. Lori is with the parents now, informing them of the decision.'

I was silent for a moment, taking it in. 'Well, I hope it all works out for them,' I said in a flat voice. 'What about Anna's belongings? They are all still here.'

'Lori wants you to pack them up and then she'll arrange to have them collected.'

'OK,' I said quietly.

'I raised the matter of you and the children having a chance to say goodbye to Anna, and Lori will ask her parents. She also said that everyone at the meeting agreed you'd helped Anna, and had helped to stabilize the situation, allowing the parents time to sort themselves out.'

'Good,' I said, without much feeling. 'I'm pleased I was of some help.'

'So have a nice weekend then. It will be a quiet one for you,' Jill added, trying to lighten the mood.

'Yes, it will, and you.'

'Take care. I'll be in touch next week.'

We said goodbye. I replaced the handset and then went slowly into the garden where Adrian and Paula were sitting in the shade of the tree, watching a line of ants. I squatted nearby. 'Jill just telephoned,' I said. 'Anna won't be returning to live with us. The social workers have decided to leave her with her parents.' Both children were quiet.

Normally when a child returns home it is good news and we are pleased for them, but of course now it was soured by the way it had been done. Usually, I would have arranged a little leaving party and bought the child a farewell gift and card. I'd still buy the card and gift, but clearly there'd be no party.

'So we won't see Anna again?' Adrian finally asked, looking up.

'Not unless her parents bring her to say goodbye,' I replied, but I wasn't hopeful.

Adrian isn't one to show his feelings and he shrugged and concentrated on the ants again as though it didn't matter. Paula said, 'That's sad for us but happy for Anna and her parents.'

'Yes, it is,' I agreed.

Having checked they were OK, I left them playing and returned indoors to make dinner. A little after 6 p.m., just as we'd finished eating, the phone rang. I answered in the kitchen while Adrian and Paula returned to the garden. I was slightly surprised to hear Lori. 'I'm with Anna and her parents now,' she said. 'Ian would like to collect Anna's belongings tomorrow. She's hardly got anything here to wear.'

And whose fault is that? I felt like saying: her mother had packed all her belongings when she put her into care and then, without any warning, had removed her. But being professional I said, 'All right, but I'll need time to pack, so can we make it in the afternoon?'

'What time?' Lori asked.

'One o'clock?'

I heard her repeat this, then she said, 'Yes, that's OK. Ian will be with you around one.'

'Will Anna be coming to say goodbye?' I asked. 'Jill thought she might.' I heard her relay this, but not the parents' reply. Lori came on the line again. 'Ian and Elaine will see how Anna feels in the morning.' Which I had to accept, and the call ended.

I went into the garden and told Adrian and Paula that Anna's father was coming to collect her belongings tomorrow afternoon and that I was going up to her room now to start packing, and to come and get me if they needed me. I could see them from Anna's bedroom window and I worked for over an hour, packing her cases, bags and boxes. Then I spent some time with Adrian and Paula. Once they were in bed, I continued packing. I wanted to get as much done as possible tonight because in the morning I planned to go into town to buy Anna a leaving gift and card.

By 10 p.m. I'd cleared her bedroom so all that remained were the bags and boxes of things she hadn't needed and I'd stowed away. I'd take those downstairs tomorrow. Anna's room looked even more sorrowful and desolate now it was empty. With a final check that I hadn't missed anything, I came out and closed the door.

Downstairs I made a much-needed mug of tea and took it into the living room where I wrote up my log notes, ending with the arrangements for tomorrow. If Anna came with her father to say goodbye then I'd add another entry; otherwise this would be the last. Closing my notes, I went to bed with a very heavy heart.

I wasn't surprised the following afternoon at one when I answered the front door to find only Ian. 'No Anna?'

'No, she didn't feel up to it,' he said awkwardly. 'Neither did Elaine.'

I nodded. 'Come in.'

'We didn't get much sleep last night,' he added. 'Anna was very unsettled.'

No surprise there either, but I didn't comment. It was

difficult enough without making the situation worse. Adrian and Paula came into the hall from the living room half expecting to see Anna, and I told them she'd stayed at home with her mother. They returned to the living room.

'Thanks for doing all this,' Ian said, referring to all the bags and boxes stacked in the hall. He picked up two and I did likewise and we began loading his car. Back and forth, the hall emptied and his car filled. There was just enough room – the boot, rear seat and passenger seat were full. Last of all I handed him the gift-wrapped box containing a girl's silver bracelet, and the farewell card signed by us all. 'A little something for Anna,' I said. 'Will you say goodbye to her from us, please?'

'Yes, of course.' He looked embarrassed. 'I suppose we should have bought you something really.'

'No need. Look after yourselves and if ever you feel like getting in touch, do.'

He nodded stiffly and, saying goodbye, left. It was the most heartless ending I'd experienced in fostering. I didn't expect to hear from them again.

CHAPTER TWENTY-EIGHT

A LONG WAY FROM HOME

N ot only had we not had a chance to say goodbye to Anna, but I hadn't been able to say goodbye to Mrs Taylor or Miss Rich. So the following week I telephoned the school and asked the secretary if she'd pass on my thanks to Anna's teacher and TA for all they had done for her while she'd been living with me. She said she would and that Anna was in school, but that was all she said.

Time passed. I didn't hear anything about Anna, but then I hadn't thought I would. When a child leaves a foster carer there is no compulsion for the social services to give the carer updates, and it relies on the child's parents or guardians to keep in touch, which Elaine and Ian didn't do. I hadn't expected them to. They hadn't even brought Anna to say goodbye, so it was unlikely they'd make the effort to keep in touch. I just hoped Anna settled down and wasn't returned into care.

The years went by. I continued fostering as a single parent and went on to adopt one of my foster children, Lucy. A big decision for us all, but definitely the right one. Then one afternoon, seven years after Anna had left, Jill telephoned.

'Do you remember a child called Anna Hudson?' she asked.

'Yes, of course. Why?' Foster carers never forget the children they've looked after.

'Her mother has been in touch with the social services. Anna would like to meet you.'

I was dumbstruck, and it was a moment before I could reply. 'Really?' I asked, amazed. 'After all this time! I don't believe it.' My eyes immediately filled. I'd had children I'd fostered before get in contact after a long time, but never in a million years had I expected to hear from Anna or her family. 'I don't believe it,' I said again. 'Gosh. She must be nearly thirteen now.'

'Yes, I believe so. Elaine told the social worker that she can remember where you live but doesn't have your telephone number. She didn't like to just turn up at your door. Shall I tell the social services to let her have your number?'

'Yes, of course. I guess it must have all worked out for them.'

'I assume so. Lori – their social worker at the time – left a few years back, sometime after their case was closed. Doubtless Elaine will tell you all.'

'Well, well, who would have thought it?' I mused. 'Just shows what an impression I made!'

Jill laughed. 'I thought you'd be pleased.'

'I am. You've made my day. I still can't believe it.'

'Speak soon,' Jill said, rounding off the call.

For the rest of the day I floated on cloud nine, immersed in a warm glow of happiness and treasured memories, for once a child leaves I only remember the good times, not their negative behaviour. I was so pleased that Anna had asked to see us, but also that Elaine had passed on her wishes and telephoned the social services. She might not have done. She could have discouraged Anna or told her it wasn't possible to contact me. But she'd done the decent thing and followed up on Anna's request. I wondered what had prompted Anna's interest in meeting me again. Possibly her age. She would be thirteen soon and young people often review and question their past as they enter their teenage years. I couldn't wait to meet her and hear all her news.

Later, when my family returned home, I told Adrian (now aged sixteen) and Paula (twelve), and they were as amazed and pleased as I was and remembered Anna clearly. The carer's children never forget their foster siblings either. I explained to Lucy (aged fourteen) who Anna was and she was happy for us. Having spent a large part of her early life before she came to me being moved between relatives and in and out of care, she appreciated the significance of Anna's wish to see us and the importance of good endings.

It was nearly another week before Elaine rang and I was starting to think that perhaps Anna had changed her mind. Then one evening, after dinner, I answered the landline in the living room and a small female voice said, 'Cathy, it's Elaine Hudson.'

'Hello, Elaine. Lovely to hear from you.'

'Thank you for agreeing to see Anna.'

'No need to thank me. We're all overjoyed you got in touch.'

'Are you?' she said as though it might not be true. 'After the way it all ended I wondered if you'd want to see us.' Clearly she had reflected on this.

'It's history,' I said. 'I'm delighted you've got in touch. I'm assuming everything worked out for you all.'

'Yes, although there are still some ongoing issues we're working on, but I won't keep you now. Anna would like to see you. Ian and I would too.'

'Great. When?'

'This weekend if you're free.'

'We're free Saturday. Afternoon would be good for us.'

'Yes, that suits us too. Around two o'clock?'

'Fine with me. You remember where we live?'

'Yes. We'll look forward to it then. Thank you, and thanks for all you did for Anna back then. I know it's a bit late.'

'You're welcome. See you Saturday.'

I replaced the handset with a smile. Talk about a happy ending! Or was it? Elaine had said she was still dealing with some ongoing issues with Anna. I hoped they were solvable and that she wasn't coming to see if Anna could stay with me again. It might sound far-fetched but I'd had experience of parents who knew I fostered stop me in the street, even knock on my door, to ask if I could look after their child or children for a few weeks, as they were struggling. I had to explain that the social care system didn't work like that and if their family was in crisis then they needed to phone the social services, who would send a social worker to assess them. If it was then decided their child or children needed to be in care then the social services would place them with a foster carer, although not necessarily in the area (it would depend where a carer was free).

Saturday afternoon, the house was spotless and a freshly baked sponge cake filled with butter icing and jam stood majestically on a plate in the kitchen, ready to be sliced. I'd told Adrian, Paula and Lucy to just carry on as normal, although obviously Anna would want to see them as they did her. But at two o'clock we were all sitting in the living room on our best behaviour and nervously awaiting Anna's arrival.

'I wonder if you'll recognize her,' Lucy said. 'It's a long time.'

I agreed. The difference between a five-year-old and a nearly thirteen-year-old would be dramatic.

When the doorbell rang a little after two o'clock I immediately left the living room to answer it, as nervous and curious as I was the first time I met Anna. Would I recognize her?

Yes, I did, but only from her clear blue eyes. When I opened the door, before me stood a tall, fashionably dressed young lady with long fair hair loosely plaited over one shoulder, and she was smiling. 'Cathy! You haven't changed at all!' she cried, clasping her hands together in delight.

'Well, thank you!' I laughed. 'Anyone who thinks I haven't changed in seven years immediately wins a place in my heart.' Elaine and Ian laughed too. It broke the ice. 'Come on in, all of you.'

I automatically kissed Anna's cheek as I welcomed her and she responded naturally and without hesitation by kissing mine. She wouldn't have done that seven years ago, I mused; she shied away from physical affection. Elaine and I cheek-kissed and then Ian presented me with a box of chocolates. 'A thank-you gift, better late than never,' he said, also kissing my cheek.

'That is kind of you,' I said. 'My favourites.'

'You've changed the colour on the walls,' Anna said, glancing around the hall.

'Yes, a few years ago. Fancy you remembering that.' I'm constantly surprised by the details children remember years after they've left us. 'We're all in the living room,' I said.

'Come through. Adrian is going out shortly but he wanted to see you first.'

'That's nice,' Anna said pleasantly.

In the living room I introduced them all to each other.

'Lucy?' Anna queried, looking puzzled.

'Cathy fostered me some years after you left, and then adopted me,' Lucy explained.

'Wow!' Anna said. 'I'm adopted too.' Which Lucy knew. 'You look like Cathy.'

'You look like your mum and dad,' Lucy said. She did. It's not imagination. Studies have shown that adopted children often grow to resemble their adoptive family in their likes and dislikes, aims, achievements, intelligence and physical appearance.

Any self-consciousness had now vanished as we settled into the chairs while the young people led the conversation. 'Which school do you go to?' Paula asked. Anna named a secondary school close to where they lived. Then followed a chat about their secondary schools, the subjects they were choosing – or in Adrian's case had chosen – to study at higher level, what they liked to do in their spare time, and the careers they were thinking of. After a while Adrian said he had to leave, and stood. 'Lovely meeting you again,' he said to Anna.

'And you. Sorry I broke your toys.'

'I'll get over it,' Adrian said dryly, which made everyone laugh.

I went with him to the front door. 'I'll see you at dinner-time then unless you phone to say otherwise,' I said. When Adrian had started going out with his friends I'd put in place some ground rules so that I knew he was safe and that food didn't go to waste.

'Yes, and save me a bit of that cake, Mum.'

'I will.'

After he'd gone I returned to the living room and offered everyone a drink. Elaine asked for tea, Ian coffee, and the girls fruit juice.

'I'll come and help you,' Elaine said, standing.

I didn't really need her help but I appreciated the chance to talk to Elaine in private, which I think is what she intended.

'Anna is a real credit to you,' I said as soon as we were in the kitchen and out of earshot. 'I'm struggling to believe it's the same child. You and Ian have done a fantastic job.'

'Oh, thank you. Do you really see that much difference?'

'Absolutely. She's sociable, warm, engaging, tactile, makes conversation and smiles! When did all this happen?'

'It was a very long process,' Elaine admitted, 'and we're still dealing with some issues.'

'Like what?' I asked, pausing from taking the cups and saucers from the cupboard.

'Mainly around control,' Elaine replied. 'Anna still likes to be in charge. She'd run our lives if we let her. But now we understand more, that it's a result of her early years' experiences, we deal with it. We're having to be firmer now she's almost a teenager.'

'That's normal,' I said. 'Most teenagers test the boundaries, but you're managing OK?'

'Oh, yes.' So I saw there'd been no need for me to worry; there wasn't an ulterior motive for their visit.

'You've done very well,' I said again, and filled the kettle.

'We had help. We were in family therapy for over a year, and Anna saw a therapist separately. Ian and I went to parenting classes – well, me mainly, as I was the main caregiver. We learned so much we wished we'd known sooner. We were incredibly naïve – we thought our love for Anna would fix everything. It played a big part, of course, but as you know we'd just been giving in to her, and giving her everything she wanted, which wasn't what she needed. Our tutor said that what a child wants can be very different from what they need.'

'Very true,' I said reflectively. 'Very true indeed.'

'That looks nice,' Elaine said as I began to slice the cake.

'Thank you. Let's hope it tastes as good as it looks.'

'I'm sure it will. I also rejoined the online group for those who have adopted,' Elaine continued. 'It helped talking to others going through something similar. I now share what we learned. I'll be honest with you, though, we had a very difficult time when Anna first returned from you. There were days when I thought I'd never be able to control her, but we got through it. We couldn't let her down again. Some of the strategies that you began here our tutor mentioned at the parenting group, and the importance of consistent boundaries.'

I nodded. I could see how confident Elaine was in her role as a parent now compared to before, and I was delighted that their family had come through the difficult times.

'Anna would like to see her bedroom here if that's OK?' Elaine said. 'She might not like to ask.'

'Yes, of course, although it's a little different upstairs now. I added an extra bedroom so we could continue fostering after Lucy stayed. So what prompted Anna to ask to visit us now?'

'We went back to the country where she was born last month and put a lot of old ghosts to rest. It was after that.'

'She decided to put this old ghost to rest,' I said, and Elaine laughed. 'Did she see her birth mother?'

'No. She didn't want to try to find her, but we did visit the orphanage. It was dreadful. It closed a year after Anna left and is a ruin now, but the atmosphere lingers. A lot of the roof has fallen in and ivy and weeds are growing inside, but those metal cots are still there, like empty cages. It sparked some very unpleasant memories in Anna, stuff she hadn't talked to us about before. She remembered children crying out for help at night and no one coming, being freezing cold in winter and hungry the whole time. She saw some sickly infants die in front of her – possibly she saw Lana, I don't know.' Elaine's eyes glistened. 'She remembers the callous attitude of the staff, as we do. Thank goodness that doesn't happen now in the orphanages there. It was shocking to hear Anna talk about it, but it helped to put the past to rest once and for all.'

I nodded. 'Will you return again?'

'No, not unless Anna wants to, and I don't think she will. She has moved on from the past; we all have.'

'Good.' I smiled and picked up the tray containing the drinks while Elaine carried the plate with the cake.

As we entered the living room Elaine joked, 'Look what I just made!'

'No, you didn't,' Anna snapped, a little disparagingly.

'She might have done,' Ian said, rising to his wife's defence. 'Your mum makes very good cakes.'

'She does,' Anna agreed, duly chastened.

'So does our mum,' Lucy said. 'Just not enough of them.'

I handed out the cake and drinks and we continued talking. The cake disappeared very quickly as Ian, Elaine and

Anna had second slices, so I put the last slice in the kitchen for Adrian. It was soon four o'clock and Ian said they would need to leave shortly as they were all going to the cinema later, so I asked Anna if she would like to look around the house now.

'Yes, please,' she said.

Ian stayed in the living room talking to Lucy and Paula while Elaine came with me. 'I've only ever seen your room in the photographs Cathy sent,' Elaine said to Anna. I always packed photographs of the child's stay when they left so they had something to look back on.

Upstairs I opened the door to what had been her bedroom, which now stood empty and ready for our next foster child. 'We had a child leave last week,' I said. 'I don't expect it will stay empty for long.'

'You've painted the walls and changed the carpet, but some of the furniture is the same,' Anna said.

'Yes, you're right.'

She went to the window and looked out to the garden beyond for a few seconds. When she turned her face was sad and her eyes glistened with tears.

'Whatever is the matter, love?' Elaine asked, going to her and putting her arm around her shoulders. 'Can you tell me?'

'I was just thinking how horrible I was to everyone. You, Dad, Cathy and her family. But I couldn't help it. I couldn't put into words what I was feeling, so I lashed out. I remember my frustration, and feeling very frightened. I knew I was a long way from home, but I couldn't work out how to get back.'

Elaine's eyes filled too as she held her daughter, and I swallowed hard. Had I appreciated back then how frightened Anna had been? No. All I saw was an angry, out-of-control child. Perhaps if I'd asked the right questions I would have discovered the frightened child within. I'll never know, but it was a lesson I learned and still remember. An angry child is a frightened child, crying out to be heard.

This is one family's account of international adoption. International adoption has been practised for many years and allows a child or children from one country (usually a developing country) to be adopted by a family in another country. The vast majority of these adoptions are very successful, with the child bonding with their new family. It should also be noted that attachment disorders can be found in children who haven't been adopted but fail to bond with their parents or primary caregiver for other reasons, usually through neglect or abuse.

For the latest on Anna and the other children in my books, please visit www.cathyglass.co.uk.

SUGGESTED TOPICS FOR
READING-GROUP DISCUSSION

———————

Elaine and Ian followed the correct procedure to adopt from abroad. Why did it go so wrong? What might they have done differently?

How far could it be said that they were simply naïve?

It is a fact that Reactive Attachment Disorder shows up as a dark mass on a brain scan where the emotion should be. Why do you think Anna was able to improve, firstly at Cathy's and then later, and more significantly, with her parents?

Elaine and Ian made the decision not to tell Anna about Lana. Was it the right decision? If she knew, what effect might it have on her? Was there anything to be gained from telling her?

Discuss the approach taken by Mrs Taylor's sister, Flo, and her husband in respect of their two boys. What indications, if any, are there that the same approach might have worked with Anna?

What do you think Elaine's and Ian's reasoning was to remove Anna from foster care when they did? Do you agree with the social services' decision to leave Anna at home with them? If not, what would you have done had you been their social worker?

What impact did fostering Anna have on Cathy and her family?

At the end Anna admits she was frightened at finding herself a long way from home and Cathy feels she should have realized this. What indicators were there, if any, that beneath Anna's challenging behaviour was a very frightened child? Would you have spotted them?

Cathy Glass

One remarkable woman, more than **150** foster children cared for.

Cathy Glass has been a foster carer for twenty-five years, during which time she has looked after more than 150 children, as well as raising three children of her own. She was awarded a degree in education and psychology as a mature student, and writes under a pseudonym. To find out more about Cathy and her story visit www.cathyglass.co.uk.

Cruel to be Kind

Max is shockingly overweight. Not only is his health suffering, but he struggles to make friends ...

With Max's mother and social worker opposing her at every turn, Cathy faces a challenge to help this unhappy boy.

Nobody's Son

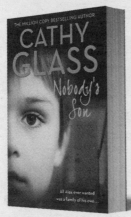

Born in prison and brought up in care, Alex has only ever known rejection

He is longing for a family of his own, but again the system fails him.

Can I Let You Go?

Faye is 24, pregnant and has learning difficulties as a result of her mother's alcoholism

Can Cathy help Faye learn enough to parent her child?

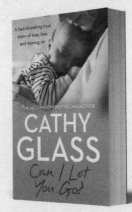

The Silent Cry

A mother battling depression. A family in denial

Cathy is desperate to help before something terrible happens.

Girl Alone

An angry, traumatized young girl on a path to self-destruction

Can Cathy discover the truth behind Joss's dangerous behaviour before it's too late?

Saving Danny

Danny's parents can no longer cope with his challenging behaviour

Calling on all her expertise, Cathy discovers a frightened little boy who just wants to be loved.

The Child Bride

A girl blamed and abused for dishonouring her community

Cathy discovers the devastating truth.

Daddy's Little Princess

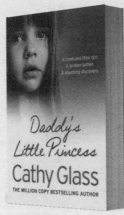

A sweet-natured girl with a complicated past

Cathy picks up the pieces after events take a dramatic turn.

Will You Love Me?

A broken child desperate for a loving home

The true story of Cathy's adopted daughter Lucy.

Please Don't Take My Baby

Seventeen-year-old Jade is pregnant, homeless and alone

Cathy has room in her heart for two.

Another Forgotten Child

Eight-year-old Aimee was on the child-protection register at birth

Cathy is determined to give her the happy home she deserves.

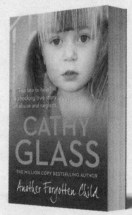

A Baby's Cry

A newborn, only hours old, taken into care

Cathy protects tiny Harrison from the potentially fatal secrets that surround his existence.

The Night the Angels Came

A little boy on the brink of bereavement

Cathy and her family make sure Michael is never alone.

Mummy Told Me Not to Tell

A troubled boy sworn to secrecy

After his dark past has been revealed, Cathy helps Reece to rebuild his life.

I Miss Mummy

Four-year-old Alice doesn't understand why she's in care

Cathy fights for her to have the happy home she deserves.

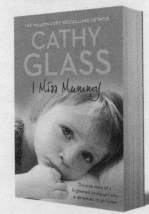

The Saddest Girl in the World

A haunted child who refuses to speak

Do Donna's scars run too deep for Cathy to help?

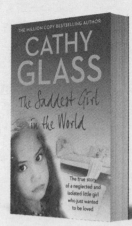

Cut

Dawn is desperate to be loved

Abused and abandoned, this vulnerable child pushes Cathy and her family to their limits.

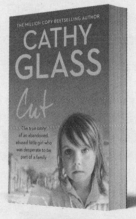

Hidden

The boy with no past

Can Cathy help Tayo to feel like he belongs again?

Damaged

A forgotten child

Cathy is Jodie's last hope.
For the first time, this
abused young girl has
found someone
she can trust.

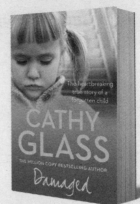

Inspired by Cathy's own experiences...

Run, Mummy, Run

The gripping story of a
woman caught in a horrific
cycle of abuse, and the
desperate measures she
must take to escape.

My Dad's a Policeman

The dramatic short story
about a young boy's
desperate bid to keep his
family together.

The Girl in the Mirror

Trying to piece together her past, Mandy uncovers a dreadful family secret that has been blanked from her memory for years.

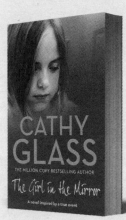

Sharing her expertise...

About Writing and How to Publish

A clear and concise, practical guide on writing and the best ways to get published.

Happy Mealtimes for Kids

A guide to healthy eating with simple recipes that children love.

Happy Adults

A practical guide to achieving lasting happiness, contentment and success. The essential manual for getting the best out of life.

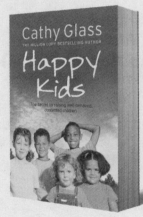

Happy Kids

A clear and concise guide to raising confident, well-behaved and happy children.

CATHY GLASS WRITING AS
LISA STONE

The new crime thriller that will chill you to the bone . . .

STALKER

Security cameras are there to keep us safe. Aren't they?

Available from
28 June 2018

THE DARKNESS WITHIN

You know your son better than anyone. Don't you?

Be amazed
Be moved
Be inspired

————

Moving Memoirs

Stories of hope, courage and the power of love…

If you loved this book, then you will love our Moving Memoirs eNewsletter

Sign up to…

- Be the first to hear about new books

- Get sneak previews from your favourite authors

- Read exclusive interviews

- Be entered into our monthly prize draw to win one of our latest releases before it's even hit the shops!

Sign up at

www.moving-memoirs.com